Luther and the Papacy

Luther and the Papacy

Stages in a Reformation Conflict

Scott H. Hendrix

FORTRESS PRESS   Philadelphia

To Emilee

Library of Congress Cataloging in Publication Data

Hendrix, Scott H
    Luther and the papacy.

    Bibliography: p.
    Includes index.
    1. Luther, Martin, 1483–1546.   2. Reformation—
Biography.   3. Papacy.   I. Title.
BR333.5.P3H46   284.1′092′4 [B]   80–2393
ISBN 0–8006–0658–2

8583K80   Printed in the United States of America   1–658

CONTENTS

CONTENTS

ABBREVIATIONS

ARG	*Archiv für Reformationsgeschichte*
CCath	*Corpus Catholicorum.* Münster, 1919 ff.
CH	*Church History*
Cl.	*Luthers Werke in Auswahl,* 3rd and 6th ed. Edited by Otto Clemen. Berlin, 1962–1967.
CR	*Corpus Reformatorum.* Halle, 1834 ff.
E var	*D. Martini Lutheri opera latina varii argumenti ad reformationis historiam imprimis pertinentia.* Frankfurt and Erlangen, 1865–1873.
HJ	*Historisches Jahrbuch*
HKG	*Handbuch der Kirchengeschichte.* Edited by Hubert Jedin. Freiburg, 1962 ff.
LJ	*Lutherjahrbuch*
LW	*Luther's Works. American Edition.* Edited by J. Pelikan and H. Lehmann. Philadelphia and St. Louis, 1955 ff.
Mirbt-Aland I	*Quellen zur Geschichte des Papsttums und des römischen Katholizismus.* Vol. I. 6th ed. Edited by C. Mirbt and K. Aland. Tübingen, 1967.
MStA	*Melanchthons Werke in Auswahl ("Studienausgabe").* Edited by Robert Stupperich. Gütersloh, 1951 ff.
NZSTh	*Neue Zeitschrift für Systematische Theologie und Religionsphilosophie*
RTA–JR	*Deutsche Reichstagsakten. Jüngere Reihe.* Gotha, 1892 ff.
SCJ	*The Sixteenth Century Journal*
ST	Thomas Aquinas. *Summa Theologiae*
TRE	*Theologische Realenzyklopädie.* Edited by G. Krause and G. Müller. Berlin and New York, 1977 ff.
WA	*Luthers Werke. Kritische Gesamtausgabe.* [Schriften]. Weimar, 1883 ff.
WABr	*Luthers Werke. Kritische Gesamtausgabe. Briefwechsel.* Weimar, 1930 ff.
WATR	*Luthers Werke. Kritische Gesamtausgabe. Tischreden.* Weimar, 1912–1921.
ZKG	*Zeitschrift für Kirchengeschichte*
ZSSR [kan. Abt.]	*Zeitschrift der Savigny-Stiftung für Rechtsgeschichte. Kanonistische Abteilung*

PREFACE

I would like to express appreciation to the following persons and institutions for their support and assistance: to the Aid Association for Lutherans for its faculty support grants; to Professor Heiko A. Oberman and his colleagues at the Institut für Spätmittelalter und Reformation in Tübingen for assistance in the early stages of my research; to the students in my courses on Luther for helping me to clarify issues; to Professor Remigius Bäumer, University of Freiburg, who graciously received my family into his home and discussed with me our different interpretations of the subject; to the administration and the Board of Trustees of the Lutheran Theological Southern Seminary for making available periods of leave for research and writing; to Professor W. Richard Fritz and the Lineberger Memorial Library for making resources available in Columbia; to the Association of Theological Schools for its Award for Theological Scholarship and Research during the final stage of research and writing; to the Church History Colloquium at the University of Göttingen and its coordinators, Professors Krumwiede, Moeller, and Mühlenberg, for the opportunity to present my views in their forum; to my colleague Carl Ficken and to Mark Edwards of Purdue University for reading the manuscript and making important suggestions; to Mrs. Walter Keller for typing the final draft; and to my family for its willingness to accompany me on the physical and mental journeys which led to this book.

Columbia, South Carolina   Scott H. Hendrix
September 22, 1980

viii

Et alijs ciuitatibus oportet me Euangeliʒare regnum Dei , quia ideo
ſuſſum . Et erat predicans in ſynagogis Galilee . Luce . iiij.

Antichꝛiſti.

Sepe contingit ꝙ Epi ,ᵱpter ſuas occupationes multiplices , vel in
ualitudines coꝛpales, aut hoſtiles incurſus, aut occaſiões alias, ne dicamus
defectũ ſcientiᷓ, ꝙ in eis reprobandũ eſt omnino , ᵱſeipſos nõ ſuffi
ciũt miniſtrare verbũ dei populo , maxime ᵱ amplas dioceſes & diffuſ
ſas Gñali conſtitutione ſancimus vt Eᵽi viros ad ſancte predicationis
officiũ ſalubriter exequendũ aſſumãt. c. inter cᷓtera de offi. oꝛdina. Hi
ſunt Eᵽi qui oꝛdinaᷟ officiᷟ ſui obliti facti ſunt anĩalia vᷓtris, dicentes,
Venite ſumamus vinũ , & impleamur ebrietate, & erit ſicut hodie ſic &
cras, & multo amplius. Eſaie. lvj.

INTRODUCTION

The relationship between Martin Luther and the papacy is hardly the subject of a tale of suspense. Everyone knows how the story turns out: Luther and the popes go their separate ways. Despite the fact that the suspense has long been over, the question of motive has remained open. That unresolved question is the reason for the publication of this book. Why did Luther oppose the papacy to the point that a lasting break with the Roman Church resulted?

Seen from the perspective of scholarship on Luther, the question is important. It is equivalent to asking why Luther became a reformer in the first place and what role his opposition to the papacy played in the development of his theology. Luther himself was not interested in individual popes or in conditions at Rome. Hence this book is not a comparison of Luther to incumbents of the papal office during his lifetime or an evaluation of the papal administration of the church in order to determine if Luther's picture of the Roman curia was accurate. For Luther the papacy was important because it was the chief pastoral office in the church, and its claims and pronouncements affected the lives of people regardless of who was the incumbent. Luther's attitude toward the papacy was directly related to his concern with the reform of the church. Therefore, the motive behind his opposition to the papacy may be expected to shed light on his development as a reformer. Taking into consideration Luther's adamant stance in his later years, as this book does in the space available, also helps us to evaluate Luther's life and reforming career as a whole.

For historians of the sixteenth century, Luther's motivation in opposing the papacy is an important concern as well. One historical question frequently leads to a larger one, and that is exactly what occurs here. Owing to Luther's dominant role at the beginning of the Reformation, an inquiry into his motive as a reformer is simultaneously an inquiry into the origins of the Protestant Reformation in general. Many factors besides Luther's decision to resist the papacy led to the Reformation. The ecclesiastical losses of the Roman Church to the Protestant movement had reverberations at so many levels, however, that the investigation of the religious origins of this movement helps us to understand the social, economic, and political dimensions of the Reformation. Luther's own motivation, for example, gives clues to the cultural factors that caused many other people to identify with his rejection of the Roman hierarchy. By the same token, the pressure applied to Luther by friend and foe alike when the papacy became the object of his criticism demonstrates the significance of that institution in the lives of the people and in the structure of society. If, as he claims, Luther tore himself away from the papacy only with difficulty and was urged by others not to take this crucial step, it is understandable that not everyone followed him and that conflict erupted between adherents of the new faith and those of the old.

The motivation behind Luther's separation from the papacy is also important to ecumenically minded theologians. They ask whether the separation was necessary and whether the division between confessions has to be regarded as permanent. A helpful discussion of such questions depends on the proper identification of the reasons behind the original division and on discovery of the extent to which it was historically conditioned and thus might be overcome in a different era. The question of the motive underlying Luther's own attitude toward the papacy is just one among many questions which theologians from Lutheran and Roman Catholic traditions have asked in their official dialogues. Not surprisingly, the statements on papal primacy which the dialogue in North America has produced give more attention to irenical attitudes expressed by other Lutherans than to Luther's own polemical remarks and final rejection of the papacy as a useful office in the church.[1] Although Luther's attitude should not necessarily determine the stance of modern Lutherans in relation to the papacy, it is important to study seriously the reasons behind Luther's position in order to gain a balanced and comprehensive historical perspective of the subject. A detailed inquiry into Luther's motivation does, in fact, reveal a consistent and significant criterion for assessing the office of the papacy, which could be considered in ecumenical discussions apart from Luther's polemic or his own historical situation.

Nevertheless, the present book has been written to aid in understanding Luther in his own setting. It attempts to follow the guideline formulated so trenchantly by Geoffrey R. Elton: "The historian's task is to understand before he approves or condemns, and understanding requires a grasp of how things looked to those we study."[2] The only lessons worth learning from history are those that are learned while taking the past with radical seriousness. In the case of Luther, a superficial look at his attitude toward the papacy might make it appear, for ecumenical purposes, obsolete. A deeper penetration of the subject, however, reveals that the development of his attitude and the stance in which he persisted were tied directly to the understanding of his task as a reformer and of the Reformation as a whole. In brief, his attitude passed through a number of stages from initial ambivalence to persistent rejection while all the time he evaluated the papacy by the criterion of whether it exercised its pastoral duty of nourishing people in the church with the word of God. The popes were to be advocates of the people, in Luther's view, and the more convinced he became that they were not willing to fill that role, the more willing he became to acquiesce in his own excommunication and in the formation of a new church.

This view of the development of Luther's attitude differs in important respects from the last two books written on the subject. In his booklet published in 1958,[3] Ernst Bizer stressed the authority of the word of God as the key to Luther's opposition to the papacy. Bizer also portrayed this opposition as a consequence of Luther's "discovery" of the word as the center of his new theology. In contrast to Bizer, this study stresses that Luther's emphasis on the word of God was crucial to his new theology and to his concept of the church prior to 1518. It also detects Luther's ambivalence about the hierarchy of the church before 1517; but, at the same time, it traces a more gradual and subtle shifting of attitude on Luther's part up to the year 1521.

Remigius Bäumer, in a study first published in 1970,[4] argued that Luther's stance in relation to the papacy should also be gauged by his view of what constituted the decisive authority for the church. Bäumer, however, described a two-step shift in Luther's view of authority during the years 1518 to 1519, which correlated with a shift in his attitude toward the papacy. Bäumer also emphasized the polemical tone of the older Luther's writings against the papacy and surmised that there must be a deeper personal hatred at work behind these treatises of Luther's later life. In contrast to Bäumer, this study proposes that Luther's attitude toward the papacy was not just linked to his views on formal authority in the church but also to the function which Luther believed the papacy and other ecclesiastical offices should exercise: to nurture the people by communicating the word of God to them. Viewed from this perspective, Luther's attitude toward the papacy did not undergo radical shifts but progressed through finely differentiated stages until he became absolutely convinced that the papacy would not fulfill its pastoral duty. In helping Luther to arrive at this conviction, doctrine and authority were less important criteria than the proper exercise of the papal office as a pastoral office. Advocacy of the people's right to hear the word, rather than personal hatred for an institution, permeated even the polemics of the older Luther.

This understanding of Luther's relationship to the papacy is not an entirely new view of Luther the reformer, although it is a view of his reforming activity which is not often stressed. It is a different view of his stance in relation to the papacy, however, and the implications of that view can contribute to a reassessment of Luther at several levels. It recalls the popular as well as the ecclesiastical and theological dimensions of his reforming work and suggests why Luther, like other reformers who saw themselves as advocates of the people, was so convinced he was doing the work of God. It also reinforces what statistics already tell us about the immense popular appeal of his early writings and the initial impact which he made. Finally, it helps to explain Luther's consistent opposition to the papacy while, on other questions such as the right of resistance to the emperor, he changed his mind. In the case of these issues, as in the case of his controversial refusal to lend theological endorsement to the demands of the peasants, Luther applied the criterion of preserving the freedom of the gospel and the people's access to it. From his perspective of the church and society in the sixteenth century, this access of people to the word was the right which most needed his advocacy. To understand this advocacy as Luther's primary concern is to see the papacy and the Reformation as Luther saw it and to form a proper basis for further assessment of his work.

1 | AMBIVALENCE
1505–1517

True, when I was a young master at Erfurt, I was often downcast due to assaults of gloominess. Thus I devoted myself mostly to reading the Bible. In this way, from the naked text of the Bible, I soon recognized many errors in the papacy. But there in the library at Erfurt many thoughts came upon me such as: "Behold, how great is the authority of the pope and the church! Are you alone supposed to be clever? Oh, you might be mistaken!" I yielded to these thoughts and suffered quite a setback in reading the Bible!

> —Luther, 1537
> (*WATR* 3, 439.2–8; no. 3593)

CHRONOLOGY

1483	November 10	Martin Luther born in Eisleben
1497	February 16	Philipp Melanchthon born in Bretten (Baden)
1501	Summer	Luther matriculates at the University of Erfurt
1502		University of Wittenberg founded by Elector Frederick the Wise
	September	Luther earns the bachelor of arts degree at Erfurt
1503		Julius II (Guiliano della Rovere) becomes pope Johannes von Staupitz becomes professor at Wittenberg and dean of the theological faculty
1505	January	Luther earns the master of arts degree at Erfurt
	May	Luther begins the study of law at Erfurt
	July 17	Luther enters the monastery of the Hermits of St. Augustine at Erfurt
1507	April 3	Luther is ordained to the priesthood
	May 2	Luther presides at his first mass
1508	Fall	Luther is sent to Wittenberg to lecture on moral philosophy

1509	October	Luther returns to Erfurt; lectures on the *Sentences* of Peter Lombard
1510		John Eck becomes professor of theology at the University of Ingolstadt
	November 13	Karlstadt obtains the doctor of theology degree at Wittenberg and joins the theological faculty
	November	Luther travels to Rome on business of his order
1511	April	Luther returns to Erfurt
	Late Summer or Fall	Luther transfers to the Augustinian monastery in Wittenberg
1512		The Fifth Lateran Council begins in Rome
	October 19	Doctor of theology degree is conferred on Luther
	October 22	Luther joins the theological faculty of the University of Wittenberg
1513		Pope Julius II dies
		Leo X (Giovanni de' Medici) becomes pope
	August	Luther begins first lecture course on the Psalms (*Dictata super Psalterium*)
1515	November	Luther begins lectures on Romans
1516	October	Luther begins lectures on Galatians
1517	Easter	Luther begins lectures on Hebrews

LUTHER LOOKS BACK

When Martin Luther's disillusionment with the papacy began is uncertain; but, by the time Luther arrived clandestinely at the Wartburg in May of 1521, his attitude toward the pope had lost all trace of ambivalence. On his way home from the Diet of Worms, where his firm opposition to the Roman Church made him a political outlaw, Luther was the victim of benevolent kidnappers who led him to the safety of the Wartburg. From this place of exile, Luther wrote to his younger colleague, Philipp Melanchthon, in Wittenberg: "Sitting here all day, I picture to myself the state of the church and I see fulfilled the word of Psalm 89 [:47]: 'Hast thou made all the sons of men in vain?' God, what a horrible picture of God's wrath is that detestable kingdom of the Roman Antichrist! . . . O kingdom of the pope, worthy of the end and dregs of the ages! God have mercy upon us!"[1]

Luther did not always feel this strongly about the papacy. Not quite a month after his letter to Melanchthon, Luther sent to his new colleague, Justus Jonas, a copy of his reply to James Latomus, theologian at the University of Louvain. Latomus had accused Luther of hypocrisy because Luther had submitted his writings to the judgment of the pope and then refused to accept the papal verdict which followed. Luther admitted with regret that he had seriously submitted his writings, but he defended himself against the charge of hypocrisy by recalling that his "sincere opinion of the pope, councils and universities was no different from the common one." Then he added, "Although much of what they said seemed absurd to me and completely alien to Christ, yet for more than a decade I curbed my thoughts with the advice of Solomon: 'Do not rely on your own insight' [Prov. 3:5]."[2]

If we take Luther at his word, his years of study and teaching prior to 1518 were filled with ambivalent feelings toward the commonly accepted church authorities. He harbored more serious reservations about the papacy than he allowed himself to express at the lectern or in the pulpit. How serious were these reservations? When did they begin? When did this ambivalence finally give way to his unambiguous rejection of the "detestable kingdom of the Roman Antichrist"?

We might expect Luther's hindsight to be of special help in answering these questions. But the proverbial advantage of hindsight is often a disadvantage for historians who have to weigh one hindsight of their subject against another. This disadvantage is evident in Luther's case. In the reply to Latomus, Luther reveals that he had harbored strong criticism of the pope, councils, and universities for more than ten years before he permitted himself to express this criticism openly. If this had been the only statement that Luther made about his attitude toward the papacy during those early years, it would be a straightforward task to examine his letters, sermons, and lectures for evidence of the accuracy of his memory. But Luther often reminisced about his early career under the pope, and some of these reminiscences reveal a different attitude toward the pope. In fact, some of his later remarks stand in such glaring contrast to his reply to Latomus that we must consider them in detail before looking back at Luther's early writings.

One notorious example is Luther's memory of the beginning of the Reformation found in the preface to his Latin writings published in 1545. Luther begs the readers of his early works to remember that he was "once a monk and a most enthusiastic papist." He continues: "I was so drunk, yes, submerged in the pope's dogmas, that I would have been ready to murder all, if I could have, or to cooperate willingly with the murderers of all who would take but a syllable from obedience to the pope." Luther compares himself to Saul (that is, Paul before his conversion) in his unrestrained enthusiasm, and contrasts his burning zeal for the pope with such "lumps of frigid ice" as John Eck, who defended the pope merely for selfish reasons.[3]

Other recollections reinforce this picture of Luther's early years as excessively propapal. Luther calls himself an "arch-papist" and a "slave of the mass" for fifteen years.[4] He immersed himself in monasticism to the point of insanity and adored the pope out of pure devotion, oblivious of ecclesiastical reward or personal gain.[5] In a sermon dating from the year 1536, Luther declares that if, thirty years earlier, anyone had preached the gospel to him as he now understands it, he would have collaborated in the persecution of Stephen himself.[6] As evidence that he did not intentionally enter the battle against Rome, he notes that he opposed even Erasmus's criticism of the papacy. It required a jolt from God to get Luther going, and even then he moved slowly. "God called me into this affair in a miraculous way and only gradually as specific occasions arose. I myself would have been the first to gather wood for the burning of any heretic who would have attacked the mass and celibacy."[7]

How seriously are we to take these testimonies to Luther's papalism? More than likely, Luther was exaggerating his enthusiasm for the pope in the early years. At least two factors account for this exaggeration. First, an apologetic motive dominates many of the recollections of the past, including the 1545 preface. Luther is worried that people will not understand why he expressed so little criticism of the papacy in his early works. Luther even notes that his contemporaries had charged him (not unlike modern critics) with contradicting himself after they had compared his bold attacks on the papacy with the meekness of his earlier works. In reply, Luther attributes his tameness both to the circumstances and to his own inexperience. He was all alone, he says, and inept at conducting such great affairs. "For I got into these turmoils by accident and not by will or intention."[8] A similar defense of Luther's early submissiveness to the pope was offered by Nikolaus von Amsdorf in his preface to the Jena Edition of Luther's works published in 1555. Amsdorf cautioned the readers of Luther's early works not to be offended when they found points on which Luther agreed with the Roman Church. In those early works neither the vision nor the pen of

Luther had yet been sharpened by the word of God and divine light to the point where he could fully and consistently expose papal tyranny. Still, Amsdorf claimed, the reader could learn from these early works how Luther grew from a papist into a true Christian and from a friend into an enemy of the pope.[9]

Second, Luther's early fidelity to the pope looked more and more zealous to Luther as his hostility to the papacy intensified during the twilight of his career. Seen over four centuries, the success of Luther's reforms appears certain at least by the time of the Diet of Augsburg in 1530. Unlike us, however, Luther never knew how the story would turn out. Notwithstanding his frequent affirmations that God was in control, Luther himself remained uncertain about how strongly the recovery of the gospel would take hold. In 1538, Luther still felt compelled to confess his "weakness and foolishness" in order that his followers would remain humble and realize that "Satan was not dead, but was still the ruler, not just of one person or of one region, but of the whole world."[10]

Luther lived out his last years under the shadow of a reinvigorated Catholic camp. Pope Paul III, Emperor Charles V, and the upcoming council at Trent posed a dark and menacing threat to Luther. His early loyalty to the pope no longer appeared neutral and harmless in retrospect. Instead of romanticizing the past, Luther vilified his early years. His life as a monk under the papacy could not simply be dismissed as the conscientious but misguided striving to lead a life of perfect humility and obedience. With the fruits of his reforming labor apparently imperiled, Luther could only view his early adherence to the pope as "arch-papalism" and insane adoration.

Adjusting Luther's remarks for these apologetic factors, we can more realistically characterize Luther's positive attitude toward the pope as sincere (but not "insane") fidelity to the Roman Church and its hierarchy. After all, this church was his spiritual and material home. As Luther later remarked, he "stubbornly and reverently" worshiped the church of the pope as the true church—"stubbornly and reverently" because he did it "with a true heart."[11]

But we have still not accounted for Luther's restrained discontent with the church, and even with the pope, in those early years. Serious disagreement, such as he describes in his reply to Latomus, does not fit well into a picture of the early Luther as an ardent son of the papacy. What did Luther mean when he said that for more than a decade he had suppressed his disagreement with much of what was taught by the pope, the councils, and the universities? Was Luther referring to the indulgence practice, specific rulings of church councils, papal pronouncements, or scholastic theology as it was taught in his day? And how could he have been disgruntled over one or more of these matters for more than ten years before the indulgence controversy? Luther must have exercised restraint uncharacteristic of his outspokenness in later years. Is it plausible that Luther was either so awed by ecclesiastical authority or so perfect in the practice of humility that he was able to contain himself and his criticism for a decade?

Luther's reply to Latomus could be dismissed as an obvious effort to save face were it not for other remarks that point to his early discontent with the papacy. In an excerpt from his *Table Talk* dated 1537, Luther said that he came to his struggle with the pope quite innocently. Twenty years prior to his realization that the pope was the Antichrist, he never would have entertained such an idea; in fact, he would have sentenced to the stake anyone who held such a teaching.[12] In this context Luther might have played down any reservations he had had about the church or its teaching in order to prove his earlier innocence. To the contrary, Luther recalled how he read the Bible as a young teacher in Erfurt and how, on the basis of the "naked text of Scripture," he soon saw "many errors in the papacy." There in the library, however, he was immediately besieged with reservations: "How great is the authority of the pope and the church! Do you think you are the only clever person? To be sure, you might be mistaken!" Luther reported that he had surrendered to these reservations and, as a result, had suffered a setback in his biblical studies. Only later, when he began to expose the abuses of indulgences and provoked the first reactions, did he come out into the open with his criticism. Even then, Luther remembered, he moved "feebly," because for three years he labored under all kinds of despair in the struggle he had undertaken.[13]

This recollection agrees in important respects with the response to Latomus. Both reveal dissatisfaction with much of what Luther read and heard during his early years as student and teacher. Both report hesitancy to express his criticism openly and attribute this hesitancy to his respect for ecclesiastical authority. Luther learned well the lesson of monastic humility: it is dangerous to elevate one's own opinion above the teaching of the church. He never forgot how well he learned that lesson. The *Table Talk* records a conversation from 1532 in which Luther recalls his self-imposed restraint. Commenting on the injunction to "obey your superiors" (Heb. 13:17), Luther says that for many years this very text deterred him from writing against the pope.[14]

The cumulative evidence of Luther's hindsight confirms that his early years were filled with ambivalent feelings toward the papacy. His positive feelings arose from loyalty and devotion to the church, although these feelings later looked exaggerated when refracted through the lens of his experience. It is impossible to date the onset of his negative feelings with precision. This is not surprising if we consider how vaguely our own memories chart the rise of feelings and opinions which have since greatly intensified. Whether looking back from 1521 or 1537, Luther remembered that reservations about church authority had been present since his early days in the monastery (1505–1507). In his reply to Latomus, Luther dated his privately held discontent from "more than a decade" prior to 1518. The twenty-year period antedating his recognition (1519–1520) that the pope might be the Antichrist would push Luther's doubts about the pope back to the very beginning of his studies. Neither reference should be taken as an attempt by Luther to pinpoint the dawning of his dissatisfaction; rather they emphasize that some long-standing discontent did haunt his early career. Dating the onset of his reservations is less important than understanding the nature and seriousness of those reservations and the ambivalence that they aroused.

SCRUPULOSITY

By the summer of 1510, when he completed the final requirement for the bachelor of theology degree, Luther had spent five years becoming a monk and studying theology. Soon after he walked into the cloister of the Augustinian Hermits in Erfurt on July 17, 1505, he was selected for advanced theological study and asked to teach in the faculty of arts as well. In 1508, he lectured temporarily on moral philosophy in the new University of Wittenberg and, after returning to Erfurt in 1509, he capped his studies by delivering the required lectures on the standard theological textbook of the Middle Ages, the *Sentences* of Peter Lombard.

During his formal preparation, Luther immersed himself in the teachings and traditions of the church; he had ample opportunity to raise questions about ecclesiastical authority. His theological mentors— William of Occam (*d.* 1350), Pierre d'Ailly (*d.* 1420), Jean Gerson (*d.* 1429), and Gabriel Biel (*d.* 1495)—had discussed church authority as intensely as they had analyzed the religious life. Luther read them thoroughly, but, as he looked back on these monastery years, his attempt to live the perfect religious life dominated his memory. Luther's later works are filled with references to the struggle he underwent trying to be an exemplary monk: "If ever a monk went to heaven through monkery, I intended to get there likewise."[15]

The monastic rule that applied immediately to Luther was the constitution written in 1504 for the Reformed Congregation of the Augustinian Order in Germany by its vicar-general, Johannes von Staupitz. According to this rule, Luther and other novices were taught to confess "purely, discretely, frequently, and humbly." All brothers were instructed to confess in secret at least once a week in addition to the daily confession of guilt in common.[16] Mortal sins were specified, and a careful distinction was made among offenses according to the degree of guilt which they incurred: "light," "grave," "quite grave," and "very grave." These offenses ranged from allowing the eyes and mind to wander during daily worship ("light") to accepting and stashing away gifts which the monks were forbidden to possess ("quite grave"). Incorrigible behavior, including the unwillingness to repent, incurred the greatest guilt.[17] In 1531, Luther reports that he strove unsuccessfully to live the monastic rule to the letter. "I was accustomed, once I was contrite, to confess and enumerate every one of my sins. Frequently I repeated my confession and I assiduously performed the penance laid upon me. Despite that, my conscience was never certain, but always doubted and said: 'You have not done this correctly; you were not contrite enough; you failed to confess this, etc.' "[18]

Much has been made of the afflictions of conscience that Luther suffered in his early years, but they have generally been divorced from the issue of church authority. Julius Köstlin, one of Luther's most thorough biographers, noted that Luther demonstrated no acquaintance with those writings of Occam, d'Ailly, and Gerson which dealt critically with papal authority. Either Luther's teachers did not dare recommend such works to him or Luther himself was too preoccupied with his private struggles to consult them, preferring more practical works on the religious life.[19] Another explanation for his lack of attention to such writings may lie in the fact that the Augustinians were especially devoted to the papacy and inculcated this devotion in their novices.[20] Some of the most avid defenders of papal sovereignty had been Augustinians. The most outstanding example was Giles of Rome (d. 1316),

8

the curialist supporter of Boniface VIII and official doctor of the Augustinian Order. Another was Johannes Zachariae, nicknamed "Hussomastix" ("scourge" of Hus) for his prosecution of John Hus. Zachariae was buried in the cloister at Erfurt, but the attitude of the Augustinians in Erfurt toward the zeal of their heroes was not totally uncritical. Luther reports, for example, that Staupitz once passed on to him a deprecating remark about Zachariae which he, Staupitz, had heard from his predecessor.[21]

In preparation for his ordination in 1507, Luther did read the *Exposition of the Canon of the Mass* by Gabriel Biel (*d.* 1495), a favorite among priests in his day. This work is a mine of medieval theology constructed around the central prayer of the mass. At that point in the canon where the priest prays for the pope, Biel comments that the pope is the head of the church as the vicar of Christ and lines up the traditional authorities for papal supremacy.[22] Biel is no rabid papist, however. He acknowledges the authority of church councils and the possibility that the pope can err;[23] he also carefully distinguishes between the pope's headship of the church and Christ's headship.[24] Despite that, it is unlikely that Biel's work weakened Luther's loyalty to the pope any more than it had weakened Biel's own. In the opinion of Otto Scheel, Luther celebrated his first mass as a "papist" not because he was a fanatical "arch-papist" and slave of the mass as he later asserted, but because Luther had committed himself to the teachings and traditions of the papal church which he was preparing to serve as priest.[25]

Although his study of the mass scarcely weakened his ties to the pope, in Luther's memory his internal struggle with confession was very much related to papal authority. The writings of Jean Gerson (*d.* 1429), mystical theologian and reform-minded chancellor of the University of Paris, played an important role in helping Luther recognize this relationship. Several times in his *Table Talk* Luther identified Gerson as the one who began to relax the reins of papal tyranny. Gerson argued that it was not a mortal sin to disobey the laws of the church unless the disobedience was deliberate.[26] When Luther applied this argument to the practice of confession, it meant that he and other Christians were not under pressure to confess every sin. This spelled relief for the scrupulous conscience of Luther and made Gerson, in Luther's memory, the great consoler among the medieval doctors and a forerunner of Christian freedom under the gospel.[27] From the perspective of the 1530s and 1540s, Gerson, as an advocate of conciliar authority in the

9

church, also appeared to be a forerunner of Luther's own opposition to the papacy. Luther added to his comments on Gerson that no one could really understand the necessity of opposing the pope unless one had lived under the darkness of the papacy.[28]

In the period of 1505 to 1510, obligatory confession of every sin may not have raised doubts in Luther's mind about papal authority per se. Potentially, however, the questions were there. The guidelines for confessing were conceivably one point at which Luther questioned the teaching of the church, especially since they touched the nerve of his own religious experience. Nevertheless, he was hardly the first to voice doubts about the degree of thoroughness required in confession. In his *Exposition* Biel, relying on Gerson, discussed quite openly the degree of certainty required of a priest who had confessed before celebrating mass.[29] According to Gerson, one should be as diligent in examining the conscience for past sins as one could be in any business where a great gain or loss is at stake.[30] Quoting Gerson in his dictionary of medieval theology, Altenstaig noted that repeated confession of the same sins might result in doubts about the efficacy of sacramental confession and thus pose a danger for scrupulous and timid consciences.[31] Luther's scruples were not unique. When, however, Luther came to recognize the connection between his internal religious struggle and the external authority of the church, his scruples sounded the keynote of his lifelong opposition to the papacy: the pope must be opposed as long as he tyrannized the consciences of faithful Christians.

Luther's internal battle with the demands of the confessional would have much more impact on his attitude toward the papacy than his trip to Rome in the winter of 1510–1511. Luther went to Rome on business of his monastery. Although he did not see the pope, Julius II, he reported that he did visit many crypts and churches, celebrated a mass here and there, and believed all the stories that had been made up for him and the other tourists.[32] But the trip was worthwhile for Luther, at least in his later years. He would not take a hundred thousand gulden in exchange for having seen Rome, said Luther in 1536; if he had not seen it, he might think he was being unfair to the city.[33] Like the tourist who, once he returns home, comments with authority on the places visited, Luther did not cease to deplore the wretched conditions in Rome. For example, he told the following story: A certain Jew about to be converted to Christianity told the priest instructing him that he would like to visit Rome before he was baptized. The priest tried to dissuade him for fear that a close view of scandal-ridden Rome would change his mind about becoming Christian. To the surprise of the priest, the Jew returned eager to be baptized. He told the priest, "I am ready to worship the God of the Christians for he is very long-suffering. If he can put up with such foolishness in Rome, then he can easily bear all the crimes of the world."[34]

Luther may have had similar thoughts about the long-suffering of the pope during that winter trip. But, more likely, he did not directly connect whatever deplorable conditions he found in Rome with the office of the papacy. At this point, he was more concerned about the state of his own soul and about the state of the church closer to home.

All the same, Luther's critical recollections of this period indicate that he was not able to divorce his internal struggles from the issue of church authority. It is impossible to determine just what Luther meant by the "many errors in the papacy" which, he says, the naked text of Scripture revealed to him during his time in Erfurt. The penitential practice of the church, however, was a likely candidate for one of those "errors." In fact, this was the discipline imposed upon him by the authorities of the church and of his order whom he was bound to obey. In his conscientious struggle to follow that discipline, questions about its wisdom and its effect on his life would spark further questions about the wisdom of the hierarchy and teachers who sanctioned and justified that discipline. The ambivalence which Luther felt toward that discipline was more than enough to spawn ambivalent feelings about its source, regardless of the loyalty that he felt toward the church to which he now committed his life as preacher and teacher.

TEACHER AND PREACHER

On October 19, 1512, the degree of doctor of theology was conferred on Luther by his "promoter" in the theological faculty at Wittenberg, Andreas Bodenstein von Karlstadt. In his doctoral oath Luther pledged not to teach strange doctrines which had been condemned by the Roman Church and, consequently, were "offensive to pious ears." In addition, as one who had received the licentiate in theology, he had to swear obedience to the Roman Church.[35] There is every reason to think that Luther took the full oath with a clear conscience, although in later years he would interpret the oath as binding him to Holy Scripture rather than to the Roman Church.[36] Regardless of this change in the object of his allegiance, Luther always regarded his doctorate as the official sanction for his reforming work: "I have often said and still say, I would not exchange my doctor's degree for all the world's gold. . . . God and the whole world bear me testimony that I entered into this work publicly and by virtue of my office as teacher and preacher and have carried it hitherto by the grace of God."[37]

Three days later Luther was formally inducted into the theological faculty of the University of Wittenberg and began to prepare the lectures that he would deliver as the successor to Johannes von Staupitz in the chair of biblical studies. From 1513 to 1515 he taught his first lecture course on the Psalms. These lectures were followed by courses on Romans (1515–1516), Galatians (1516–1517), and Hebrews (1517–1518). From this earliest phase of his teaching career we also possess sermons Luther delivered, marginal notes to medieval theological works, letters, and theses prepared for academic debate. Luther was a busy man. In a letter to John Lang, the prior of the Augustinian monastery in Erfurt, Luther revealed the many demands on his time in 1516:

> I am a preacher at the monastery, I am a reader during mealtimes, I am asked daily to preach in the city church, I have to supervise the study [of novices and friars], I am a vicar (and that means I am eleven times prior), I am caretaker of the fish [pond] at Leitzkau, I represent the people of Herzberg at the court in Torgau, I lecture on Paul, and I am assembling [material for] a commentary on the Psalms. . . . The greater part of my time is filled with the job of letter writing. I hardly have any uninterrupted time to say the Hourly Prayers and celebrate [mass]. Besides all this there are my own struggles with the flesh, the world, and the devil. See what a lazy man I am![38]

During these years Luther was hardly preoccupied with the papacy. His writings, in fact, contain surprisingly few references to the pope and the Roman curia. What he says explicitly about Rome is positive for the most part. In his first Psalms lectures, Luther notes that Christ seems to have forgotten all other churches in the world except the Roman Church, which he addressed in the person of Peter: "Your faith will not fail" (Luke 22:32).[39] The Roman Church is the chief part of all the churches.[40] Within the church the hierarchy occupies a necessary place and the authority of the pope at the summit of the hierarchy is not challenged by Luther. In a sermon for the festival of St. Peter in Chains, August 1, 1516, Luther argues that the church would not have been perfect unless Christ had given all his power to humankind; otherwise there would be no order in the church and everyone would claim to have been tapped by the Spirit.[41] Even Roman Catholic historians have disagreed to what extent this sermon refers to the pope. Few have questioned, however, that Luther recognized the necessity of a visible human hierarchy, established by divine right, to guarantee the stability and permanence of the church.[42]

For this reason, it is difficult to evaluate why, especially in his first lectures on the Psalms, Luther never interpreted the "rock" of Matt. 16:18 as the pope, but rather as Scripture, Christ, or faith. It may be, as Hans Preuss said, that his failure to acknowledge this traditional proof text for papal authority shows where Luther's particular interest did not lie, namely, in the papacy. Other scholars have been quick to point out that Luther's interpretation was by no means unique; in fact, it was rather common in the medieval exegesis of Scripture. In spite of this, Preuss found it significant at least that Luther chose not to apply Matt. 16:18 to the pope.[43]

A sermon preached by Luther in 1517 gives support to Preuss's suspicion that Luther's lack of reference to the papacy was intentional. In this sermon Luther stressed orally what he would write down months later in the *Explanations of the Ninety-five Theses*: the power of the priests to bind and loose sins based on Matt. 16:19 was given to them for our comfort and certainty. Their tongues are the keys to the kingdom of heaven. Whenever we hear the word of absolution from their mouths, we should believe firmly in that word and no longer trust in our own contrition and repentance.[44] But, complained Luther, this word of comfort has been twisted into a tyrannical word. For a long time, Luther recalls, Matt. 16:19 tormented his soul because he had thought it meant that the pope could do with him whatever he wanted; and, indeed, the keys are still being used to terrify and vex the people. The priests are madly mistaken if they think they absolve only those Christians whose genuine contrition can be proved. On the contrary, faith in Christ through the word of the priest brings forgiveness to whoever trusts in that word.[45]

By 1515, Luther could have decided not to apply the rock in Matt. 16:18 and the power of binding and loosing in Matt. 16:19 to the pope because he felt himself to be a victim of the misuse of that power in the penitential practice of the church. Consequently, he decided to adhere to the safer traditional exegesis of which he was certain. Even if Luther made such a decision, there is no reason to assume that he was questioning anything more than the misuse of papal and priestly power.

On the other hand, Luther's neglect of the pope could mean that he was not yet concerned about any misuse of the keys prior to 1516 or 1517. Arguments from silence are notoriously unreliable. Silence may speak louder than words, but it is frequently impossible to determine what that silence is saying. Still, Luther's handling of Matt. 16:18–19 does fit into the ambivalence about the papacy which his recollections about this period reveal.

No ambivalence can be detected in the importance Luther attached to the priesthood during these years. Throughout his early writings Luther extols both the power and the authority of the hierarchy. The mouth of the priest is the mouth of God, and even preachers of the gospel who do not possess the Spirit serve God.[46] Priests and prelates are the seats from which Christ exercises his rule in the church. Obedience is owed to these seats when they sit in judgment no matter how inappropriate their judgment might be, as long as it is not against God.[47] It is precisely because Luther valued the priesthood and obedience to the hierarchy so highly that he could criticize them as sharply as he did in his early works.

Both in his lectures and in his sermons Luther censures the improper conduct of the clergy because of its destructive impact upon the church. He scores the laxity which pervades the church and, even prior to 1517, criticizes indulgences for encouraging this laxity among both priests and people. Priests and prelates pour out indulgences from the treasure of the church, accumulated for us by the blood of Christ and the martyrs, without taking responsibility for restocking that treasure.[48] They mislead the people by paving the way to heaven with indulgences, although the presence of tribulation rather than the lack of it is the sign of a healthy church. In these remarks Luther is not questioning the validity of indulgences, but the consequences of their widespread use. Because their very purpose is to release Christians from works of satisfaction—alms, prayers, fasting, and so on—indulgences teach Christians to take their sins less seriously than they should and beguile them with false security. Even the pope is censured, along with the priests, for seducing the people from true worship of God by cruelly exacting through indulgences a price for the pardon which they have received freely.[49] Indulgences are not the only abuse, however. Luther frequently bewails the poor quality of the preachers whom bishops approve for the pulpit, and he regards the proliferation of loquacious preachers as a punishment of God on the church.[50]

Luther's criticism of the priests and higher prelates has been dismissed as within the bounds of what was typical in the Middle Ages. He was certainly not the first, nor even the last, to criticize the use of indulgences, the immorality of the clergy, and bad preaching. Luther did indeed echo the complaints of many medieval reformers and even borrowed their arguments. For example, he adopted the historical perspective of Bernard of Clairvaux to condemn the lack of persecution in the church of his day as the most serious persecution of all because it lulled the church to sleep.[51] Furthermore, none of Luther's criticism directly impugned the authority of the Roman hierarchy or the authority of the pope himself. Luther's criticism was not revolutionary.

Nevertheless, Luther's sharply critical remarks do reveal a typical concern for the church which would remain the driving force behind his more explicit attacks on the papal hierarchy to come later. That concern is for the people of the church and for their access to the genuine word of God through the words of their pastors. He criticizes indulgences because they direct the attention of the people away from their need for forgiveness and the source of that forgiveness in the words of their priests. He criticizes poor preaching and abuse of the keys because they fail to feed the people with the promises by which Christ feeds his people. This concern for the proper execution of the church's pastoral duty is expressed forcefully by Luther at two points in his early writings.

The first is a sermon that Luther prepared for delivery by George Mascov, the archdeacon of Brandenburg, at a synodical gathering in 1512 or 1515.[52] Luther's text is 1 John 5:4–5: "Whatever is born of God overcomes the world. . . ." In the first part of the sermon, Luther uses James 1:18 to define the birth from God which is mentioned in the 1 John text: "Of his own will he brought us forth by the word of truth. . . ." As Luther assesses the church of his day, the most urgent need is that priests abound in that word of truth. It is no wonder that so many superstitions and false opinions flourish among the people since they are being taught the words of men instead of the word of God. As Luther puts it, the quality of the birth depends upon the quality of the word that is taught, and the people in turn reflect their birth.[53] The moral degradation of the clergy is bad, of course, but incomparably worse is their failure to teach the word of truth. Worst of all, the priests do not realize that they adulterate God's word. In this crucial matter a priest thinks he cannot sin, whereas it is precisely in his failure to teach the word of truth that the priest sins qua priest.

Even if a priest were to live a blameless life, for this one sin alone he should be counted among wolves and not among pastors.[54]

For Luther, only that priest who stands before the people with the word of truth and brings about their divine birth is also a pastor, an angel of the Lord of hosts (Mal. 2:7). The people of Christ multiply only through the word of truth, and by this word alone are they fed and perfected. Even if the synod should pass superb regulations and provide for good order, if it does not command the preachers to proclaim the gospel to the people, then it will have accomplished nothing. This is the hinge of any real reform and the foundation of all piety. "This statement stands firm: the church cannot be born or exist (in its own nature) except through the word of truth. 'He bore us,' he says, 'by the word of truth.' Therefore, no other [word] is to be sought, taught or received unless you wish to take away this divine truth, extinguish the church and drown the people of Christ, like Pharaoh, in the rivers of Egypt, that is, to destroy it with the words of man."[55]

Finally, Luther extols faith as "our victory which overcomes the world" (1 John 5:5). But only the person who calls upon the Lord can believe. And only that person believes who hears the word of truth. To hear the word of truth one must hear the gospel. And to hear the gospel, one must listen to a priest who is an angel of God.[56] The priest holds the fate of the people in his hand. Only he can give birth to a believing people and guarantee the continued existence of the church. Because faithful priests are so crucial to the survival of the church, Luther does not hesitate to upbraid them in severe tones.

No passage in Luther's early lectures stresses the crucial nature of the pastoral office as forcefully as this early sermon. Nevertheless, at one place in his early lectures on the Psalms, Luther takes a swipe at the clergy in a way that ominously foreshadows his rejection of the Roman hierarchy. In Ps. 119:98–100, the psalmist rejoices in his love of the law and asserts that "thy commandment makes me wiser than my enemies. . . . I have more understanding than all my teachers. . . . I understand more than the aged." Applying these verses to the church of his day, Luther argues that many believers who are taught by the anointing of the Spirit (John 6:45) are wiser than prelates and doctors and "literal Christians," because they are spiritual and their meditation on the law of Christ is spiritual. To be spiritual is to recognize that the commandment of God is eternal and promises an eternal righteousness. Luther cites a biblical text which was frequently used in the Middle

Ages to support the supreme authority of the pope. That text is 1 Cor. 2:15: "The spiritual man judges all things but is himself to be judged by no one." Instead of applying this verse to the prelates and doctors of the church, however, Luther uses the text to support the superior judgment of all those who understand the law of Christ in a spiritual way. In contrast to these spiritual Christians, many prelates and doctors enforce human traditions against the spiritual people, and thus become enemies of the church who think less wisely than the church itself.[57]

John 6:45 and 1 Cor. 2:15 will later serve as key components of Luther's concept of a priesthood of believers. In these early Psalms lectures, Luther has not yet solidified such a theological foundation. By no means does a spiritual priesthood replace the clerical priesthood of the Roman Church. Neither is the authority of the papacy directly challenged. This harsh criticism should be read in light of the crucial importance that Luther attaches to a faithful and properly functioning priesthood. Nevertheless, important ingredients of a later rejection of the Roman hierarchy are being utilized to underscore the failure of many priests and teachers to provide for the nurture and subsistence of their people. It would be only one more step in the same direction, albeit a revolutionary step, for Luther's criticism to culminate in rejection and for that rejection to touch even the papacy. Prior to 1517 Luther did not envision that revolutionary consequence.

THEOLOGY AND REFORMATION

As Luther made the formal transition from student to teacher, his sense of responsibility expanded to include the welfare of the church in addition to his personal religious welfare. This expansion is evident in his concern for the proper functioning of the priesthood just discussed. Yet, this concern is frequently neglected in discussions of Luther's early theological development. The attempts to fix the date and nature of Luther's "Reformation discovery" have understood it as an exegetical and theological solution to Luther's personal religious problems. To be sure, this solution is seen as possessing revolutionary potential for Luther's involvement in church reform, but the discovery itself is generally divorced from his view of the church and his feeling of responsibility for it. The discovery has been regarded either as a prelude to his conflict with the papacy or as a result of this conflict—depending upon the date which is finally assigned to it.

Luther does present his discovery to us as the solution to his own struggle to live faithfully the monastic life.[58] His conclusion that the righteousness of God is a gift to believers instead of a standard by which God judges them is both an exegetical insight into the text of Rom. 1:17 and a correction of Luther's own former view of God, which he holds responsible for the anguish under which he labored. The extent to which this insight alone constitutes a "Reformation" discovery has been questioned by many scholars.[59] Other theological motifs play significant and lasting roles in Luther's mature thought, e.g., the cluster of insights which fall under the label "theology of the cross." It would be necessary to consider their place in Luther's early writings in order to describe the genesis of his Reformation theology as a whole. How one defines what that Reformation theology is will determine the point at which Luther is seen to have arrived at it.

If, however, Luther's new theology is defined in such a way that his concern for the state of the church and its leadership is excluded, it does not deserve the name "Reformation" theology in the fullest sense. One necessary element in any definition of Reformation must be the break of Luther with the papacy. As a result, his Reformation theology must also include a view of the Christian life and of the church which leads to and can survive this break. Here, important questions for any discussion of Luther and the papacy are raised. Was the conflict between them only a corollary of some purer Reformation insight which could have subsisted on its own without causing this conflict? Or did Luther's Reformation theology include at its core a view of the church that led directly to this conflict? Was the break with the papacy an essential part of the Reformation, or was it only an unfortunate consequence of Luther's religious views caused by events that could have been prevented?

Luther's writings prior to the outbreak of the indulgence controversy in 1517 do contain a view of the church that could support a new ecclesiastical structure separate from the Roman hierarchy. This new ecclesiology is integrally related both to his new insights into the Christian life and to his harsh criticism of the priesthood. It can be summed up by Luther's statement in his lectures on Hebrews that Christ rules the church by no power other than the word of God.[60]

Luther's early lectures and sermons exhibit the same view of Christian life and of the church that is stated so forcefully in his sermon prepared for the prior at Leitzkau. Genuine Christians are defined as those who do not put their trust in the things of this world but who live in faith and the Spirit.[61] It is the word of God, the gospel, that feeds the faithful with promises of spiritual goods which they cannot now see or grasp. These words for which the faithful long are the food with which Christ feeds them in the church.[62] The faithful are fed through the preaching of faithful priests and bishops. All power resides in the bishop. If he is blind, the people are blind; if he sees, then the people can see. The greatest care should be taken to see that the people have a good bishop, especially one who is a preacher, because it is the office and duty of a bishop to preach.[63]

Whether or not this view of the Christian life entails Luther's full Reformation theology, the ecclesiology contained here can definitely be labeled "Reformation." The church which arose after Luther's break with the papacy was able to base itself on this principle: the true church is the place where Christians are fed by the faithful preaching of the word. Although not every element of Luther's later ecclesiology is contained in his earliest writings, the theoretical basis for the continuation of the church apart from the papacy is present. To this extent, Luther's early theology is Reformation theology, in spite of the fact that Luther in 1517 had no intention of establishing a new church in opposition to the papacy.[64]

To assess Luther's attitude toward the papacy before the outbreak of the indulgence controversy, it is appropriate to distinguish between the unconscious potential of his theology and his conscious attitude toward the pope. In order to recognize the antipapal potential of the former, it is not necessary to arrive at a definitive answer to the question whether Luther's Reformation theology was "discovered"—either partially or completely—by late 1517. It is enough to recognize that he did view the Christian life in terms of word and faith and regarded it as the responsibility of the church to nourish that faith by the preaching of the word. His denunciation of the priesthood for not fulfilling this responsibility shows to what extent he had made the theology of word and faith his own.

Luther's conscious attitude toward the papacy, however, is more difficult to determine. His criticism of the church would apply only indirectly, if at all, to the papal office. And it is only the papal office, not the person of the pope, which Luther might have regarded with ambivalence during this period. Luther does not even mention Pope Leo X by name before 1518. At least this much is certain: Luther is not an insane papalist at the time of his early lectures and sermons. Furthermore, given the difficulty of distinguishing between moderate papalism and conciliarism in the late Middle Ages, Luther cannot be termed a papalist with any degree of certainty.[65] Luther's attitude toward the pope may have been basically positive, as Remigius Bäumer says;[66] but Luther was not necessarily a papalist in the sense that he attributed absolute and unquestioned authority to the pope. The later Middle Ages supply evidence that many reformers expressed a positive attitude toward the papacy without attributing absolute authority to the papal office. They recognized the legitimacy of a papal office in the church; but they also harbored ambivalent feelings about the pope and sometimes built these reservations into their ecclesiologies so as to limit papal authority in specific cases.

Bäumer also labels Luther's attitude toward the papacy as positive because there was no "decisive criticism" of the papacy by Luther prior to the indulgence controversy.[67] True, Luther directed little specific criticism against the papacy as such. However, the fundamental view of the church which he articulated in his lectures would prove to be more decisive in Luther's eventual break with the papacy than any explicit, but superficial, critical remarks about the papacy could have been. For example, in his first lectures on the Psalms, Luther interprets Ps. 122:5 without referring to the pope at all. The "seats which sit in judgment upon the house of David" are the vicars of Christ, the priests, in whom Christ, the true king, prince and president of his people, sits. Although hidden, Luther says, Christ is eminently and immediately present in the seats of his bishops and priests.[68] In 1519, however, this same interpretation of Ps. 122:5 is used by Luther against John Eck in the Leipzig Debate to reject the monarchy of the pope in the church. Luther maintains that Christ cannot be forced outside the church militant into the church triumphant in heaven only to be replaced in the earthly church by the monarchy of the pope. Rather, the church militant is a kingdom of faith in which Christ its head is present, though hidden, according to Ps. 122:5: "There thrones for judgment were set, the thrones of the house of David." "There are many seats namely in which the one Christ sits. We see the seats, but not the sitter or the king."[69]

Again, in 1520, Luther presses the argument of Christ's presence in the militant church against the pope. In his *Open Letter to Pope Leo X*

Luther ridicules the idea that the pope is the vicar of Christ since this title describes all too well the absence of Christ from his church:

> See how different Christ is from his successors, although they all would wish to be his vicars. I fear that most of them have been too literally his vicars. A man is a vicar only when his superior is absent. If the pope rules while Christ is absent and Christ does not dwell in his heart, what else is he but a vicar of Christ? What is the church under such a vicar but a mass of people without Christ? Indeed, what is such a vicar but an Antichrist and an idol? How much more properly did the apostles call themselves servants of the present Christ and not vicars of an absent Christ?[70]

The absence of specific references to the papacy prior to 1517 hardly supports a view that Luther held inordinately strong feelings in favor of papal authority. The ease with which Luther could use his early theology to criticize papal authority in 1519 and 1520 raises questions about the depth of any positive feelings which he might have held.

Before 1517, Luther spent his academic life lecturing and preaching on the Bible, not writing ecclesiological treatises or taking stands on the relative authority of pope and council. Insights into his thinking must be gained indirectly from his exegesis, his sermons, and from the recollections of his early years. Although these works do not allow one to pin on Luther a papalist or a conciliarist label, they do yield strong clues that Luther's feelings about the papacy were at best ambivalent. First, the hindsights, when adjusted for perspective, document the presence of negative feelings about the Roman hierarchy and teachings of the church. Second, numerous passages criticize directly contemporary prelates and indirectly, perhaps, the papacy itself, especially in relation to an issue dear to Luther's own scrupulous conscience: the power of the keys. Third, these early works establish the feeding of the faithful with the word of God as the criterion for claiming legitimate authority in the church. This criterion is a key building block in Luther's construction of a new ecclesiology.

The pope was not a dominant figure in that ecclesiology; perhaps he was more ignored than intentionally excluded. Ambivalent feelings about a subject do result in lack of attention to it until one is forced to face the matter head-on. Perhaps that is what Luther meant when he said later that, while he was engaged in teaching and preaching, the papacy crossed his path.[71] If so, the Reformation had begun, even if unintentionally, in the mind of Luther himself.

21

2 | PROTEST
October 1517 to June 1518

While all the rest remained spectators and let me alone
take the risks, I was neither happy, confident nor certain.
For then I was ignorant of many things which I now
know. I had no idea what indulgences were, but after all
the whole papacy did not know anything about them.
They were venerated only because of custom and usage.
Therefore, I did not debate in order to abolish them; but,
since I knew perfectly well what they were not, I wanted
to learn what in fact they were. And since the dead and
mute masters, namely the books of the theologians and
jurists, were not satisfying me, I decided to consult the
living and to listen to the church of God itself, so that if
organs of the Holy Spirit were left anywhere, they would
have mercy on me and, also for the common good, make
me more certain about indulgences!

—Luther, 1538
(WA 39/I, 6.22–31)

CHRONOLOGY

1514	March 9	Albert of Brandenburg elected archbishop of Mainz
1515	March 31	Pope Leo X grants Albert authority to offer the St. Peter's indulgence in his territories
1517	January 22	John Tetzel, O. P., enters the service of Albert as subcommissary for the St. Peter's indulgence in the province of Magdeburg
	February 24	Luther criticizes indulgences in a sermon on Matt. 11:25 ff.
	April	Tetzel in Jüterbog
	September 4	Luther: *Disputation against Scholastic Theology*
	October 31	Luther invites a debate over indulgences with his *Ninety-five Theses*

22

1517	December 13	Albert reports he has sent the *Theses* to Rome with a denunciation of Luther
1518	January 20	Tetzel defends himself with theses authored by Wimpina at Frankfurt on the Oder
	February 13	Luther writes to Bishop Jerome of Brandenburg explaining the nature and purpose of his *Theses*
	February 15	Luther announces he will publish explanations of his *Theses*
	Mid-March	Tetzel-Wimpina theses are seized and burned by students in Wittenberg Luther: *A Sermon on Indulgence and Grace*
	March 24	Luther reports he has seen the *Obelisci* of John Eck; responds shortly thereafter with his *Asterisci*
	March	Luther concludes his lectures on Hebrews
	April	Tetzel: *Rebuttal of a Presumptuous Sermon Containing Twenty Erroneous Articles on Papal Indulgence and Grace Which Is Necessary for All Faithful Christians to Know—by Brother John Tetzel, Inquisitor of the Order of Preachers*
	April 9– May 15	Luther defends theses on philosophy and theology at a chapter meeting of Augustinians in Heidelberg
	Late April or Early May	Tetzel issues a second set of fifty theses dealing with papal authority
	May	Karlstadt issues 380 theses against Tetzel and Eck
	May 30	Luther dedicates the *Explanations of the Ninety-five Theses* to Pope Leo and writes a letter to Staupitz requesting him to forward the *Explanations* to Leo
	June	Luther: *A Defense of the Sermon Concerning Papal Indulgence and Grace*

INDULGENCES

In the early sixteenth century, a debate over the power of indulgences did not have to escalate into a controversy over papal authority. Strictly speaking, indulgences had to do with the sacrament of penance, and only with one part of that: the works of satisfaction which the penitent sinner was required to perform in order to pay the penalty of sin. Medieval theologians distinguished between the guilt incurred by sin and the penalty that had to be paid, since no sin could go unpunished. When the guilt was forgiven by God through the absolution of the priest, the penalty of eternal condemnation was commuted into works of satisfaction which the priest then imposed upon the repentant sinner according to the seriousness of the sin committed. An indulgence was the additional prerogative of the church to release penitents from these works of satisfaction. Since the thirteenth century, the power to permit such a relaxation or "indulgence" of the penitential obligation was derived from the "treasure of the church." This treasure contained the accumulated merits of Christ and the saints which, since they were superfluous for those who had originally acquired them, stood available for ordinary sinners in the church. An indulgence applied these merits to the penitent sinner and canceled the debt he would otherwise be obliged to pay off with works of satisfaction.[1]

As frequently happens, the practice of the church outran its original theological justification. Four developments in the late Middle Ages made indulgences a sensitive issue in the church and the subject of frequent criticism. The first development was the rise of the so-called full or plenary indulgence. Originally, indulgences were granted for the relaxation of specific penalties and corresponded in duration to the sentence imposed by these penalties. For example, an indulgence of 100 days canceled an ecclesiastical penalty that would have required 100 days of satisfaction to pay. In the year 1095, however, Pope Urban II granted a full or plenary indulgence to all those who participated in the first crusade for religious reasons. This indulgence guaranteed both the cancellation of all temporal penalties imposed by the church and the forgiveness of all sins. Such plenary indulgences became common during the late Middle Ages, especially after they were granted for pilgrimages to Rome during the jubilee years proclaimed by the pope. It also became customary for these plenary indulgences to release one from the guilt as well as from the penalty of sin.

Second, indulgences became the prerogative of the popes. Thomas Aquinas taught that the power of granting indulgences resided completely in the pope "because he is able to do as he wishes provided that a legitimate reason exists."[2] Both the custom of granting plenary indulgences and specific papal rulings on indulgences anchored this practice firmly in the Roman curia. For example, in 1343 Pope Clement VI

24

made the concept of the treasure of the church an official dogma. Luther's selection of indulgences rather than another practice as the target of his first public protest increased the chance of conflict with the papacy.

Two additional developments made the practice of indulgences both popular and more subject to abuse. The extension of indulgences to souls in purgatory provided relief for deceased Christians who were still paying the penalty of their sins after death. It also provided an additional market for indulgences among their survivors. Furthermore, letters of indulgence could be obtained by the contribution of money to a specific cause of the church. Instead of going on a crusade, one could stay at home, help finance the cause, and thus become eligible for an indulgence. The effects which these developments had on the people and on the penitential practice of the church are not difficult to estimate. The necessity of true contrition for one's sin could easily be replaced by the attitude that forgiveness of sin was available for purchase.

All the negative features of the indulgence practice came to a head in the particular indulgence that sparked Luther's protest in the *Ninety-five Theses*. On March 31, 1515, Pope Leo X authorized Archbishop Albert of Mainz to sell a plenary indulgence in his provinces of Germany. The proceeds from this indulgence were designated for the construction of the new Basilica of St. Peter in Rome. The proceeds were also being used to pay off debts which Albert had incurred to the pope for his elevation to the Archbishopric of Mainz and for papal permission to hold simultaneously two additional ecclesiastical offices. Although Luther did not know about this private arrangement between Pope Leo and Albert when he wrote the *Ninety-five Theses*,[3] the scandalous details are a good illustration of the way in which the indulgence practice had become a flexible fund-raising device of the church.

What irritated Luther were the claims being made for this particular indulgence and the effects that these claims had on the people who came to him for confession. These claims were contained in an instruction manual called the *Summary Instruction*,[4] which Albert had prepared for the preachers who would promote his indulgence. The heart of the *Instruction* consisted of four principal benefits to be enjoyed through the acquisition of the indulgence. The first benefit entailed the complete remission of all sins both here and in purgatory.[5] The second benefit was the confessional letter and all the privileges it granted, such as the right to select one's confessor and to receive from him full remission of sins at any time when death might be imminent. This second benefit retained its power even beyond the eight-year period of the indulgence's validity.[6] The third principal benefit was participation in all the "goods" of the church for oneself and one's deceased parents. By this means one could share in whatever benefits were produced by the prayers, almsgiving, fasting, and pilgrimages that were performed anywhere in the universal church.[7] Finally, the *Instruction* again promised full remission of sins for souls in purgatory when an indulgence was acquired for them. The persons obtaining the indulgence need not themselves give evidence of contrition or go to confession. Preachers should be as diligent as possible in explaining this benefit so that both departed souls and the building of St. Peter's Basilica could be promoted as quickly as possible.[8]

The Franciscans, who were normally responsible for the sale of the St. Peter's indulgence, declined Albert's invitation to work for him in Germany; hence, John Tetzel, a Dominican and an experienced indulgence preacher, was chosen by Albert as his subcommissary.[9] Tetzel began to sell the indulgence early in 1517, and by April he had arrived in Jüterbog, just outside the territory of Electoral Saxony. The preaching of the St. Peter's indulgence was forbidden in Saxony because the Elector Frederick was afraid that his own indulgence business, based on his massive relic collection at the Chapter of All Saints in Wittenberg, would suffer from the competition. But nothing could prevent the people of Wittenberg from crossing the border to Jüterbog, purchasing the indulgence letters from Tetzel, and bringing them back to their confessors in Wittenberg. One of these confessors was the university professor and Augustinian monk, Martin Luther.

THE NINETY-FIVE THESES

In 1541 Luther recalls that, upon discovering that many Wittenbergers were going to Jüterbog and Zerbst to purchase the St. Peter's indulgence, he began to preach very gently that they could do something better and more reliable than acquire indulgences.[10] He notes accurately that he had already criticized indulgences in his preaching and had thereby earned the disfavor of the Elector Frederick who, of course, was proud of his relic collection and wanted to see it prosper.[11] In these sermons Luther had expressed his doubts about indulgences, and some of these doubts would reappear in the *Ninety-five Theses*. He deplored the false understanding of penance and contrition taught by the indulgence preachers, but he asserted that the intention of the pope was right and true and even the words of the preachers were true in some sense.[12]

The rumors that he heard about Tetzel's preaching together with the *Summary Instruction* exacerbated his irritation to the point that Luther took stronger action. Both of these sources confirmed Luther's fears that the people were being sold indulgences under false pretexts and that their salvation was in danger. In the letter he wrote to Albert of Mainz on October 31, 1517, Luther admitted that he could not directly accuse the preachers, since he had not heard their sermons. Among the false notions which the people derived from them, however, were the following misguided presumptions: the purchase of an indulgence letter would assure one of salvation; in the words of the famous rhyme, "as soon as the coin in the coffer rings, the soul from purgatory springs"; there was no sin so great—not even the rape of the mother of God—that it could not be forgiven through these indulgences; finally, these indulgences released one from all punishment and guilt.[13]

Luther summed up his concern when he told Albert that souls committed to his care were being led straight to death.[14] Luther said he had put off writing for a long time; but his duty to the archbishop and now the peril to which the faithful were being exposed made it imperative to inform Albert of what was happening.[15] In these words Luther revealed the real motivation that led him to take such a bold step. As a solitary Augustinian monk, though a doctor of theology, he was exhibiting considerable temerity by writing directly to Albert.[16] Part of Luther's temerity was due to his natural assertiveness, which became more pronounced in the struggle that followed. Nevertheless, his heart probably did quake within him[17] as, conscious of his unimportance, he addressed this polite but pointed letter to Albert. The genuine conviction that the people were perishing led Luther to extend the protest which up to now he had confined to lectern and pulpit.

In his letter, Luther makes two points that demonstrate his solicitude is grounded in theological convictions. First, it is not possible to be secure about one's salvation either through an official episcopal act or through the grace which God infuses into the soul. If the Lord himself proclaims vigorously the difficulty of being saved, how can this be claimed for indulgences which only remit a penalty for sin imposed by the church?[18] Second, works of love and devotion are infinitely more valuable than indulgences, but they are discouraged by the preaching of indulgences. The first and only duty of bishops is to see that the people learn the gospel and the love of Christ. Jesus never ordered the preaching of indulgences, but he did forcefully command the proclamation of the gospel. How great an abomination and danger to the bishop, therefore, if the gospel is silenced and only the clamor of indulgences is permitted to reach his people. Albert appears to care more for indulgences than for the gospel![19]

Both the danger of false security and the indispensability of the word of God were themes that had echoes in Luther's works and formed key elements in his early theology. Here they converge to undergird a crucial ecclesiological step which Luther takes in theory and in practice. In theory, Luther states clearly that the most important duty of a bishop is to see that his people learn the gospel and the love of Christ. This statement underscores the centrality of the word in the church which had become a prominent theme in his ecclesiology. In practice, Luther now directly requests the withdrawal of a major obstacle to the preaching of that word. He asks Albert to withdraw his *Instruction* from circulation and to give the preachers another guide before someone else forces the archbishop to it by writing against the *Instruction*.[20] Luther brings the element of pastoral duty in his early ecclesiology to bear on a specific abuse in the church. The proper duty of the church's leaders is to feed the people with the word of God, and indulgences are preventing them from fulfilling that duty.

With his letter Luther enclosed ninety-five theses in order to show how debatable Albert's view of indulgences was, even though the preachers were claiming absolute authority for it.[21] Whether Luther only mailed the theses to Albert and to some of his acquaintances or also nailed them to the door of the Castle Church in Wittenberg has been hotly debated. Luther reports only that he published the theses and mailed them privately to the best scholars; Melanchthon claims that Luther had the theses posted on the church door.[22] Since the door of the church served as the bulletin board for university events including academic debates, the purpose of the theses remains the same in either case: to provide the basis for a theological debate over the nature and effects of indulgences. Luther later assured Pope Leo X that the theses were not doctrines or dogmas, but propositions he had formulated enigmatically to spark debate.[23] As he reexamined the theses in his *Explanations*, Luther distinguished those theses which he asserted from those which were still up for discussion and even decided that he had to reject a large part of one thesis.[24]

In spite of the formally tentative nature of the theses, Ernst Kähler appropriately emphasizes their forceful character.[25] The theses have a double thrust. In the first place, Luther directly challenges both Albert's *Instruction* and the claims of indulgence preachers such as Tetzel which he had heard from the people. For example, Luther carefully distinguishes between the penalty and the guilt of sin and the pope's right to remit in each case (Th. 5–6). He also questions the application of indulgences to purgatory (Th. 8, 20), since the pope's power to impose and to remit penalties does not extend that far. To the claim that the soul flies out of purgatory as soon as the money clinks in the chest,[26] Luther replies that indeed grace and avarice are increased, but the request of the church that the soul be released remains in God's hands alone (Th. 27–28). Those who teach that persons about to purchase indulgences need not be contrite do not teach Christian doctrine (Th. 35). Blessed is one who guards against the lust and license of the indulgence preachers (Th. 72), especially when they claim that papal indulgences are so great that they forgive even the sin of raping the mother of God (Th. 75), that St. Peter could not grant greater graces if he were alive (Th. 77), or that the cross erected by the indulgence preacher is equal to the cross of Christ (Th. 79). Luther's warning to Albert is broadened in Thesis 80: "The bishops, curates and theologians who permit such talk to be spread among the people should be made to answer for it."

In the second place, Luther sets forth his view of penance and the Christian life in terms that do not sound at all tentative. From the beginning, when he interprets the command of Jesus to repent as that inner repentance which never ceases (Th. 1–4), Luther emphasizes the seriousness and duration of sin that he stressed in his *Lectures on Romans* (1515–1516). The consequences for indulgences are stated with equal clarity. It is impossible for even the most learned theologians to extol the benefits of indulgences and the truth of contrition simultaneously. They obviously work at cross purposes. True contrition loves and seeks out punishment whereas indulgences relax punishment and cause it to be hated (Th. 39–40). Writing specifically against the first and third principal benefits of the St. Peter's indulgence cited in Albert's *Instruction*, Luther maintains that every Christian who is truly contrite has full remission of guilt and punishment even without indulgence letters. Furthermore, every true Christian, whether living or dead, shares in all the goods of Christ and the church apart from the acquisition of indulgence letters (Th. 36–37). Against the admonition of the *Instruction* that other sermons not conflict with the preaching of indulgences,[27] Luther asserts that whoever commands this is an enemy of Christ and of the pope. The pope would wish for the gospel to be proclaimed with a hundred times more pomp and ceremony than indulgences (Th. 53–55). The true treasure of the church is the holy gospel of the glory and grace of God, not the merits of Christ and the saints (Th. 62). Christians are to be taught to follow their head, Christ, through pains, death, and hell, and they should be more confident of entering heaven through many tribulations than through the security of peace (Th. 94–95).

Although Luther's primary opponent in the *Ninety-five Theses* remained the indulgence preachers and commissaries, he was well aware that the St. Peter's indulgence was a papal indulgence sanctioned by the bull that Leo X had issued on March 31, 1515. In 1520 Luther said that he had seen this bull "against which he had first taken action in this matter" (of indulgences).[28] Whether or not Luther had seen the bull by 1517, he was well aware of its existence from the references to it in Albert's *Instruction*, and he knew that Albert based much of the *Instruction* on its authority. It has been argued, therefore, that next to indulgences "the pope is the second great theme of the theses."[29]

Luther treats the theme of the papacy from two perspectives. First, he deals with the proper limits of papal authority in granting indulgences according to the laws of the church. The pope can grant indulgences only for those penalties he has imposed by the rules of the church (Th. 5, 20). Nor does his authority extend to souls in purgatory; the pope can only apply the intercession of the church to them (Th. 26). These restrictions on papal authority were not unknown in the late Middle Ages even though they were seldom adhered to in practice, as Albert's *Instruction* testifies.

Second, Luther deals with the personal intention of the pope. He attempts to uphold what he says would be the genuine desire of the pope against the distortion created by the preachers. Christians should be taught that if the pope were aware of the excessive demands of the indulgence preachers, he would rather see St. Peter's Basilica disintegrate than have it built with the skin, flesh, and bones of his sheep (Th. 50). The pope would also prefer that St. Peter's be sold and that the proceeds be distributed to those from whom the preachers now solicit contributions (Th. 57). Just as the pope justly thunders against those who contrive to hinder the sale of indulgences,[30] he intends to lash out even more against those who under the pretext of indulgences contrive to cheapen holy love and truth (Th. 73–74). Finally, Luther claims that the licentious preaching of indulgences makes it difficult even for learned men to save the reputation of the pope from the slander and shrewd questions of the laity (Th. 81). For example, why doesn't the pope empty purgatory for the sake of holy love and of the souls themselves, rather than for the puny reason of raising money to build a church (Th. 82)? Or why doesn't the pope, rich as the legendary Croesus, build the church with his own money rather than with the money of believers (Th. 86)? To suppress these questions without giving good reasons in reply is to expose the pope and the church to the ridicule of their enemies and to make Christians unhappy (Th. 90). If, therefore, indulgences were preached according to the spirit and intention of the pope, all these problems would be resolved (Th. 91).

Nowhere in these remarks did Luther indicate that he meant to attack the pope in the sense of a frontal assault. In fact, he said later that, when his opponents could not refute his position on indulgences, they pretended that he had attacked papal authority.[31] Luther was not attacking; rather, he was protesting and testing. By recalling the limits on papal authority according to canon law, he was protesting the ignoring of this law and testing the intention of the church to abide by its own rules. By contrasting the pope with the indulgence preachers, Luther was protesting the false claims of the preachers and testing the intention of the pope himself.

This testing was an outgrowth of Luther's ambivalence about the papacy and a reexamination of his own earlier assertion that the intention of the pope was true.[32] Luther now knew that Albert's *Instruction* specifically named Leo's bull of 1515 as the source of the four principal benefits which were promised through the St. Peter's indulgence[33] and which Luther rejected in the *Theses*. According to his remarks in 1520, however, Luther thought that the bull contained falsifications[34] and did not, perhaps, reflect the pope's true thinking on indulgences. Although Luther was not naive about the involvement of Leo X at this point, he was not sarcastically attacking that involvement with his contrast between the pope and the indulgence preachers. At most he was using irony and hyperbole to test the pope's true intentions and to dramatize his concern for the misguided people.

Even though the pope is the "second great theme of the theses," he is still only the second. Luther is concerned with the pope only because indulgences, and in particular the St. Peter's indulgence, were primarily the prerogative of the popes. Luther's first concern is with the effect of indulgences on the people who are being led to buy them. Kähler is correct, therefore, in calling the *Theses* an "appeal"[35]—not, of course, directly to the people, because the *Theses* were written in Latin and prepared for academic debate, but to scholars and church leaders to restore to the people the right perspective of indulgences. Theses 42 through 51, with their introductory words "Christians are to be taught . . . ," reveal more than any others the real purpose of the *Theses*. Christians should be taught that works of charity are better than indulgences, and even the pope himself would rather have the prayers than the money of the people (Th. 48). He would rather see St. Peter's Basilica burn to the ground or be sold than have it built with the kind of sacrifices the preachers were expecting from the people (Th. 50–51).

The *Ninety-five Theses* constitute a crucial ecclesiological step forward for Luther. By asking Albert to curb the excesses of the indulgence preachers and by asking scholars to debate even the extent of papal power in granting indulgences, Luther appealed to responsible parties in the hierarchy of the church to remove a specific threat to the faith of the people. The protest against the indulgence preachers delivered to Albert was direct and would receive a direct reply. The testing of the pope, which revealed the persistence of Luther's ambivalent feelings about the pastoral sensitivity of the pope, was indirect and ironically expressed. This indirect method of testing the pope's true intentions would not be appreciated with equal subtlety by Luther's readers.

FIRST REACTIONS

The *Ninety-five Theses* did not find the reception that Luther intended. The various persons who responded to them did in fact construe them as an attack upon the papacy. This is illustrated by a legend that arose probably after 1600, concerning a dream which Frederick the Wise is supposed to have had on October 31, 1517. The legend was portrayed in a cartoon[36] which shows Luther writing the *Ninety-five Theses* on the door of the Castle Church in Wittenberg. The quill pen he uses extends far in the distance to the city of Rome, where it has knocked the papal tiara off the head of the pope. The German princes are shown running toward the pen and trying to break it. According to the legend, Frederick the Wise asks Luther why the pen is so strong. Luther replies that the feather comes from a hundred-year-old Bohemian goose and receives its strength from the soul of the goose. He is referring to a prophecy attributed to John Hus which Luther later applied to himself: "Today you may burn this goose (= Hus) but after one hundred years will come a swan whose song you will be unable to silence."[37] True to the legend, the cartoon depicts in the background the burning of John Hus and Jerome of Prague at Constance in 1415, while in the foreground a swan (singing?) watches Luther write.

Although this legend arose much later, it helps to explain why Luther's contemporaries could jump to the conclusion that his criticism of a papal indulgence was an attack on the papacy itself. John Hus had attacked papal indulgences a century earlier, and the memory of his condemnation was still very much alive in Saxony, especially in Leipzig where the German masters had immigrated after they were ejected from the University of Prague by the supporters of Hus. In opposition to Luther's Thesis 37, John Eck in early 1518 raised the specter of Hus by labeling the implications of Luther's position "Bohemian poison."[38] Eck would also push this identification between Luther and Hus at Leipzig a year later.

Eck's reaction was symptomatic of the hostile reception the *Theses* received. Albert's *Instruction* had already threatened persons who hindered the sale of the St. Peter's indulgence with serious ecclesiastical censures.[39] Accordingly, Albert took steps to apply these censures. He sent Luther's *Theses* to the theological faculty of his territorial university at Mainz and requested an evaluation. On December 17, 1517, the university replied to Albert that some of Luther's *Theses* limited the power of the pope in the matter of indulgences and therefore it could not deliver a verdict since canon law allowed no one to judge or dispute the question of papal power. It also recommended that the *Theses* be sent to Rome to be tested by the "source of power and wisdom," keeping in mind the admonition of canon law "that the statute of the pope be regarded as if it came from the mouth of God or of St. Peter himself."[40] Albert, however, did not wait to receive this response. He had already sent the *Theses* and other documents to the pope with a note that the Wittenberg monk was spreading "new teachings" among the people. Thus, the first official reaction to Luther's *Theses* judged them to be an affront to papal authority, and by early 1518 they were in the hands of the pope.[41]

By early 1518, copies of Luther's *Theses* were also in the hands of at least a dozen persons, friends and potential foes alike.[42] Among the latter was John Tetzel, who took up Luther's challenge by defending 106 theses at a meeting of the Saxon Dominicans which began on January 20, 1518, at Frankfurt on the Oder. These theses were written by Conrad Wimpina, a professor of theology at the University of Frankfurt. Wimpina's authorship was not due to Tetzel's ignorance or inability, as has been charged. It was common practice in university debates for theses to be written and defended by different persons.[43] The theses attempted to refute Luther's positions on indulgences; they designated all his statements as erroneous and claimed all the power for papal indulgences which Luther had questioned.

In so doing, the theses naturally disputed the limit Luther had placed on the pope's power in granting indulgences. For example, Tetzel claimed that the pope did have power to remit all satisfactions and not only those imposed by himself, that a papal indulgence released persons from all penalties, and that the pope's authority to remit satisfactions to souls in purgatory was valid, though it did not take place through the power of the keys but by means of interceding for souls as Luther had emphasized.[44] More important, Tetzel rejected Luther's attempt to dissociate the intention of the pope from the practice of indulgence preachers. In response to Luther's assertion that the preachers were enemies of Christ and of the pope if they prohibited the preaching of the word of God in order that indulgences could be proclaimed, Tetzel contended that a bishop had the right to impose silence on other preachers if he himself wished to preach. Therefore, it was the vilest mistake to call the pope an enemy of the cross if he wished to have his indulgence preached under the same right.[45] Tetzel blamed Luther for trying to flatter the pope, after having insulted him in prior theses, when Luther accused the indulgence preachers of failing to safeguard reverence for the pope against the embarrassing questions of the laity.[46]

Tetzel and Wimpina understood Luther's irony to be intentional sarcasm and construed the theses to be antipapal. The debate between Tetzel and Luther did not stop there, however. The Tetzel-Wimpina theses were brought in mid-March to Wittenberg, where students seized copies and burned them in the marketplace. Luther disapproved of this demonstration, and several days later he published in German A Sermon on Indulgence and Grace, which was designed to explain his position on indulgences in a way better suited for public consumption than the Ninety-five Theses had been. Luther did not mention papal authority in the treatise but concentrated on refuting the opinions of the "new" scholastic doctors concerning the efficacy of indulgences: "I do not have any doubt about these points and they are sufficiently grounded in Scripture. Therefore, you also should not have doubts about them and let the scholastic doctors be scholastics; all of them together with their opinions are not enough to give solid ground for one sermon."[47]

In April 1518, Tetzel replied to Luther's sermon with a treatise of his own explicitly entitled *Rebuttal of a Presumptuous Sermon Containing Twenty Erroneous Articles on Papal Indulgence and Grace Which Is Necessary for All Faithful Christians to Know—by Brother John Tetzel, Inquisitor of the Order of Preachers.* By identifying the indulgence in question as a papal indulgence and himself as "inquisitor," Tetzel indicates the point on which he will concentrate in his rebuttal. The claims made for indulgences are to be accepted as true because the Roman Church makes these claims and grants indulgences on the basis of these claims. For example, Luther prefers not to believe that indulgences release souls from purgatory since the church has not made such a ruling.[48] Tetzel replies that the holy Roman Church nevertheless supports this view by erecting altars and chapels in Rome at which the pope does in fact grant such indulgences. The pope and the Roman Church would not permit this to be done unless it was well founded, that is, unless the pope and the papal office did not err in matters pertaining to faith—which indulgences are. Therefore, whoever does not believe that the pope can grant indulgences to both the living and the dead also does not believe that the pope has received from Christ the fullness of power over the faithful.[49] Furthermore, said Tetzel, Luther's teaching would undermine all authority in the church, including that of the pope, and would result in great danger for souls in Christendom because everyone would believe what he or she pleased.[50] Even Tetzel possessed a concept of pastoral duty, although it was based on a formal claim of authority rather than on the content of the church's teaching.

But Tetzel did not stop here. In a second set of fifty theses published in late April or early May 1518 he explicitly accused Luther of attacking the authority of the papacy.[51] Each of the theses begins with the phrase, taken from Luther's Theses 42 through 51, "Christians are to be taught." In these theses, Tetzel states the claims of papal superiority and infallibility in the strongest possible terms. Christians are to be taught that, since papal power is supreme and instituted by God alone, it can be restricted or amplified only by God (Th. 1). Furthermore, in matters concerning faith, only the pope has the power of determination, and he alone can interpret authoritatively the sense of Scripture (Th. 4). The church also holds many catholic truths which are not found verbatim in Scripture, and Christians should reckon to these all observances in matters of faith defined by the apostolic see (Th. 16 and 18). Tetzel directs his warning not only against those who teach contrary to papal authority, but he charges with heresy those who intentionally spread their teachings among the people and those who willingly listen to such teachings.

By this time, Luther was aware that in Rome he was under suspicion of heresy. At the end of his *Sermon* he had noted that some people wanted to label him a heretic because the truth about indulgences was bad for business. He did not take it too seriously, however, since his detractors were a few fuzzy brains who had never smelled the Bible, read Christian teachers, or understood their own teachers. If they had, they would have known that they should not slander anyone who had not been heard or proven wrong.[52] In his response to Tetzel's *Rebuttal*, published in June 1518, Luther reminded Tetzel that he knew what went on in Rome since he himself had read some masses there for souls in purgatory. But, in a dangerous matter such as indulgences, a Christian writer should support every position with Scripture, canon law, or appropriate reasons, not with statements that any bumpkin could give, such as that "it is done in Rome" or that "the pope allowed it."[53] Only if the church made a firm decision would he believe that indulgences release souls from purgatory. Until then, Luther said he would keep his hands off the indulgence abuse so that he would not deceive himself or other poor souls.[54]

The main line of Luther's argument is still clear in this final rejoinder to Tetzel. The nature and effect of indulgences are debatable as long as the church renders no clear decision. Since Christians are easily deceived into believing that indulgences are more valuable than repentance and good works, it is better not to recommend them to the people regardless of the church's support of them. Luther's main concern is with the effect of the indulgence traffic on the people, just as it was in his letter to Albert and in his *Theses*. Tetzel, on the other hand, expresses concern about the effect of questioning a practice that theologians and the pope himself have endorsed.[55] Nonsense, replies Luther. Eck's claim that his attack on indulgences undermines the authority of the church and the faith of the people is a false alarm, equivalent to crying out that the sky will fall. To make such a claim is to show that self-interest and not love for the people is the main motivation behind indulgences.[56]

Tetzel insisted that Luther bring his *Sermon* to the attention of the pope, but Luther says he can smell Tetzel's real purpose; before long, says Luther, he will submit his case to the pope, perhaps more than Tetzel would like. Now is not the time to burden the pope with unnecessary sermons, much less with plain texts of Scripture which are preached and understood uniformly in all of Christendom.[57] Luther knows that Tetzel wants to get him in trouble with the pope, but he apparently has no qualms about submitting his case in due time. This is borne out by his comments on Tetzel's second set of fifty theses. Luther first puts them down by saying that sun and moon marvel at the great light of their wisdom. But then he affirms that he holds most of them to be true. He only wishes that in place of "Christians are to be taught" Tetzel had written "sellers of indulgences and inquisitors of heresy are to be taught."[58]

SEARCHING FOR CONSENSUS

Luther refused to take seriously Tetzel's accusation that he was attacking papal authority. He was aware that he was contradicting the teaching of Thomas Aquinas and other medieval theologians, but there was no reason for him to equate this theological disagreement with an attack on the papacy. Luther had come out strongly against the teaching of the medieval nominalist theologians on sin and grace in his lectures on Romans and again in his *Disputation against Scholastic Theology* (1517). The entire program of curricular reform at the University of Wittenberg was shaped around the replacement of an Aristotelian-based theology with the study of the Bible, biblical languages, and the church fathers. This reform had been underway for some time in Wittenberg[59] and no one had thought to challenge it as an attack on the papacy. When the Dominicans introduced Thomas and the scholastic theologians as authorities on indulgences, Luther regarded the issue as another encounter between the theology of the schoolmen on the one side and the Wittenberg theology of Scripture and the church fathers on the other. Coupling this theological debate with his concern for the exploitation of the people through indulgences, Luther insisted that the salvation of the people was far more directly at stake than the authority of the pope. In the first half of 1518, Luther repeatedly asserted that the attempt of Tetzel and others to shift the ground of the debate to papal authority was only a ploy to conceal the weakness of their own arguments in favor of the indulgence preachers.[60]

The reaction of Luther's colleague, Karlstadt, to Tetzel's theses lends credence to Luther's assertion that his protest against indulgences did not mean that he was attacking the pope. On May 9, 1518, Karlstadt completed 380 theses in reply to both sets of theses produced by Tetzel-Wimpina and to the *Obelisci* of John Eck. Eck had contacts with the circle of humanists in Nuremberg and had recently made the acquaintance of Luther through correspondence encouraged by a prominent member of the circle, Christoph Scheurl. Scheurl sent Eck a copy of Luther's theses; and a copy of Eck's response, intended privately for the Bishop of Eichstätt, reached Luther through his friend and fellow Augustinian in Nuremberg, Wenceslaus Link.[61] Luther was surprised by the sharpness of Eck's rebuttal. Eck applied to Luther's theses such adjectives as "false," "frivolous," and "impudent." He accused Luther of subverting the entire ecclesiastical hierarchy and of showing irreverence toward the pope. More volatile was Eck's aside, already mentioned, that one of Luther's theses was tantamount to pouring out "Bohemian poison," a remark which associated Luther with the heresy of John Hus.[62]

Before Luther could reply to Eck, and without Luther's knowledge, Karlstadt rushed his theses onto paper and announced an academic debate. In addition to treating the immediate issue of penance and indulgences, Karlstadt confronted the more serious question of ecclesiastical authority which both Tetzel and Eck had raised.[63] Karlstadt had already handled this question in a disputation in 1516 in Rome, where he had earned a doctorate in civil and canon law. At that time, before the outbreak of the indulgence controversy, Karlstadt opposed the infallibility of church councils by using the argument of the canon lawyer, Panormitanus (Nikolaus de Tudeschis, *d.* 1445), that the judgment of an individual Christian in matters of faith, when based on Scripture, takes precedence over all other church authorities. Naturally, this argument could be employed just as well against the infallibility of the pope as against the authority of a council.

In May 1518, however, as in 1516 at Rome, Karlstadt did not draw this conclusion in spite of the claims of Tetzel-Wimpina and Eck for papal authority. Instead, Karlstadt adhered to the traditional canonistic position that the objective authority of Scripture only supersedes that of the pope in the single instance when a pope has fallen into heresy and thus lost all authority. Although both Luther and Karlstadt were challenging the understanding of penance and indulgences set forth by Tetzel and Eck, neither had any intention of accusing the pope of heresy. In fact, later in his theses, Karlstadt even agreed with Tetzel that the interpretation of Scripture belonged to the prerogatives of the pope in his "fullness of power." Like Luther, Karlstadt attacked only the flatterers of the pope, implying that in their ignorance of canon law they would uphold the pope even when he contradicted Scripture.

Owing to his special positions as papal viscount[64] and as archdeacon of the Chapter of All Saints in Wittenberg, Karlstadt had a more conservative attitude than Luther toward indulgences.[65] Nevertheless, the theses of Karlstadt in May 1518 help to explain how Luther could attack the theological and canonistic basis of indulgences while simultaneously professing loyalty to the pope and the willingness to subject his opinions in the *Ninety-five Theses* to a papal judgment. This parallel is instructive for the examination of Luther's *Explanations of the Ninety-five Theses*, which he had finished writing by March 5, 1518, but which were not published until August of the same year.

In the *Explanations* Luther attempts to clarify his stance in relation to the papacy by distinguishing between the person and the office of the pope. Luther makes this distinction in reference to his twenty-sixth thesis, which proposes that the pope does not possess the power of the keys over souls in purgatory. Luther first supports his position by referring to papal decrees in canon law and by stressing the word of Christ: "Whatever you loose *on earth*" (Matt. 16:19, emphasis added). Then he answers the objections to his position that he has heard. First, he says, it is well known that a pope granted remission of sin after death to a certain Parisian master who taught that the pope had power over purgatory. The pope seemed to approve the master's teaching by this action. In reply, Luther makes the bold assertion that it does not matter to him what pleases or displeases the highest pontiff. "He is a man like all others. Many popes have been pleased not only by errors and vices but even by monstrosities. I listen to the pope as pope, i.e., when he speaks in and according to the canons, or when he makes a decision in accordance with a council. I do not listen to him, however, when he speaks merely his own opinion; otherwise, I might be forced to say with those who know Christ only poorly that the horrible murders committed by Julius II against Christian people were really benefits conferred on the sheep of Christ by a devoted pastor."[66] What at first sounds like impudence on Luther's part is in reality an attempt to take the pope seriously: listening to the pope's own words in papal decrees as opposed to what Tetzel and others claimed about the pope on the basis of Albert's *Instruction* and of rumors such as the one which Luther here recounts.[67]

In the next objection to his thesis, Luther is forced to confront a papal decree which seems to contradict his position. According to a bull of Sixtus IV in 1476, the pope could extend the effect of indulgences to purgatory by interceding for souls instead of directly applying to them the judicial power granted to him by the canons. Sixtus IV was also supposed to have decided that this "mode of intercession" did not detract from the power of indulgences.[68] Luther responds that the latter interpretation would be a new article of faith, and it is not the pope's prerogative, but the right of a universal council, to establish such articles. Otherwise, he says, since the pope is a man who can err in faith and morals, the faith of the whole church would constantly be in danger if it were mandatory to affirm whatever seemed pleasing to the pope. Furthermore, says Luther, even if the pope together with most of the church should hold a correct opinion, it is not sin or heresy to believe the contrary, especially in a matter not necessary to salvation, until that opinion is approved or rejected by a universal council.

In this response, Luther reveals that he is certainly no papalist on the issue of church authority. In fact he shows healthy respect for conciliar authority, although he does not take an extreme conciliar position which would elevate a council polemically above the pope. Rather he acknowledges the authority of ecclesiastical decisions clearly established by both pope and council in the canons of the church. This respect for legitimate ecclesiastical authority has led K.-V. Selge to conclude that in the *Explanations* Luther operated with a "mixed" principle of authority.[69] Another ingredient must be added to the mix, as Selge rightly points out. This ingredient is the authority of Scripture and of the church fathers, to which Luther appeals in the traditional declaration preceding the *Explanations*. Luther testifies that he wishes to hold and say nothing which cannot be held first on the basis of Holy Scripture, next on the basis of the church fathers, and, finally, on the basis of the canons and papal decrees.[70]

Luther applies this testimony in Thesis 58; he denies that the treasure of the church, from which indulgences draw their efficacy, is composed of the merits of Christ and the saints. To the objection that St. Thomas, the pope, and the church must have erred in defining the treasure, Luther responds that truth is on the side of himself and many others who have harbored doubts about the power of indulgences. Even the pope is on his side, and that means the church is on his side since the church thinks as the pope does.[71] To be sure, Luther cites an opinion from canon law which supports his position while passing over in silence the decree *Unigenitus* of Clement VI, which clearly interprets the treasure of the church as the merits of Christ and the saints. But this preference for one papal decree over another shows how he is employing the first two criteria, Scripture and the church fathers, to decide which papal opinion should be followed. In response to Eck's designation of his position as "shameless error," Luther says it is far more shameless to assert something in the church which Christ did not teach. Where is this found in the Bible or in the church fathers or, except for our teachers, in the whole world? In accord with his remarks on the mode of intercession, Luther says that it is one thing for the pope to say something, but another thing for him to establish it, and something far different for the pope to establish a position *and* for a council to approve it.[72]

Just as it was possible for Karlstadt to set the opinion of the individual Christian grounded in Scripture over the decision of a council and at the same time to honor the power of the pope to interpret Scripture, it was possible also for Luther to recognize simultaneously the authority of Scripture, church fathers, pope, and council. Popes and councils were expected to rule in accordance with the first two criteria, to be sure, but given the conflicting decrees in canon law, especially in the confusing case of indulgences, Luther sought a consensus of all his authorities and reserved the right to hold his own opinion until a definitive decision was forthcoming from the church.

As part of his search for consensus, Luther hoped for a just and favorable verdict from Pope Leo when he submitted his *Explanations* to him. To Staupitz Luther wrote, "Christ will know whether my words are his or my own. Without Christ's command not even a pope can speak, nor is the heart of a king in his own hand. This Christ is the judge whose verdict I am awaiting through the Roman see."[73] Luther implored Leo himself, "Holy Father, I cast myself at your feet with all that I am and possess. Raise me up or slay me, summon me hither or thither, approve me or reprove me as you please. I will listen to your voice as the voice of Christ reigning and speaking in you."[74] These words did not contradict what Luther said in the *Explanations*.[75] Like Karlstadt, Luther directed his attack at the flatterers of the pope rather than at the pope himself. In fact, Luther expressed his highest respect for the person of Leo X, a respect shared in many humanist circles, and believed that Leo deserved to be pope in better times.[76] At the end of the *Explanations*, Luther did express his regret that he could not support the pope's suspension of previously granted indulgences for the sake of the St. Peter's indulgence. But if he were to judge the intention of the pope apart from his mercenary hirelings, then he would say with brevity and confidence that one should presume the best about him.[77] In other words, the results were still out on Luther's testing of the pope's real intentions. Meanwhile, Luther could express respect for Leo and hope for an opinion from the pope that would fit into his consensus of authorities.

Luther had reason to believe that Leo would rule in his favor, since he could invoke a papal decree in support of his overriding concern that indulgences should not be used to deceive the people. Both in the *Explanations* and again in reply to Eck, Luther cited the warning of Clement V (1312) that indulgence preachers were not allowed to proclaim anything to the people other than what was contained in the indulgence letters themselves.[78] In his reply to Tetzel's second set of theses in June 1518, Luther cited this decree to reject the claims of the indulgence preachers that their words were God's word and their abuses the accepted practice of the church.[79]

The same commitment to the people that led him to challenge such claims in the *Ninety-five Theses* was voiced by Luther both in the *Explanations* and in the letters to Staupitz and Leo. In the letter to Leo, he placed the blame for the controversy on the indulgence preachers who were oppressing the people with false hopes and were tearing the flesh off the bones of the people and fattening themselves on it.[80] In the *Explanations* Luther's distress at the deception in the church led him to call for reformation. This deception made even good preachers ineffective and prevented God, in his wrath, from giving the church shepherds after his own heart who, rather than selling indulgences, would feed the people with proper food.[81]

This concern for the faithful execution of the church's pastoral duty was consistently and unambiguously expressed by Luther in all the important documents issuing from the indulgence controversy. Neither au-

thority per se nor the pope was his primary concern, although his opponents made them the dominant issues. His search for consensus was
undertaken to bolster his basic ecclesiological conviction that the responsibility of the church at all levels was to feed the people with the
word of God and that his responsibility as a doctor of the church was
to call false preachers to account for their failure to do this. "Even if my
friends have been decrying me as heretical, ungodly and blasphemous
for many days because I do not interpret the church of Christ and the
Holy Scripture in a catholic sense, nevertheless, relying on my conscience, I believe that they are the ones deceived, while I love the
church of Christ and its honor."[82] As the first round of the indulgence
controversy reached its close, this honor still included the honor of
the pope.

3 | RESISTANCE

June to December 1518

If the cardinal had acted more modestly in Augsburg and had accepted me as a suppliant, things would never have gone so far, for at that time I still knew little of the errors of the pope!

—Luther, 1538
(WATR 3, 662.12–14; no. 3857)

CHRONOLOGY

1518	April 26	Cardinal Cajetan named papal legate to the Diet of Augsburg
	Before June	At the order of Pope Leo, Jerome Ghinucci prepares a summons of Luther to Rome and Sylvester Prierias writes a theological response to Luther: *Dialogue Concerning the Power of the Pope*
	Before July 10	Luther: *Sermon on the Power of Excommunication*
	July	The summons and Prierias's *Dialogue* sent to Cajetan at Augsburg to be forwarded to Luther in Wittenberg
	August 5	Emperor Maximilian, in a letter composed by Cajetan, denounces Luther as a heretic to Leo X and offers to enforce church sanctions against Luther
	August 7	Luther receives the summons and the *Dialogue*
	August 8	Luther petitions Frederick, who is in Augsburg, to see that his case is heard in Germany
	August 23	In *Postquam ad aures* Pope Leo directs Cajetan not merely to hear Luther, but to demand a recantation and to arrest and deliver Luther to Rome if he refuses
	August 29	Philipp Melanchthon delivers his inaugural lecture in Wittenberg

1518 August 31   Luther's *Sermon on the Power of Excommunication* is published and he sends his *Response* to Prierias's *Dialogue* to Spalatin

Early
September   In Augsburg Frederick persuades Cajetan to treat Luther in a fatherly way and afterwards not to detain him

September 11   In *Cum nuper* Leo directs Cajetan to judge Luther in the pope's stead, but not to enter into debate with him

September 22   Frederick leaves Augsburg

September 25   Cajetan completes the first of fifteen theological tracts (the last is dated October 29) on issues which Luther raised in the *Theses* and *Explanations*

September 26   Luther leaves Wittenberg for Augsburg

October 7   Luther arrives in Augsburg

October 12   Luther appears before Cajetan for the first time

October 13   Luther offers to prepare a written statement

October 14   Luther presents statement to Cajetan; writes letters to Spalatin, Karlstadt, and Cajetan

October 16   Luther appeals from a badly informed pope to a pope who should be better informed

October 20   Luther leaves Augsburg at night

October 23   In Nuremberg Luther sees a copy of the papal directive to Cajetan, *Postquam ad aures*, dated August 23

October 25   Cajetan demands that Frederick turn over Luther or drive him out of Saxony

November 9   Leo X issues the bull *Cum postquam*, drafted by Cajetan, in which he reaffirms and enforces papal teaching on indulgences

November 12   Augsburg *Proceedings* (*Acta Augustana*), written by Luther, are in press

November 19   Frederick receives the ultimatum of Cajetan (October 25) and forwards it to Luther for his response

November 28   Luther appeals to a "legitimate" council of the church

December 7
or 8   Frederick refuses Cajetan's ultimatum to turn over Luther and sends Cajetan a copy of Luther's response

PRIERIAS

By June of 1518 no direct encounter between Luther and the pope had yet taken place. Luther's letter and *Explanations* were on their way to Rome. A legal proceeding against Luther was already underway, but the details surrounding the beginning of Luther's case at the curia are cloudy. The denunciation of Luther by Albert had at least placed Luther under suspicion of heresy in Rome and, on February 3, 1518, Pope Leo may have ordered the future general of the Augustinians, Gabriel Venetus, to impose silence on Luther, who was allegedly spreading "new teachings" in Germany.[1] Luther was aware that he was suspected of heresy and responded that he was only debating theological opinions and not making dogmatic statements. "I might be mistaken, but I will be no heretic, no matter how much those who think and wish otherwise might rage and be consumed with anger."[2]

Sometime before June 1518, Pope Leo ordered the chief legal officer of the curia, Jerome Ghinucci, to prepare a summons for Luther to appear in Rome within sixty days. At the same time, Leo directed the official curial theologian, Sylvester Prierias, the master of the sacred palace, to write a rebuttal of Luther's *Theses* which could serve as the basis of charges against him. Although the summons was the first official step in moving the case of Luther toward trial, Prierias's treatise was the first theological response to Luther from the papal court itself. Its title, *Dialogue Concerning the Power of the Pope against the Presumptuous Positions of Martin Luther*,[3] shows that the question of papal authority, which Tetzel had brought to the forefront, would be the issue on which Luther and the curia would collide.

Sylvester Mazzolini (1456–1527), called Prierias after his birthplace, was a renowned Thomist scholar in Italy. He also earned a good reputation as a canon lawyer through the publication in 1514 of his *Summa Sylvestrina*, a very popular casebook on moral theology and canon law.[4] Prierias was a Dominican, like Tetzel and Cajetan. Although this triad of black and white habits looked to the Augustinian Luther like a Dominican coalition against him,[5] Prierias was at the time involved in a controversy with Cajetan and other "modern" Thomist scholars over the question whether Aristotle had taught the immortality of individual human souls.[6] This controversy had more to do with their common scholarly vocation as interpreters of Thomas Aquinas than with their fraternal bond as Dominicans. An awareness of this disagreement helps to avoid the hasty conclusion that a Dominican conspiracy was behind the curial opposition to Luther.

Prierias's *Dialogue* against Luther was not his first encounter with a member of the Wittenberg faculty. In 1515 Prierias had joined the theological faculty of the city university in Rome (the Sapienza) and in December of that year was appointed master of the sacred palace, the theological adviser to the pope and censor of books in Rome. Prierias was present when Karlstadt debated his theses in Rome in 1516 and earned his degree in civil and canon law. Karlstadt obliquely recalled a face-to-face encounter with Prierias. As Karlstadt supported one of his arguments with the authority of Scripture, the master of the sacred palace reproached him with the sharp rejoinder, "Do you come here with the book of faith?"[7]

Prierias was therefore not unaware of the small, new university in Germany when, at the request of Leo, he tore himself away from his work on Thomas Aquinas and dashed off his answer to Luther in three days. In the dedication of his *Dialogue* to the pope, Prierias depicted himself as a shield doing battle for the honor and majesty of the Roman see and of the truth. He completed his three days of labor with such blitheness of spirit that love gradually imparted the truth to him, and this truth in turn steadily penetrated his spirit.[8] Prierias gave Luther himself part of the credit for this infusion of life. Although unaccustomed for a long time to literary tasks, and with his powers weakened by age, Prierias reports that he was nevertheless stirred by the words with which Luther, like a new Dares (a reference to Vergil's *Aeneid*), was calling athletes from all sides into the contest. Therefore, he, Prierias, had decided to enter unfamiliar arenas to defend the truth and the apostolic see.[9]

The *Dialogue* is directed against Luther's *Ninety-five Theses* alone. Prierias has Luther present each of his *Theses* and then himself defends the opposite, and correct, position. In this way, says Prierias, he will teach Luther on which fundamental positions he should rely, since the bases for Luther's own *Theses* are not apparent. To be sure that these *fundamenta*, or basic premises, are clear, Prierias states them at the beginning of the *Dialogue*.[10]

All four premises are related to papal power and infallibility. First, Prierias defines the universal church virtually as the Roman Church, the head of all the churches, and the Roman Church virtually as the pope who is head of the church, although in a different way from Christ.

Second, Prierias determines that neither a true council of the church, the Roman Church, nor the pope himself, when he rules in his office as pope and seeks the truth to the best of his ability, is able to err. Third, Prierias asserts that anyone who does not rely on the doctrine of the Roman Church and of the pope as the infallible rule of faith, from which even sacred Scripture draws its strength, is a heretic. Finally, in the premise that is most crucial to his case against Luther, Prierias argues that it is improper to distinguish between the teachings and the practices of the Roman Church. Custom assumes the power of law since the will of a prince is expressed either through what he allows or what he in fact does. Therefore, just as it is heretical to hold a false opinion concerning the truth of Scripture, anyone who contradicts the doctrines *and the practices* of the church in matters pertaining to faith and morals is likewise a heretic. To be sure that Luther does not miss the point, Prierias adds a corollary which declares anyone to be a heretic who says that in the matter of indulgences the Roman Church cannot do what it de facto practices. Now Martin, says Prierias, bring forth your theses.

As Luther presents his *Theses*, Prierias wastes no time in applying his premises to them. Typical is his rebuttal of Luther's fifth thesis. Luther proposes that the pope is not willing or able to remit any penalties for sin besides those that he has imposed by his own will or through the canons of the church. Prierias responds simply that the church does otherwise according to the teaching of the holy fathers when it grants plenary indulgences. Luther's position is therefore heretical because, according to the fourth premise, Luther contradicts the practice of the church in a matter concerning faith and morals. Prierias cites Thomas Aquinas as one of the holy fathers, the only authority to which he refers by name in the *Dialogue*.[11] Since Prierias had not seen the *Explanations* with its *protestatio*, in which Luther explicitly challenged the authority of Thomas, he had no way of knowing that his own appeal to Thomas would have little impact on Luther.

This summary rejection of Luther's position does not mean that Prierias fails to give serious theological attention to Luther's *Theses*. He does argue, for example, that the demands of divine justice prevent the pope from releasing all souls from purgatory gratis.[12] Still, Prierias does not extend his arguments substantially beyond the teaching and practice of the church. In accord with his third premise, he writes that indulgences are not made known by the authority of Scripture but by the greater authority of the Roman Church and of the pope.[13] In response to Luther's attempts to dissociate the intention of the pope from the claims of the indulgence preachers, Prierias accuses Luther of a procedural error. If in fact the preachers were guilty, which Prierias does not believe, then Luther has violated the rule of fraternal correction by divulging their mistakes to the public.[14] On the question of papal intent, so crucial and still uncertain for Luther, Prierias responds summarily, "If the mind of the pope were as you have described it, it would be a mind badly instructed and far astray from the truth, as is clear and will be clearer now that we have to do not with conclusions [Luther's *Theses*] but with worthless trifles."[15]

Luther received a copy of the *Dialogue* on August 7, 1518. The next day he wrote to Spalatin that he was already at work on his reply to the *Dialogue*, which was truly overgrown with woods (a pun on "Sylvester" which has this meaning in Latin) and thoroughly uncultivated.[16] At the end of his *Response*, Luther claimed that it took him only two days since Prierias's arguments were trifles and he could answer them extemporaneously.[17] These words give the impression that Luther did not take the *Dialogue* very seriously. Recalling in 1533 his first look at the work, Luther says,

> The pope never hurt me, except at first when Sylvester wrote against me and put this legend in the front of his book: "Master of the Sacred Palace." Then I thought: "Good God, has it come to this that the matter will go before the pope?" However, our Lord God was gracious to me, and the stupid dolt wrote such wretched stuff that I had to laugh. Since then I've never been frightened.[18]

Luther did take the *Dialogue* seriously at the time, however. In compliance with Prierias's request that he state the basic premises of his position, Luther listed three. First, two verses from Paul: "test everything; hold fast to what is good" (1 Thess. 5:21); "if . . . an angel from heaven should preach to you a gospel contrary to that which we preached to you, let him be accursed" (Gal. 1:8). Second, Luther quoted from a letter of Augustine to Jerome in which the Bishop of Hippo asserted the superiority of the biblical books over all other writings, no matter how outstanding they might be, since only the authors of Scripture had never erred. Third, Luther cited his favorite papal decretal, *Abusionibus* of Clement V, which forbade preachers of indulgences to make any claims for their letters that were not stated in the letters themselves. Turning the tables on Prierias, Luther added that the prohibition of Clement V should be included among those "practices" of the church to which Prierias had attributed infallible validity.[19]

In the body of his *Response*, Luther applies his premises just as thoroughly to Prierias's arguments as Prierias applied his premises to Luther's *Theses*. The most crucial confrontation of authorities occurs in reference to Luther's fifth thesis. Luther rejects the appeal of Prierias to Thomas and to the practice of the church.[20] Luther asks how a universally valid practice of the church is to be recognized. Which boundary of the church is to be used to define this practice? To illustrate the difficulty, Luther cites the disagreement over the immaculate conception of Mary which Thomas and the Dominicans opposed even though the church celebrated it. If Prierias can contradict such a "practice" of the church as long as a council has not ruled otherwise, then why is Luther not permitted the same privilege on the question of indulgences?[21] Luther also refuses to acknowledge that the church's remission of penalties imposed by God is a legitimate practice of the church since, according to Panormitanus, both pope and council are able to err. After citing this new authority from canon law, about which he probably learned from Karlstadt, Luther maintains that Prierias's definitions of the church in his premises are invalid. Virtually, says Luther, I do not know the church except in Christ and, representatively, in a council. If whatever the pope does is called a practice of the *church*, then how many monstrosities must be accepted as beneficial acts of the church![22]

Although Luther does show respect for the authority of a general council, his major concern is not to plead conciliar authority but to challenge Prierias's facile identification of papal practice with the practice of the *church*. This challenge complements Luther's argument in the *Explanations*. There he distinguishes clearly the personal opinion of a pope, even established by decree, from the same opinion established and approved by a general council. In his *Response*, Luther says that he does not believe that pope or council has ever decreed those things which Prierias labels "practices" of the church.[23] The argument from Panormitanus that pope and council can err remains on the theoretical level, however. Later in the *Response*, Luther even agrees with Prierias that the Roman Church is the rule of faith, if that refers to the church's fidelity in the past:

> I give thanks to Christ that he preserves this one church on earth by so great a miracle which alone could prove our faith to be true, namely, that never in any of its decrees has it departed from true faith. Nor has the devil, even in the nadir of so many ruinous customs, been able to prevent the authority of the canonical books and of the church fathers . . . from enduring since the beginning of the church, although there may be many persons who privately have no faith at all in those books or who do not even care to read and understand them.[24]

The first literary encounter between Luther and Rome has not significantly altered the stance which Luther took in the *Explanations*. On the question of church authority, Luther's principle of consensus is still in force; he seeks to base his own position inclusively on Scripture, the church fathers, and decrees of the church.[25] The only new wrinkle in Luther's consensus is the citation of Panormitanus's opinion that a pope as well as a council can err. The theoretical fallibility of church councils, however, is overshadowed by the respect which he still shows for their authority against the papalist Prierias; the most potent parts of his consensus remain Scripture and the church fathers.[26]

Prierias is unable to break down Luther's respect for Leo and Luther's hope that the pope would not condone the abuses of the indulgence preachers. Luther repeats his opinion that Leo X is the best pope, like Daniel in Babylon. He assures the doubting Prierias that the abuses of the preachers really do occur but are no reflection on Leo since the pope's own innocence cannot prevent others from acting reprehensibly.[27] To Prierias's charge that he is an unjust detractor of the pope, Luther responds once and for all that he honors the highest pontiff, as is fitting, while he condemns the opinions and flattery of Sylvester.[28] Prierias accuses Luther of irony in saying that the pope has greater gifts to bestow than indulgences; Luther retorts that he is not speaking ironically, but plainly, since the pope has the gospel, the gifts of ministry, and all the gifts enumerated in 1 Corinthians 12. "For the pope does better if he places one good pastor at the head of one church than if he should grant all indulgences at once."[29]

Luther is still able to hold together his concern for the faithful execution of pastoral duty and his confidence in the pope. The response of

Prierias, coming from the curia itself, did nothing to buttress Luther's confidence in Leo, but it did not noticeably shake that confidence.[30] As late as 1520, Luther still hesitated to identify Prierias unequivocally with the pope and cardinals.[31] Prierias may have forced only one small wedge between Luther and the Roman Church. Luther charges that Prierias threatened him with curses and censures. But you cannot hurt me, says Luther. "Christ lives and he not only lives but also reigns, not just in heaven but also in Rome, no matter how much she rages. If I am cursed for the truth, I will bless the Lord. The censure of the church will not separate me from the church if the truth of the church joins me."[32] Even in this confession Luther equates his truth with the truth of the church, although it may not be the view of everyone in Rome. He is not yet convinced that the pope is among those who would deny that truth.

THE ROAD TO AUGSBURG

When Luther received the summons to Rome on August 7, 1518, he urgently sought the help of his closest confidant at the electoral court, Georg Spalatin (1484–1545), the private secretary, adviser, and occasional confessor of the Elector Frederick.[33] Spalatin was already in Augsburg with Frederick for the Diet of the Empire, and Luther's letter reveals that he felt at a loss with both his friend and his prince being so far away at this crucial time. Spalatin was to use his influence to have both Frederick and the Emperor Maximilian petition the pope to allow Luther's case to be heard in Germany. Behind the plea stood Luther's fear that the Dominicans, "those murderers who seek my destruction," would prejudice his case if it were heard in Rome. In addition, Luther expressed concern for the honor of the University of Wittenberg, a concern which he knew would be dear to the elector's heart. Time was so short, Luther told Spalatin, that he also wrote directly to Frederick.

Although Luther could reasonably expect favorable action from Frederick, the chance of gaining support from Emperor Maximilian was, unknown to Luther, slim. Two days before Luther received the summons to Rome, the emperor had dispatched a letter to Leo in which he denounced Luther as a heretic and offered to use imperial power to enforce whatever steps the church took against Luther. This denunciation, probably composed by the papal legate Cajetan,[34] was based in part on excerpts from a sermon Luther had preached on the subject of excommunication sometime before July 10.[35] According to Luther, hostile hearers had taken notes on the sermon and disseminated them in the form of theses taken out of context in order to discredit him.[36] Luther was confronted with these theses while visiting in Dresden, and they had also caused consternation in Augsburg where Cajetan presumably became aware of them. The occasion for the sermon was apparently not Luther's personal difficulty but false allegations about excommunication which were misleading the people.[37] Although Luther regarded the sermon as sufficiently orthodox that it might even find favor with his critics, Spalatin, aware of the sensitive situation in Augsburg, begged Luther not to publish it or anything else while the negotiations surrounding his request were underway. It was too late. On August 31, Luther wrote to Spalatin that both his sermon and the *Response* to Prierias had already appeared.[38]

The main point of the sermon was the distinction between ecclesiastical excommunication, which excluded one from the sacraments, and spiritual excommunication, which alone could separate one from God and the church as the internal, spiritual communion of the faithful. The purpose of the distinction was to teach the people that, even if they were unjustly excommunicated by the church, they still remained in the spiritual communion of the faithful as long as they were bound to God by faith, hope, and love. In case of unjust excommunication, the people should not worry but bear their sentence with patience and with respect for the power of "mother church," which was none other than the power of Christ.[39] This injunction to obedience was the basis of Luther's claim that the sermon "magnificently extolled the sacred power of the church." But the distinction between the external church and the spiritual communion of the faithful was more than enough to arouse his critics.

Before Spalatin had a chance to hear from Rome that his attempt to have Luther's hearing moved to Germany had been successful, Leo X instructed his legate in Augsburg, Cardinal Cajetan, to take Luther into custody. In the papal brief *Postquam ad aures*, dated August 23, 1518,[40] Leo directed Cajetan to arrest Luther, with the help of secular force if necessary, and to hold him until further orders arrived from Rome. If Luther should demonstrate a change of heart, then Cajetan was empowered to receive him back into the church. But if Luther should persist in his beliefs and not submit to arrest, then Cajetan was likewise empowered to declare Luther a heretic and to excommunicate both him and his supporters. The brief is obviously not a response to Spalatin's request, but a harsher step taken by Leo on the basis of evidence that Luther had published additional heretical works since the original summons to Rome had been issued.[41] In terms of his legal standing, Luther was no longer merely under suspicion of heresy with the right to have his case heard. He was now a declared heretic whose options were narrowed to recantation or excommunication.[42] There was to be no hearing in Augsburg, only a decision on Luther's part.

The political situation dictated otherwise. An important item on the agenda of the diet was the designation of an heir to the imperial throne. Frederick had long opposed the election of Maximilian's grandson, Charles of Spain, as king of the Romans and thus heir to the throne. The papacy shared this opposition, preferring instead the aspiring king of France, Francis I, to counterbalance Hapsburg power in Europe. As elector, Frederick was one of the princes who had the right to choose the imperial successor. Leo and Cajetan did not want to risk losing Frederick's political support through a theological quarrel. Therefore, when Frederick appeared before Cajetan in early September to request that Luther's case be heard in Germany, the papal legate agreed that Luther should appear before him and that he would treat Luther in a fatherly manner and search for a satisfactory resolution of the matter.[43]

According to Frederick, Cajetan also promised to release Luther, although Cajetan was only authorized to do this if Luther recanted. A second papal brief issued to Cajetan on September 11 (*Cum nuper*) did not alter Cajetan's mandate in this regard. The pope officially appointed Cajetan to act as judge in his stead and, after hearing Luther, to absolve or to condemn him. Although the language is milder than in the brief of August 23, the new order neither granted the objective hearing before German judges which Luther sought through Frederick nor gave Cajetan explicit permission to release Luther regardless of Luther's response.[44] When Frederick left Augsburg on September 22 to return to Saxony, he apparently thought that Luther would have the opportunity to present his case and then return home. On the other hand, Cajetan was caught in a squeeze between his instructions from Leo and his promise to Frederick. Obviously, Cajetan would feel pressured to bring Luther to recant in order to avoid conflict with the curia.

While these delicate negotiations were underway in Augsburg, Luther waited in suspense in Wittenberg. On August 29, he heard with enthusiasm Philipp Melanchthon's inaugural lecture as professor of Greek. "If he remains healthy, I do not wish to have another professor of Greek as long as I live," remarked Luther; but he feared that Melanchthon's frail constitution would collapse under the rough conditions in Saxony, and he worried that the salary might be too small to hold him.[45] In a letter to Staupitz, Luther expressed his determination to persist in his study of Scripture despite the summons and the threats aimed at him. "I suffer incomparably worse things, as you know, which force me to regard these temporal and momentary storms as trifles, except that I sincerely desire to show reverence to ecclesiastical power."[46] Luther accused Roman flatterers such as Prierias of obstructing the preaching of the truth in Christ's own kingdom and reported that the people yearned for the voice of their pastor Christ, and even young people were fervent in their zeal for Scripture. He announced happily that Greek was now being taught (with the arrival of Melanchthon); "we are all studying Greek in order to understand the Bible." He also noted that the elector was to see to it that Hebrew would soon be taught. That hope was realized in early November.[47]

Perhaps buoyed by his progress in the study of Scripture and the response of the people, which had been his first concern in Wittenberg, Luther left for Augsburg on September 22. On October 7, exactly two months after he had received the summons to Rome, Luther arrived in Augsburg, as he said later, "afoot and poor."[48] That was accurate enough since he had first climbed aboard a wagon only three miles outside the city. He recovered quickly from the trip in his quarters at the Carmelite monastery (there was no Augustinian cloister in Augsburg). The advisers and friends of the elector took care of him, and he dined with local notables such as Conrad Peutinger. They all advised Luther not to appear before Cajetan until he had received a safe conduct from the emperor. While this was being prepared, Cajetan sent a member of his Italian entourage, Urban of Serralonga, who had been in Wittenberg, to persuade Luther to recant and to return to the church. Urban tried to dissuade Luther from arguing his case before Cajetan with the remark, "Do you want a tournament?" Luther replied that if he were shown that his teaching departed from what the Roman Church believed, he would be his own judge and sing his recantation. Since Urban placed more value on the opinions of Thomas than the decrees and authority of the church would bear, Luther said he would not recant until the church had revoked its earlier decree on which he relied (*Abusionibus?*). Then, according to Luther, Urban made some wild claims: he denied that papal power could be debated and praised it to the skies for its ability to abrogate even matters of faith. At this Luther sent him away.[49]

Urban returned the next day to find out why Luther had not yet appeared before Cajetan. When Luther said his friends had advised him to wait for a safe conduct, Urban blew up and asked, "Do you suppose Prince Frederick will take up arms for your sake?" Luther replied, "This I do not at all desire." "And where will you stay?" asked Urban. "Under heaven," answered Luther. Then Urban asked, "If you had the pope and cardinals in your power, what would you do?" "I would," said Luther, "show them all respect and honor."[50] Luther was thus prepared for the topic of papal power to come up when he finally met Cajetan for the first time on October 12. But he was not entirely afraid. As he said after his first encounter with Urban, "Thus I hover between hope and fear. For this inept mediator has given me not a little confidence."[51]

CAJETAN

Thomas de Vio (1469–1534), called Cajetan after his birthplace Gaeta, possessed a "small body and a frail build, but an immense mind and wealth of learning; he was afraid of no one when justice was required."[52] At the age of sixteen he entered the Dominican cloister in his hometown and assumed the name Thomas in honor of the greatest theologian of the order, Thomas Aquinas. Cajetan rose rapidly in Dominican ranks, finally becoming general of the order at the age of thirty-nine. He held the office for ten years, and during that period he sent the first Dominican missionaries to Central America. Cajetan also continued to build his reputation as the outstanding Aquinas scholar of his day. His commentary on the *Summa Theologiae* of Thomas was included in the famous nineteenth-century Leonine Edition of the *Summa*. When Leo X created thirty-one new cardinals on July 1, 1517, Cajetan was named cardinal priest of St. Sixtus in Rome. His permanent ecclesiastical benefice was the bishopric of his hometown, but he spent most of his years in Rome or as the representative of the pope on special missions, such as the legation to the Diet of Augsburg in 1518. Cajetan had not been sent to Augsburg to meet with Luther. In fact, he had only been appointed papal legate to the diet in April 1518 as a last-minute substitute for Cardinal Farnese, who excused himself as sick. As the representative of the pope at the annual meeting of the emperor with the German estates, his foremost assignment was to lobby for a tax to be levied on the German territories to support campaigns against the Turks.[53]

Cajetan was well-prepared, however, when the complex course of events called for him to confront the young Augustinian monk, fourteen years his junior. In addition to his expertise on Thomas Aquinas, Cajetan was well grounded in the ecclesiological issues that had come to the forefront in Luther's case. In 1511 he defended papal supremacy against the resurgence of conciliarism at the Council of Pisa with a treatise entitled *The Authority of the Pope Compared with the Authority of a Council*. Cajetan argued that the pope held supreme power in the church by divine right, that is, by virtue of the words of Christ to Peter in Matt. 16:18 ("you are Peter, and on this rock I will build my church") and in John 21:17 ("Feed my sheep"). Through this divine institution, Christ made Peter the one head of the whole body of the church and entrusted all power in the church to his successors.[54] With these classic proof texts of papal supremacy, Cajetan excluded any version of conciliar authority that would attribute to the pope only that power delegated to him by the church or that would give other members of the hierarchy an equal share in the power given by Christ directly to the successors of Peter. In addition, since all power in the church was derived from the papacy, it was impossible for the pope to err when he made a definitive judgment in matters of faith. Otherwise the whole church would err, and that would contradict the promise of Christ that "when the Spirit of truth comes, he will guide you into all the truth" (John 16:13).[55]

While the Council of Pisa requested a rebuttal of Cajetan's treatise from the University of Paris, the late medieval stronghold of conciliarism, Cajetan himself was chosen to deliver the opening sermon at the second session of the Fifth Lateran Council in Rome in 1512.[56] For this sermon Cajetan chose a subject he had passed over in the 1511 treatise: the symmetry between the earthly and the heavenly churches. This symmetry was an ancient ecclesiological theme which owed its popularity to the anonymous fifth-century author known as Dionysius the Pseudo-Areopagite.[57] The purpose of this comparison between the two churches was to demonstrate that the earthly or militant church was the true church because it conformed to the perfection of the heavenly or triumphant church. Specifically, the comparison showed that the hierarchy of the militant church was a faithful representation of the perfect order of the triumphant church. For Thomas and for

Cajetan, this corresponding order dictated that just as Christ was the only lord of the triumphant church in heaven, so the pope was the only prince of the church on earth whom all citizens of the militant church should obey. The thrust of the sermon was to show that the Council of Pisa, with its conciliaristic view of the church, could in no way conform to this divinely given model of the true church.[58] In contrast, the Fifth Lateran Council would demonstrate the correspondence of the Roman Church to this model through its decree of 1516, *Pastor aeternus*, in which Leo X reasserted the supremacy of the papacy as a mark of the true church.[59]

As forceful as Cajetan's papalism was, it "was not without nuance."[60] Like many papalist theologians of the late Middle Ages, Cajetan admitted that a general council could declare that a pope had fallen into heresy and depose him. But Cajetan was careful to emphasize that the power a council would exercise in this case was a "ministerial power," itself subject to the papacy. That power only dissolved the bond between the office of the papacy and the officeholder and therefore did not assert itself over the papal office.[61] On the question, which was becoming acute in Luther's case, of what constituted a schismatic break with the church, Cajetan had already expressed himself clearly in his commentary on Thomas's *Summa*. According to Cajetan, membership in the militant church was judged by two criteria: first, the presence of the theological virtues faith, hope, and love, which the Holy Spirit effected in all faithful Christians; and, second, the subordination of all members to the bishop of Rome who was the head of the church. The failure to meet either criterion was enough to make one a schismatic.[62] Cajetan appreciated the fine points of the ecclesiological debates which had been raging for years between papalists and conciliarists, but there was no question on which side he stood.

Cajetan did not depend aloofly on his papalist principles, however, when it came to his confrontation with Luther. He took time to read the works of Luther that were available to him. On the day before Luther left Wittenberg for Augsburg, Cajetan completed the first of fifteen theological tracts on the subjects of penance, indulgences, and excommunication. Luther never saw these works, which were completed by the end of October, but he soon encountered the fruits of Cajetan's labor in the meetings that began on October 12. Although not authorized to debate Luther, Cajetan was well-prepared to argue with Luther in order to bring about a recantation, which would enable him to fulfill both his responsibility to the curia and his promise to Frederick. Owing to Cajetan's thorough preparation, the hearing at Augsburg did not bog down in nonessentials but quickly focused on the decisive issues between Luther and Rome.

According to Luther's brief account of what happened in Augsburg, published after his return to Wittenberg in November, Cajetan received him "with kindness bordering on reverence" and explained that he did not wish to debate Luther but to settle the affair in a gentle and fatherly manner. Following the orders of the pope, Cajetan proposed that Luther recant his errors and promise henceforth to abstain from them and from anything else that might disturb the church.[63] He could have done that in Wittenberg without a perilous journey, thought Luther, and he asked Cajetan to teach him where he had erred since he was not conscious of any error on his part. Cajetan was ready to oblige, and promptly named two points. First, he cited in opposition to Luther's Thesis 58 the papal decree *Unigenitus* of Clement VI (1343), popularly known as the *Extravagante*, which defined the treasure of the church as the merits of Christ. Second, he referred to the explanation of Thesis 7 as a new and erroneous doctrine. Luther had asserted that the person about to receive the sacrament of penance should trust with certainty in the words of absolution, or else it would be received to the person's condemnation; Cajetan argued that anyone going to the sacrament remained uncertain of obtaining grace.[64] In both cases what impressed Luther, besides the smiles and giggles of the Italians in Cajetan's retinue, was the self-assurance with which Cajetan presented his arguments. Luther did not know that two of the eleven rebuttals to his positions which Cajetan had written by that date dealt specifically with these points.[65]

On the first point Cajetan was certain that he had caught Luther in contradiction to an explicit papal decree. Luther guessed that Cajetan presumed that he had not seen *Unigenitus*, since it was not contained in all the collections of canon law (hence the nickname *Extravagante*, "wandering outside" the lawbooks). Luther responded quickly that he had seen it but that it did not convince him because it distorted the Scriptures by citing them out of context.[66] Cajetan appealed to the power of the pope, which he placed above that of a council, Scripture, and everything in the church. Such assertions were new to his ears, said Luther, and he rejected them by citing the recent appeal of the University of Paris to a church council.[67]

Luther may have regarded Cajetan's papalism as the opinion of one party in the church, an opinion which he did not expect to hear from the papal legate.[68] Luther's own words, however, suggest that what surprised him was not the claim for papal authority as such, but the way in which Cajetan seemed to state that claim exclusive of Scripture and the councils of the church. Formulated in this way, Cajetan's position violated the principle of consensus which Luther had been using and which he had assumed to be normative in the church. Up to this point, Luther had not objected to papal authority itself, but to the way in which flatterers of the pope such as Tetzel and Prierias had made claims for that authority which could not be supported by the other elements in the consensus: Scripture, church fathers, councils, and clear reasons. In his explanation of Thesis 58, Luther had written that he did not accept the merits of Christ as the treasure of indulgences because it could not be proved by Scripture or by good reasons. If the Roman Church would decide the contrary, said Luther, it would become vulnerable to the criticism of heretics who demanded probable reasons and authority, not merely the will of the pope and the Roman Church. "This is most certainly my only goal in the whole matter," Luther had said, namely, to shield the church from ridicule and to ensure that the church could defend itself with more than mere opinions.[69]

Luther was therefore not likely to be impressed by the way in which Cajetan tried to intimidate him with the fact of *Unigenitus* alone without arguing its merits, as the descriptions of their encounter attest.[70] He elaborated on his rejection of *Unigenitus* in a written response presented to Cajetan on the third and last day of their meeting (October 14). Luther confessed that he knew about *Unigenitus* when he wrote his explanation of Thesis 58. Since, however, it was most certainly the "unanimous opinion of the whole church" that the merits of Christ could not be committed to humankind or passed on through human agents, Luther decided to ignore *Unigenitus* and leave to more ingenious minds the difficulties and embarrassment which he was suffering in silence in order to preserve reverence for the pope.[71] Luther was sure that the consensus of authorities supported his doubts about *Unigenitus*. Therefore, he was surprised that even a supporter of papal supremacy such as Cajetan would deny his right to debate its merits, since Luther shared his concern to uphold the credibility of the papacy.

The response to *Unigenitus* helps to clarify the stance which Luther took in relation to the papacy from the beginning of the indulgence controversy. First, it confirms the sincerity of his express desire to respect and safeguard the honor of the papacy. Second, it demonstrates that this honor is not preserved by the naked assertion of papal authority but by the establishment of the pope's credibility. That credibility does not depend on the demonstration that prior papal decrees have never been erroneous but on the willingness of the reigning pope to give justifiable reasons for his own rulings. This last point explains why Luther could submit his positions to the judgment of the reigning pope, Leo X, while at the same time questioning the rulings of previous popes.

Third, Luther's response clarifies the relationship between these earlier papal rulings and Luther's consensus of authorities. Luther did not understand past papal rulings such as *Unigenitus* to be isolated dicta of popes which must be accepted without question. They were part of the corpus of canon law, which contained decrees not always in harmony with one another and therefore had to be sifted and reexamined by canon lawyers and theologians. This reexamination had to rely on clearly defined criteria, and Luther's consensus exercised this evaluative function. Luther did not fail to notice that canon law itself recognized the need for such criteria, especially since the criteria it mentioned formed the core of his own consensus. Referring to the paragraph in canon law that said the decrees of the Roman pontiff were to be received as if coming from the mouth of Peter himself, Luther pointed to a gloss which limited this reception to those decrees that agreed with Scripture and did not dissent from judgments of the church fathers.[72] He also cited (as he had against Prierias) the comment of the canon lawyer Panormitanus that the opinion of any Christian, when supported by better arguments, was preferable to the opinion of the pope. Luther was not setting himself categorically above any ruling which Leo might render but affirming the tentativeness of all prior papal decrees and the right of doctors of the church to challenge them on the basis of better arguments, such as the criteria contained in his consensus. Consequently, Luther noted that perhaps the time had come for *Unigenitus* itself to be corrected, since many decrees in canon law had been corrected by subsequent papal rulings.[73]

Although the controversy over *Unigenitus* clarified the already existing disagreement between Cajetan and Luther over papal authority and credibility, Cajetan's second objection revealed a substantial difference which had serious consequences for Luther's ensuing attitude toward the papacy. Luther had asserted that Christians approaching the sacrament of penance should not trust in their own contrition but in the words of Christ spoken by the priest in the absolution. If they believed in these words, then they could be certain of forgiveness, because these words were absolutely reliable, whereas the sufficiency of their contrition was never certain. In reply, Cajetan upheld the prevailing theological opinion: although it was true that contrition was never perfect, its presence made one worthy to receive the grace conferred by the sacrament. Still, one could never be certain that one's contrition was sufficient to effect the forgiveness one hoped to receive. To hold the contrary, said Cajetan, was to teach a new and erroneous doctrine and to "build a new church."[74]

Part of the reason for Cajetan's sharp reaction lay in the different concepts of faith which he and Luther espoused. For Cajetan, faith was one of the virtues infused with grace, and it entailed belief that the doctrine of penance itself was correct. For Luther, faith was not this general confidence in the correctness and power of the sacrament but "special faith" in the certain effect of the sacrament on the penitent Christian who trusted the word of Christ.[75] Cajetan quickly perceived the difference but failed to appreciate Luther's underlying concern.[76] To him Luther's "special faith" appeared to be a subjective human assessment which undermined the objective power of the keys at work through the priest's pronouncement of the absolution. It imposed a new condition on the efficacy of the sacrament beyond that most recently defined at the Council of Florence; therefore, Luther was again challenging an explicit decree of the church.[77] Luther, however, was striving for just the opposite: to put the sacrament on a more objective basis. He was trying to remove the uncertain, subjective element of human contrition as a basis for the efficacy of the sacrament and to replace it with the objective, certain words of Christ pronounced in the absolution.

Luther's reaction to Cajetan's objection indicates how much was at stake. "I heard this objection with grief," he reported, "because I had misdoubted nothing less than that this matter would be called into question."[78] In his report to Karlstadt on October 14, Luther maintained that he would not become a heretic by recanting the opinion that had made him a Christian. He would rather die and be burned, exiled, or cursed.[79] And, finally, in his commentary on the proceedings at Augsburg, Luther wrote that the whole of salvation depended on his response to this objection. "You are not an evil Christian regardless whether you recognize or ignore the *Extravagante;* you are nothing but a heretic, however, if you deny faith in the word of Christ."[80] Obviously, the question at stake was not merely the formal issue of authority in the church, but the essence of the Christian life and the heart of Luther's own religious experience. Replying to Cajetan's objection, Luther summed up his understanding of justifying faith which formed the core of his "Reformation" theology: "No disposition [on your part] makes you worthy, no work makes you fit for the sacrament, but only faith. For only faith in the word of Christ justifies, makes alive, makes you worthy and prepares you; anything else is an exercise in presumption or despair."[81]

The commentators on Luther's encounter with Cajetan have agreed on the personal, theological, and Reformation significance of these words and of the thirteen authorities, mostly biblical, which Luther ticked off in favor of his position. The question remains, however: How did the objection of Cajetan and Luther's confession affect his attitude toward the papacy? What is the relation between the controversy over the *Extravagante* and this theological dispute over worthy preparation for the sacrament?

The answer lies in two comments Luther made following this summary of his theology. First, he appealed to Cajetan to deal clemently with him, to have compassion on his conscience and not to force him to recant those things to which his conscience compelled him to consent. He also asked Cajetan to intercede with Leo since he was ready to retract anything which he had expressed improperly and would be overjoyed to let truth be the victor—unless he should be forced to go against the opinion of his conscience.[82] Long before his famous reply at the Diet of Worms in 1521, Luther appealed to his conscience and to the necessity for him to obey God rather than men (Acts 5:29). This appeal to conscience, however, should not be mistaken for an assertion of autonomous individual rights against the religious establishment.[83] For Luther, a doctor of the church, an appeal to conscience included a heightened sense of responsibility for the proper exercise of the church's duty to nourish the faith and life of the people. His appeal to his own conscience was also an appeal to the conscience of the church.

This point is undergirded by the second comment. After noting that Cajetan, in his passion to bring him to recant, completely ignored Scripture, Luther said he was not upset by this omission since he knew that

Cajetan was merely following the procedure which he was accustomed to use in the Roman curia and in scholastic debates. For, Luther continues,

> it has long been assumed that whatever the Roman Church has said, damned or desired would be said, damned and desired by everyone, and that no other reason needed to be given except that the apostolic see and the Roman Church felt this way. Therefore, since sacred letters have been ignored and the traditions and words of men accepted, it has come to pass that the church of Christ is not fed with its portion of food [Luke 12:42], i.e. with the word of Christ, but is frequently ruled by the temerity and will of some unlearned flatterer. And the extent of our misfortune is shown by the fact that they begin to compel us to reject and deny the Christian faith and the most sacred Scripture.[84]

Behind Luther's appeal to his own conscience stood his concern for the church: both for the people of the church whom, all along, he had sought to protect from the deception of the indulgence preachers, and for the hierarchy of the church, which was not fulfilling its responsibility to feed the people with the word of Christ.

Cajetan's objection to Luther's theology of faith and the sacrament touched not only the nerve of Luther's own religious experience but also challenged the motivation behind his criticism of indulgences in the first place. He had hoped that the pope would speak out clearly on the abuse of indulgences for the sake of the people; but Cajetan's rejection of what Luther understood to be the essence of the Christian life, the indispensable nourishment of the people with the word of Christ, must have dealt his hope a severe blow. The impact of Cajetan's rejection is reflected in his harsh judgment on the Roman Church and the explicit inclusion of the apostolic see in this judgment. Luther does not attack Leo X personally. But, coming from the best qualified representative of Leo that Luther had encountered so far, Cajetan's inflexibility not only confirmed his judgment that past papal decrees such as *Unigenitus* were in error but also warned him that a favorable ruling from Leo himself was hardly to be expected. Luther gradually became aware of the possibility that he might have to maintain the truth of his position on the basis of Scripture, church fathers, and good reasons against the opinion of the reigning pontiff. After Luther returned to Wittenberg and had time to reflect on the encounter, he asserted the theoretical legitimacy of such a step. Commenting on his appeal to Cajetan and Leo at the end of his written response, Luther assured the readers of his *Proceedings* that his submission did not reflect any doubts about his stance or a willingness to change his mind, but only the necessity of showing reverence to the pope and his legate. "Divine truth is lord even of the pope; I do not await the judgment of a man when I already know the judgment of God."[85]

LOYALTY UNDERMINED

When he left Augsburg, Luther did not yet feel this skeptical about a favorable decision from Leo. Before his departure, his friends advised him to prepare an appeal from Cajetan to Pope Leo. Luther thought such an appeal was unnecessary since he had twice before submitted his positions to the holy see, once in the dedicatory letter to Leo accompanying his *Explanations* and again at the end of his written response to Cajetan. But he allowed the appeal to be notarized on October 16, and two days after he left Augsburg it was formally posted on the cathedral door. The appeal contained nothing new. It reaffirmed Luther's stance as a disputant seeking the truth and cited his favorite decree from canon law, *Abusionibus*, as the legal basis for his right to challenge the indulgence preachers.[86] Luther submitted his position to Leo in the same terms he had used in the dedicatory letter, and he recapitulated the consensus of authorities to which his teaching ought to conform. Finally, he appealed from a pope ill-informed to a pope who should be better informed.[87] In other words, Leo was a good pope but the victim of bad advice.

Whatever misgivings Cajetan's inflexible attitude aroused in Luther, the appeal was not inconsistent with his attitude toward the papacy at this time.[88] Luther's hesitation about the appeal was not owing to his having given up on Leo but to the redundancy of another appeal. Nor did Luther's hasty departure from Augsburg betray a lack of seriousness about the appeal. Luther had received no response to a letter in which he had taken formal leave of Cajetan, and rumors were flying that the cardinal was about to have Luther arrested. Luther's advisers became nervous and arranged for him to leave town at once. During the night of October 20, Luther was roused from sleep and sent half-clothed on a horseback ride that he would long remember.

In the weeks following his departure from Augsburg, however, two events made Luther more pessimistic about receiving a favorable response from Leo. On his return to Wittenberg, Luther stopped in Nuremberg where he saw for the first time the papal instruction to

Cajetan, *Postquam ad aures* (August 23), which had originally ordered Luther's arrest and recantation. Luther called this brief "diabolic" instead of apostolic (i.e., papal); and he maintained that it was a forgery since it was "incredible that such a monstrosity should have been issued by the supreme pontiff, especially one like Leo X." He promised Spalatin that he would include it, along with a commentary, in his account of the proceedings at Augsburg. If it did come from the Roman curia, he said, then he would teach those people something about their shameless temerity and wretched ignorance.[89] In that commentary, Luther presumed that Leo was innocent and that the Dominicans were behind the falsified brief which distorted Leo into his accuser.[90] Although Leo himself was still exempt from Luther's displeasure, the Roman curia came under increased suspicion.

Before Luther arrived in Wittenberg, Cajetan wrote to the Elector Frederick that he had discharged his duty in Augsburg, as promised, in a fatherly and not a judicial manner. It was no use, however. Luther had refused to be instructed in person, and his sermons and German tracts did not state his positions tentatively, but assertively and affirmatively. These positions were in part contrary to the teaching of the apostolic see and in part deserving of condemnation. Alluding to his thorough study of Luther's writings, Cajetan claimed that his judgment was based on certain knowledge and not merely on opinion. Therefore, he exhorted Frederick to deliver Luther to Rome or to banish him from Saxony. Delay would not help, warned Cajetan, since the case would be prosecuted promptly at Rome as soon as he had washed his hands of the matter and referred it to the pope.[91]

Frederick forwarded Cajetan's letter to Luther for a response. Luther answered in a long letter, which Frederick eventually sent to the cardinal along with his own refusal to comply with Cajetan's request. Luther protests again that he desires to be shown where he has erred, not just for his own sake, but also for the sake of truth and for the honor of the church, of the pope, and of Cajetan himself.[92] He supports, however, the distinction which Cajetan made between teachings that were contrary to the apostolic see and those that were worthy of condemnation. The distinction is valid, says Luther, because they are indeed different things. One who speaks contrary to the teaching of the apostolic see does not necessarily deserve condemnation. This applies precisely to his own case, since he has been cited for the former, but has not yet spoken in a manner deserving condemnation.[93]

This distinction amounts to an admission that the pope can err, an admission which Luther had already made about past papal decrees both in theory (citing Panormitanus) and in the specific case of *Unigenitus*. In the aftermath of Augsburg, Luther expands this admission to include the possibility that a reigning pope may err. First, he adduces examples of error in other past decrees. In the *Proceedings at Augsburg*, which began to appear in print about the same time that Luther responded to Cajetan's letter, Luther takes umbrage at Cajetan's reproach that he did not spare the holiness of the pope when he accused the *Extravagante* of distorting Scripture. Luther says that the popes are accustomed in their decretals to violating Holy Scripture. As an example, he selects the decree of Gregory IX (1227–1241) which interprets Heb. 7:12 to mean that the priesthood has been transferred from Moses to Christ and from Christ to Peter. Luther argues that this interpretation violates the text and protests that he would not be terrified by human threats that he was not sparing the holiness of the pope. "I will honor the holiness of the pope," he says, "but I will worship the holiness of Christ and of truth."[94]

Then Luther cites a potentially more dangerous example, which touches the divinely endowed authority of any pope: the words of Christ to Peter in Matt. 16:18–19. Suppose he were to argue, says Luther, that this text does not prove that the Roman Church is superior to the other churches of the world, and suppose that Cajetan cited the decree of Pope Pelagius II (579–590), which uses these words from Matthew to support such superiority. Would he abandon the sense of the gospel and embrace the interpretation of Pelagius? The answer is no, although Luther protests that he is not condemning "the new rule of the Romans in our age." He wants instead to prevent the power of Scripture from being reduced to mere words and to resist those insipid persons who have tied the church of Christ to a certain time and place and who deny that one can be Christian without being subject to the Roman pontiff and being oppressed by his decrees.[95] These people would eject from the church of Christ all those Christians in the East and in Africa who, for eight hundred years, were never subject to the Roman pope or never interpreted Matt. 16:18–19 to mean that they should be.[96] For the first time, Luther reveals his own interpretation of this crucial supporting text for papal primacy. According to the church fathers, he says, Peter receives the keys of the kingdom from Christ on behalf of all the apostles, not as one who is set above the other apostles. If papal rule can be proved, says Luther, then it should be based on Paul's words in Rom. 13:1 that all authority is from God. By virtue of this, "we are subjected to the Roman See as long as it pleases God, who alone, and not the Roman pontiff, transfers and establishes kingdoms."[97]

Luther does not yet challenge the divine authority of the papacy, although, by quoting Rom. 13:1, he does place the authority of the papacy on the same level as other human authorities instituted by God. Still, he has questioned the validity of Matt. 16:18–19 as the key proof text for the divine right of papal rule. Luther has also begun to challenge the identity of the church of Christ with the Roman Church and papal decrees. Though still an historical argument, it possesses more relevance to his own situation than the same argument did in his *Explanations*. By attempting to force him to accept the interpretation of Scripture contained in papal decrees, Cajetan and others are binding the church to the decrees of the pope and making subjection to all papal decrees a condition for being in the church. This church can only equal the Roman Church. Luther resists this subjection and this identification as expressed in earlier papal decrees; the evangelical sense of Scripture must take priority over any papal decree that is not based on this sense, even a decree from the reigning pontiff. Although referring to the *Extravagante*, Luther states this priority now in categorical terms: "The truth of Scripture comes first; then one ought to see if the words of man are able to be true."[98]

Within Luther's consensus of authorities, the weight has shifted in favor of Scripture at the expense of papal decrees. One should not, however, jump to the conclusion that Luther has abandoned his consensus in favor of an exclusive Scripture principle or a conciliaristic viewpoint. Either conclusion is tempting, because Luther does resist both those who elevate the pope over councils and those "who brazenly state in public that the pope cannot err and is above Scripture."[99] His opposition to both misconceptions should be a warning against labeling Luther either a "scripturalist"[100] or a conciliarist.

The strongest evidence against the "scripturalist" label is Luther's appeal to a council of the church on November 28, 1518. He is no longer appealing from an ill-informed pope to a pope who should be better informed but from "our most holy lord Leo who is not correctly advised" to a "legitimate future council assembled in a safe place."[101] This appeal alone, however, does not make Luther a conciliarist. A council has long been part of his consensus of authorities. Even in the

Explanations, where Luther requires the confirmation of papal decrees by a council, he does not argue the conciliaristic thesis that the pope derives his authority from a council or that the council derives its authority from Christ. Luther's appeal to a council is still anchored in his consensus principle of church authority. Even the verdict of a council must be supported by Scripture, the church fathers, and clear reason.[102]

At this point Luther is not formulating in positive terms an exclusive principle of authority. Rather, he concentrates on resisting those flatterers of the pope who abuse his authority by seeking to make the pope's decisions the exclusive principle of authority in the church. For example, Luther expands the circle of flatterers to include canon lawyers who elevate tradition above Scripture in sharp contrast to "us theologians" who guard the purity of Scripture. The lawyers elevate the authority of the pope above councils and above Scripture. If these monstrosities are swallowed, then Scripture and the church will perish and nothing will remain but the word of human beings. They promote ill will against the church and seek its ruin and destruction.[103] "But I swear to you, my reader," says Luther in the *Proceedings,* "that I worship and follow the Roman Church in all things. I resist only those who in the name of the Roman Church strive to erect a Babylon among us; they desire that whatever they think up, as long as they can move their tongues to pronounce the words 'Roman Church,' be immediately and *in toto* accepted as the opinion of the Roman Church, as if Holy Scripture were not supreme."[104]

For Luther, this loyalty to the Roman Church no longer included loyalty to the pope, unless Leo unexpectedly issued a justified verdict. Not only have past papal decrees been in error, but now, for Luther, the pope is placed categorically on the same level with all erring humanity. Not even the pope is exempted from the verdict of the psalmist: "Every man is a liar" (Ps. 116:11).[105] This text, which Luther had quoted so confidently from Nuremberg on the eve of his departure for Augsburg, has now become a polemical barb against the pope.

But it is not just the pope's fallibility and rejection of his appeal that undermine Luther's loyalty. He no longer expects that Leo will exercise the pastoral duty of his office, which Luther sought from the beginning. Since through Cajetan the pope has demanded that Luther deny faith in Christ and the true understanding of the clearest Scriptures, he has abused his office. "The pope has not received power to destroy his sheep or to cast them into the throats of wolves and to abandon them to falsehood and to teachers of falsehood, but to recall them to the truth as befits a pastor and bishop, the vicar of Christ. . . . I foresee that no one will dare to confess Christ or to profess the sacred Scriptures in his own church. And I will be wrenched from a true, wholesome Christian faith and understanding, thrust into the empty and lying opinions of men, and forced to accept the fables which seduce Christian people."[106] Luther's dedication to the proper instruction of the people by a hierarchy faithfully exercising its pastoral office has at last led him to resist the papacy and even Leo himself. Luther's concern for the church has remained intact, and the papacy becomes its first major casualty.

At the time of his appeal, Luther did not yet realize the accuracy of his foresight. On November 9, Leo at last issued the definitive papal ruling which Luther had sought. In the bull *Cum postquam*, addressed to Cajetan and presumably drafted by him, Leo reaffirmed the papal teaching on indulgences which Luther had protested and ordered that the bull be published in Germany. Leo specifically decreed that his understanding of indulgences be held and preached under a penalty of excommunication which could only be lifted by the pope himself.[107] Luther would certainly take these words as the fulfillment of his prophecy that he would be forced to accept the fables that seduced Christian people and as justification for his resistance to Prierias and Cajetan. Even before he saw these words, Luther prepared for the worst. On November 25 he wrote to Spalatin: "I expect anathemas from Rome any day. Therefore, I am putting everything in order so that, when they arrive, I will be girded and ready to leave, like Abraham not knowing where I will go, but absolutely certain of the way because God is everywhere."[108]

4 | CHALLENGE
1519

Here, in my case, you may see how hard it is to struggle out of and emerge from errors which have been confirmed by the example of the whole world and have by long habit become a part of nature, as it were. . . . For that reason I can bear with a less hateful spirit those who cling too pertinaciously to the papacy, particularly those who have not read the sacred Scriptures, or also the profane, since I, who read the sacred Scriptures most diligently so many years, still clung to it so tenaciously.

—Luther, 1545
(WA 54, 183.21–23, 8–11)

CHRONOLOGY

1518	August 14	John Eck defends himself against the *Apologetic Conclusions* of Karlstadt and proposes a debate between them for April 1519
	December 13	Official publication of the papal bull *Cum postquam* takes place in Linz, Austria
	December 28	Karl von Miltitz meets with Frederick at Altenburg
	December 29	In Augsburg, Eck publishes in placard form twelve theses for the debate
1519	January 4–6	Miltitz negotiates with Luther at Altenburg. Luther drafts a letter to Leo which is not sent
	January 10	Emperor Maximilian dies
	Between January 13 and 19	Luther responds to the papal bull *Cum postquam* in a letter to Frederick
	February 19	Luther petitions Duke George for permission to appear in Leipzig as a disputant
	End of February	Luther publishes an *Instruction* for the laity as he promised Miltitz (*Unterricht auf etliche Artikel*)

1519	March 14	Eck issues a revised set of thirteen theses and an open letter in which he names Luther as his opponent
	By May 16	Luther has revised his set of countertheses to correspond to Eck's thirteen theses
	May 17	Luther declines the invitation of Miltitz to appear before the archbishop of Trier
	After June 6	Publication of Luther's explanation of his thirteenth thesis against Roman primacy (*Resolutio Lutheriana super propositione sua decima tertia. . . .*)
	June 10	Duke George grants a safe conduct for Karlstadt "and his party" to come to Leipzig
	June 21	Eck arrives in Leipzig
	June 24	Karlstadt, Luther, and their party arrive in Leipzig
	June 27	Debate between Eck and Karlstadt begins
	June 28	Charles V elected holy Roman emperor in Frankfurt
	July 4–14	Eck and Luther debate
	July 21	Melanchthon sends Oecolampadius his account of the debate; Eck immediately publishes a reply
	August	Melanchthon publishes a *Defense* against Eck
	August 30	Luther is condemned by the University of Cologne
	End of August	Luther publishes an explanation of the theses debated at Leipzig
	September 30	Luther: *Addition to Goat Emser*
	October 3	Luther receives a copy of Hus's treatise, *The Church,* from two Prague Utraquists
	October 9–10	Luther meets with Miltitz in Liebenwerda
	End of October	Luther's *Sermon on the Sacrament of Penance*
	November 7	Luther is condemned by the University of Louvain
	November 9	Luther: *Sermon on the Sacrament of Baptism*
	Early December	Luther: *Sermon on the Blessed Sacrament of the Holy and True Body of Christ and on the Brotherhoods*
	December 8	Miltitz warns Frederick that the curia will take severe steps against him unless he delivers Luther

1519   December   Frederick responds that Luther's case is still pending

AN INTERIM SOLUTION

The last month of 1518 and the first two months of 1519 were a critical period in Luther's relationship to the papacy. This was true no less for his legal standing with Rome than for his private attitude toward the Roman curia. It was also a critical period for Luther's personal future. Others recognized the decisive point at which Luther stood. From Salzburg, Staupitz wrote that he saw only a cross ahead for Luther. From his vantage point, the prevailing opinion was that no one should examine the Scriptures without consulting the pope. Luther, on the other hand, had few defenders. Therefore, wrote Staupitz, "it would please me if you would leave Wittenberg for a while and come to me, that we might live and die together."[1]

While Luther prepared for the worst, Frederick and his advisers deliberated how to respond to Cajetan's ultimatum to deliver Luther to Rome or to banish him from Saxony. At one point it looked as if Luther would have to leave Wittenberg. Spalatin advised Luther to flee, and on December 1, 1518, Luther invited his friends to the Black Cloister for a farewell dinner. During the meal, however, a letter from Spalatin arrived indicating that the elector wished Luther to remain.[2] Thus, Luther stayed in Wittenberg, marveling at the solicitude of his friends and confident now that the elector and the university were on his side. Luther's confidence was justified. On December 8, Frederick dispatched to Cajetan his refusal to comply with the ultimatum and attached to his letter a copy of Luther's response.

In persuading Frederick to make this crucial decision in favor of Luther, Spalatin might have appealed to the imminent visit of Karl von Miltitz to the Saxon court. Miltitz was a young Saxon nobleman who had studied in Bologna and pursued his fortune at the papal court in Rome. He became attached to the papal household and was available to provide the services of an intermediary between Rome and Saxony. In the fall of 1518, his services were needed. On September 3, the consistory of cardinals had approved the awarding of the Golden Rose to the Elector Frederick in order to win his support for their opposition to Charles of Spain as heir to the imperial throne. Miltitz was chosen to deliver the award to Frederick, and in mid-November he set off for Germany. Miltitz was instructed only to sound out Frederick on his attitude toward Luther; he was under strict orders to take no action without the approval of Cajetan, and he deposited the Golden Rose in Augsburg until Cajetan gave permission for the award to be presented.[3]

As soon as he reached Germany, Miltitz began to conceive of his mission in more grandiose terms: to bring about reconciliation between Luther and the pope.[4] In Nuremberg he convinced Christoph Scheurl that Luther should submit to the pope, and Scheurl, in turn, sent Luther detailed accounts of his conversations with Miltitz. Scheurl acknowledged that Luther had intimidated Rome, but now Luther should strive to reach an understanding with the pope that would avoid scandal and alienation on all sides.[5] The impression that Miltitz made on Scheurl reflects the eagerness of many of Luther's sympathizers to prevent a break between him and the papacy.

Miltitz pursued his plan when he arrived at the electoral court in Altenburg on December 28, 1518. Spalatin remarked that he came loaded with seventy official briefs, including several that granted new indulgence privileges in connection with Frederick's relic collection at the Castle Church in Wittenberg.[6] Two of the letters were intended for Spalatin himself. Pope Leo appealed to the priestly duty of Spalatin to obey the holy see and asked Spalatin to persuade his prince to be obedient as well, so that Frederick would not bring dishonor on the noble house of Saxony.[7] After discharging the authorized duties of his mission, Miltitz asked if he could meet with Luther and, upon reviewing Miltitz's proposal, Frederick summoned Luther to Altenburg. Both Frederick and Spalatin were willing to risk this attempt at rapprochement, whatever they thought of Miltitz, since its success would relieve Frederick of the necessity of continuing his difficult and embarrassing resistance to Leo.

In terms of Luther's trial, the impact of Miltitz's visit was negligible. Miltitz was unable to persuade Luther to appear before the archbishop of Trier even though Luther had agreed that this archbishop might be an acceptable arbiter for him.[8] Still, Miltitz's encounter with Luther did have an important effect on his stance in relation to the papacy; it forced Luther to reconcile his growing private reservations about the papacy with his desire to uphold publicly the honor of the Roman Church and of the pope. Because of the agreement reached in Altenburg, Luther was pushed to work out an interim solution to this dilemma.

The private reservations about the papacy had grown more serious since he had completed the *Proceedings at Augsburg*, and Luther had apparently been putting his feelings on paper. On December 18, 1518, he promised Wenceslaus Link that he would send him some of his worthless trifles so that Link might judge whether the true, divine Antichrist predicted by Paul was reigning in the Roman curia. "I think," said Luther, "I can demonstrate that today Rome is worse than the Turk."⁹ A few days later, Luther criticized the bishops of the church, and particularly the pope, for failing to exhibit the form of a servant. Instead, they sat like Antichrists in the temple of God (2 Thess. 2:4), exploiting the power they received and extorting the submission of everyone else.¹⁰ Before he met Miltitz at Altenburg, Luther had begun to voice the suspicion that the Antichrist might be at work in the midst of the Roman hierarchy.

The meeting took place in Spalatin's quarters on January 5 and 6, 1519. It began, according to Luther, with Miltitz accusing him of having brought dishonor and shame on the church. Luther offered to do all that he could, short of recanting, to settle the matter, and he submitted four proposals to Miltitz and to the elector.¹¹ In the second of these, he volunteered to write humbly to Leo in order to explain why he, a faithful child of the church, had fought the blasphemous preaching which brought the Roman Church scorn, dishonor, and scandal from the people.¹² Probably on the same day, Luther prepared a draft of this letter to show to Miltitz. The explanation Luther promised was the same as he had given before. The indulgence preachers promoted avarice with their insipid sermons preached in the name of the pope; then they blamed Luther for their own brashness.¹³ Quite to the contrary, says Luther, he sought only to prevent the Roman Church, "our mother," from being polluted with avarice and to prevent the people from being led astray and taught to prefer indulgences over works of charity.¹⁴ He never intended to touch the power of the pope or of the Roman Church. The power of this church was above all things and it ought to be honored above everything else in heaven or on earth except Jesus Christ, Lord of all.¹⁵

In this letter Luther does not retreat from anything he had said before. He cannot recall or recant his *Theses* because the indulgence preachers are to blame and the proper instruction of the people is at stake. Nevertheless, Luther does not criticize Leo for failing to restrain the indulgence preachers or for refusing to grant the impartial hearing he had requested. This lack of criticism, alongside Luther's bold affirmation of the church's power, has raised questions about Luther's sincerity in this draft. How could Luther honestly affirm the supremacy of the Roman Church and refrain from all criticism of Leo when less than a month earlier he had voiced the suspicion that the Antichrist might be at work in the Roman curia?[16]

Luther was trying to maintain a position over against the papacy on two levels simultaneously. Privately, he was expressing his growing disillusionment with the pope. This disillusionment would intensify through the next several months as he studied past papal decrees in preparation for the Leipzig Debate. For example, in a letter dated February 20, Luther said that he would uphold and confess the power and majesty of the pope, but he could not bear the corruption of Holy Scripture. For a long time, Luther said, he had wanted to write against papal decrees, but he had not dared. Now the Lord was drawing him and he was following not unwillingly.[17] By mid-March Luther would whisper confidentially to Spalatin that he did not know whether the pope was the Antichrist himself or only his apostle, so miserably did he corrupt and crucify Christ in his decrees.[18] In early January, Luther had not yet speculated on a personal identification between the pope and the Antichrist;[19] but it is unlikely that he privately expected Leo to change his mind and to take his side against the indulgence preachers.

Publicly, Luther was complying with the wishes of the elector and of friends such as Spalatin and Scheurl not to adopt an irreconcilable stance. Accordingly, the draft of the letter contained no criticism of Leo and defended Luther's good intention in the whole affair. The affirmation of the power of the Roman Church which Luther made did not contradict his earlier statements. In the *Proceedings at Augsburg* he had criticized the presumption of the Roman Church to be the only true church and its right to demand unqualified acceptance of its decrees. But it was still possible for him to affirm the supremacy of Rome among Western churches as long as Rome subordinated itself to Christ, as he stated in the letter to Leo. Even his suspicion that the Antichrist had invaded the curia did not yet cause him to reject the authority of the Roman Church.

The tension between his public statements and his private fears was severely tested in January and February when the papal bull, *Cum postquam,* finally came to Luther's attention. In this bull, officially published on December 13, Leo laid down the definitive justification for the indulgence practice of the church. Luther professed astonishment at the decree. It said nothing new, restated old positions even more obscurely than earlier decretals, and failed to resolve contradictions between past and present decrees. Finally, and most important, the bull did not cite any saying of Scripture, teachers, or laws of the church, nor did it offer any compelling arguments.[20] Since the church should give reasons for its teaching, as St. Peter (1 Pet. 3:15) and St. Paul (1 Thess. 5:21) had commanded, Luther said he could not recognize the decretal as a legitimate and sufficient teaching of the holy church. Instead, he must obey God's commands and prohibitions. "Although I will not reject it, I will also not bow down before it."[21]

In effect, Luther did reject it, although he did not condemn it publicly, and this rejection was the turning point in his case. Luther now refused to accept an explicit papal ruling on a matter which he had claimed was still open to debate because no such ruling existed. When Luther demanded that the pope give responsible reasons for his ruling, he subjected the papal decree to the same conditions he imposed upon the academic arguments of his opponents. This "revolutionary step," as one historian has called it,[22] was based on the same arguments Luther had previously used to justify his questioning of papal teaching. Since the whole world was now asking not only *what* was said (by the church), but also *why* it was said, the Roman Church would suffer dishonor and ridicule if he were now to recant, although that church was not able to offer any convincing arguments against his position.[23] Those arguments, as Luther outlined them, would have to come from the same consensus of authorities that he had been proposing for almost a year. The only "revolutionary" aspect of his reaction to *Cum postquam* was that Luther did now oppose the decree of a reigning pontiff. The ground for this step had already been well prepared in the *Proceedings at Augsburg.*

In spite of its importance, Luther's rejection of *Cum postquam* was not a public rebuke of the papacy. It occurred at the semiprivate level in a letter to the Elector Frederick. It did not, therefore, destroy the delicate balance between his private misgivings about the papacy and his public affirmations of loyalty to the Roman Church. Indeed, in the same letter to Frederick, Luther repeated his determination to honor the Roman Church in all humility and not to allow anything in heaven or on earth to take precedence over it except God and his word.[24] In the *Instruction* for the people, which he issued in late February as part of his agreement with Miltitz,[25] Luther argued that issues such as the power and authority of the Roman see should be left to the scholars because the blessedness of souls did not depend on that at all. Christ did not build his church on external power and authority over worldly matters but on internal qualities such as love, humility, and unity. Let power be as great or as small as God chooses to distribute it. We should be content and, for the sake of unity, not resist papal commands.[26]

These words reveal the strain to which Luther's interim solution was being subjected. He could maintain respect for the papacy only at the cost of dissociating the salvation of the people from the question of papal authority. The salvation of the people had long been Luther's main concern. In his letter to Frederick, Luther said that he had been strengthened by the conviction that the Roman Church would not tolerate the damaging sermons of the indulgence preachers and allow the poor people of Christ to be seduced by indulgences.[27] Papal decrees, especially the most recent, *Cum postquam,* had dashed that hope as far as the papacy itself was concerned. Still, Luther had not given up on the Roman Church as a whole, and he attempted to salvage that hope and his concern for the people by temporarily excluding the question of papal authority. This was the first occasion on which Luther stated explicitly that the salvation of the people was independent of the papal see and its power. Under such tension, Luther could not remain silent much longer.

ECK

More than any other person, John Eck provoked Luther to issue his first public challenge to the papacy. Eck was the catalyst who finally changed Luther's uneasy alliance of public loyalty and private disillusionment into public opposition. At the same time, Eck began his own tenacious opposition to Luther and the Protestant movement which lasted until his death in 1543.

Although he died three years before Luther, John Eck was three years his junior. Like Luther's colleague, Philipp Melanchthon, Eck had been a precocious student. At fourteen he earned his master of arts degree at the University of Tübingen. He then pursued the study of theology at Freiburg while giving lectures in the arts faculty. "Thus I made progress teaching and learning at the same time," recalled Eck of his years in Freiburg.[28] In 1508 he was ordained to the priesthood and in 1510, at the age of twenty-four, he was awarded the doctor of theology degree. In the same year he accepted a call to become professor of theology at the University of Ingolstadt in Bavaria. Eck had been recommended for the chair in Ingolstadt by the prominent Augsburg humanist Conrad

Peutinger, who was adviser to the powerful banking family of Jacob Fugger. Here Eck may have benefitted for the first time from Fugger influence, which was to help him become one of the most prominent and best-connected theologians in Germany.[29]

Eck established his theological reputation with a work entitled *Chrysopassus*, published in 1514. It contained the results of his studies and lectures on predestination and demonstrated his thorough knowledge of both classical and scholastic authors. In the front of his work, Eck compiled an index of authors he had consulted directly or indirectly, many of whom had nothing to say on the subject of predestination. In spite of this tendency to extol his own learning, Eck never exchanged his given German name, Hans Maier (Eck was his birthplace), for a more elevated classical form after the manner of humanists such as Philipp Melanchthon or Urbanus Rhegius (1489–1541).[30] Rhegius, who had been a pupil of Eck in Freiburg, praised his former teacher as a man without equal in a poem that was also printed in the front of *Chrysopassus*. By 1534, however, Rhegius would extol Luther as the greatest man he had ever met.[31] In 1514 neither he nor Eck could imagine how radically things would change over the next twenty years.

Eck consolidated his fame in a disputation held in Bologna in 1515. The subject of the disputation was the legitimacy of charging interest. The church had long opposed usury, but it was not clear whether this prohibition applied to interest being charged by the large banking houses in Germany such as the Fuggers. Many humanists were opposed to the practice, and, when Eck emerged as its defender, the prominent circle of humanists around Christoph Scheurl in Nuremberg persuaded the chancellor of the University of Ingolstadt and bishop of Eichstätt, Gabriel von Eyb, to forbid Eck to debate the matter in Ingolstadt. To them, Eck appeared beholden to the Fuggers, and they were afraid that a public debate would scandalize the laity. As a doctor of theology, Eck protested that he had the right to put the matter up for debate. A debate would not cause offense, but would instead counter misconceptions harbored by laity and clergy alike. The argument that Eck used was strikingly similar to Luther's defense of his right to debate the merits of indulgences until the church ruled otherwise. An ironical switch occurred when Eck declared Luther's theses on indulgences dangerous for the common folk and Luther protested that it was his right as a doctor of theology to debate the theses, especially since they were written in Latin and intended only for scholars.[32]

Both Eck and Luther, therefore, had exhibited concern for the enlightenment of the laity before they came to blows over the papacy. They disagreed, however, over what was best for the people in their religious life. In opposing Luther's *Ninety-five Theses*, Eck appealed to the devastating effect they would have on the people's respect for the church hierarchy and the pope. This defense of the hierarchy at all costs united Eck, the young sophisticated humanist, with such contrasting types as the indulgence seller, Tetzel, and the older curialists and distinguished Thomists, Prierias and Cajetan. Awe of the pope and respect for the ancient and venerable institution founded upon his see cut across all barriers of age and theological traditions in the opposition that faced Luther by early 1519.[33]

It fell to Eck in particular to provoke Luther's first public challenge to papal authority because of Eck's prior involvement with the Wittenbergers and the prospect of another prestigious debating victory for himself. After he read Luther's *Proceedings at Augsburg* and his appeal to a council, Eck was convinced that Luther had rebelled against the papacy and was guilty of heresy and schism.[34] An opportunity to call Luther to public account was already at hand. Eck used an upcoming disputation which he had arranged to hold with Karlstadt as the opportunity to bring Luther out into the open. At the end of December, he published in Augsburg twelve theses for the debate, which were directed primarily against Luther instead of Karlstadt. Eck aimed his twelfth thesis specifically against a statement made by Luther in his explanation of the twenty-second of his *Ninety-five Theses*: "Suppose the Roman Church were such as it was at the time of Gregory I when it was not over the other churches, at least not over the churches of Greece. . . ."[35] In opposition to this historical judgment, which Luther used to prove another point,[36] Eck posed the thesis: "We deny that the Roman Church was not above the other churches before the time of Sylvester; rather, we have always acknowledged the one who occupied the see of the blessed Peter and held his faith as the successor of Peter and as the general vicar of Christ."[37] Eck singled out this historical argument devoid of polemical intent as the culmination of his theses in order to focus his attack on the issue of papal authority. Eck later defended his action as taken on behalf of the faith and in defense of the apostolic see.[38]

At first, Luther expressed dismay that Eck chose for discussion matters related to his own *Theses* instead of the weightier subjects of sin and grace over which Eck and Karlstadt had planned to debate.[39] But he was also visibly relieved that the question of papal authority would be debated openly. In a letter to Scheurl on February 20, 1519, he said that for a long time he had been playing, but now serious steps would be taken against the Roman pontiff and Roman arrogance.[40] Those steps were called for by Luther's study of canon law, which had been underway since the controversy with Cajetan over the *Extravagante*. Now he intensified his study of past papal decrees in order to counter Eck's thesis, and this study led on March 13 to his whisper to Spalatin that the pope himself might be the Antichrist.[41] Luther had apparently made copious notes on the decrees; he promised to send them to Spalatin so that "he too could see what happens when laws are made without regard for Scripture, merely from a desire to exercise tyranny, not to mention all the other works of the Antichrist in which the Roman curia abounds."[42]

This negative reaction of Luther to his study echoes two familiar themes. First, papal decrees have had a tyrannical effect upon the people. Luther tells Spalatin that he is tormented by the deception of the people of Christ under the guise of laws and of the "Christian" label.[43] This concern for the people of the church is accompanied by the increasing importance of Scripture. "Daily greater and greater help and support by virtue of the authority of Scripture well up in me."[44] The immediate impact of Eck's challenge was to confirm Luther's suspicions, already voiced at Augsburg, that the deception of the people against which he had protested was anchored in a false theory of papal authority contained in papal decrees which abused Scripture. His study led to this conviction; the upcoming debate caused him for the first time to express the conviction publicly. It was time to write against the pope.[45]

PROPOSITION THIRTEEN

Luther's first public challenge to papal authority was formulated against Eck's twelfth thesis and soon became the famous "Proposition Thirteen."[46] Luther maintained that only "the most unconvincing [literally, most frigid] decrees of the Roman pontiffs issued within the last four hundred years prove that the Roman Church is superior to all others; against these stand the accepted history of the last fifteen hundred years, the text of divine Scripture and the decree of the Council of Nicea, the holiest of all councils."[47]

When this thesis was issued in mid-May as number thirteen in his

Disputation and Defense of Brother Martin Luther against the Accusations of Dr. John Eck, Luther blamed Eck for raising the question of papal authority and noted accurately that he had never dealt with this material or thought of making it the subject of debate.[48] He also disclosed the new confidence, gained through his studies and his readiness for the battle: "I am convinced that the apostolic see neither will nor can do anything against Christ. Furthermore, in this matter I fear neither the pope nor the name of the pope, much less those little popes and puppets. I am concerned about one thing, namely, that the despoiling of my Christian name does not bring with it the loss of the most holy doctrine of Christ."[49] The tension of the previous months was finally released. "In this matter I do not want anyone to expect patience of me. . . . I not only want to bite vehemently, to the discomfiture of Eck, but I want to prove myself invincible in devouring so that, to use Isaiah's phrase [Isa. 9:12], I could swallow in one gulp all Sylvesters and Civesters, Cajetans and Ecks and the other brothers who are adversaries of Christian grace."[50]

Luther had to bite sooner than he expected. In spite of three requests, he did not receive official permission to go to Leipzig for the debate. In order to defend himself publicly, therefore, he published in June *Luther's Explanation of Proposition Thirteen Concerning the Power of the Pope*. It was his first treatise on the subject of the papacy, and it came just twenty months after the *Ninety-five Theses*.

In spite of Luther's readiness to "bite vehemently," the *Explanation* stopped short of a complete rejection of papal authority. Luther sought to refute only the claim that the Roman bishop was head of the church by divine right, that is, that Christ established Peter and his successors as the head of the universal church. Luther was quite willing to admit that the pope was head of the Western church by human right and that he enjoyed authority given to him by God just as all earthly rulers did. Luther made this point emphatically, citing Rom. 13:1 in support of his argument as he had done in the *Proceedings at Augsburg*.[51] If the popes would accept this basis of their rule, their monarchy in the church would rest on a much firmer foundation. As long as they claimed to rule by divine right, however, and enforced their rule with terror, they would only arouse hatred in their subjects and harden their own rule into tyranny.[52]

Indeed, in Luther's eyes papal rule had degenerated into just such tyranny, and hence the remainder of the treatise refuted the claim of the popes to rule by divine right. As the thirteenth thesis indicated, Luther based his refutation on both exegetical and historical arguments. Crucial to his argument was the treatment of two biblical texts that served as the foundation of the papal claim. The first was Matt. 16:18–19: "You are Peter, and on this rock I will build my church. . . . I will give you the keys of the kingdom of heaven. . . ." The second was the command of Christ to Peter in John 21:16: "Feed my sheep." Luther noted that not all commentators on canon law agreed that the primacy of Peter was based on the Matthean text. For example, Panormitanus argued that the primacy was more properly based on the second text than on the first.[53] Hence Luther also reserved the right to reject the first text as proof of papal primacy by divine right. In the first place, Luther emphasized that Peter did not receive the keys for himself alone but for all the apostles, just as Peter had responded for them all when Christ inquired who they thought he was.[54] All the apostles received the keys equally and, consequently, they belonged to the whole church and not to successors of Peter alone. In the second place, Luther interpreted the rock on which Christ promised to build his church as the confession of Peter and not as the person of Peter. As a result, the church was present anywhere that the same lordship of Christ was confessed and not merely where Peter's successors, the popes, reigned.[55]

The superiority of the Roman Church could only be based upon Matthew 16 if this text were interpreted as confirming the superiority of the person of Peter, as in fact the papal decrees had done. Luther, however, chose to follow a different exegetical tradition which regarded Peter as the representative of all the apostles and applied the text to the whole church and its faith instead of to the Roman Church alone. Luther adopted this interpretation because it better fit the context of the passage,[56] but his decision was not based on exegesis alone. The exegesis that Luther adopted coincided with his conception of the church's nature. The church was not tied to any one person or place but extended as far as the circle of all believing Christians extended and was knit together by their faith in the word. Or, as Luther now expressed it, the church is the communion of saints and the "daughter of God, born by the word of God, which hears the word of God and perseveres to the end in confessing that word."[57] This conception of the church was not new for Luther.[58] He had held it prior to the *Ninety-five Theses,* and he had already employed it briefly against the claims of the Roman Church to be exclusively the church.

A theory of the church by itself, however, did not cause Luther to reject the main proof text for the divine right of papal primacy. As was true in the case of the *Ninety-five Theses,* the convergence of theory and practice made this ecclesiological application necessary. The exclusive claim of the papacy to rule the church by divine right had led to devastating consequences for the people who made up the church. This theme was paramount in Luther's rejection of the second main proof text of divine right, the command of Christ to Peter in John 21:16: "Feed my sheep." Aside from the fact that Christ did not tell Peter to feed all the sheep by himself, the popes and their decrees completely misunderstood the meaning of "feed." It did not mean to be the chief over others but to preach and teach the word of God. If this were applied to the Roman pope, he would have to immerse himself day and night in Scripture and labor for the word in the face of danger and death. Rome would then present quite a different face.[59]

Furthermore, Christ gives Peter the command to feed only after he ascertains that Peter loves him. Therefore, this command of Christ is not meant to exhort the sheep to be subject to their pastors but to exhort the pastors to love Christ and to feed the people. "If only the Roman pontiffs would believe that this word applied to them!", exclaims Luther. They leave the feeding to others while they lord it over the people and reserve the honor and profit of their office for themselves. All ranks in the hierarchy do the same. They all want the honor and reward, but none wants to do the work of feeding the people; hence, the people are not fed. If this text is forced to apply to the pope, then the Roman Church has had no pastor since Gregory the Great (*c.* 600), who was virtually the last pope to study and interpret Scripture.[60]

Luther's opposition to papal claims to rule by divine right, therefore, is based upon the same concern for the feeding of the people by faithful pastors that sparked his protest against indulgences. That concern echoes throughout the *Explanation* as he refutes individual papal decrees and adduces reasons in addition to Scripture for his opposition. Justifying his rejection of papal decrees issued within the last four hundred years, Luther complains that they have been put on the same level with the chief articles of faith. This adulation of the decrees has led to confusion of ecclesiastical order, terrible torment of consciences, ignorance of the gospel, crime with impunity, and the despicable tyranny of the Roman flatterers. As a result, no name under heaven is more detestable and abominable than the name of the Roman curia.[61] Not papal rule as such, therefore, but the effects of that rule as undergirded by the claim of divine right caused Luther to challenge the papacy publicly.

This first public work on the papacy does not contain a new view of the church or even a different motivation and concern; these remain the same as they were before the controversy over indulgences erupted. The new element is that Luther now holds the official theory underlying papal primacy, as espoused by the popes themselves, responsible for the failure of the church's pastors and bishops to execute their office properly. Luther has discovered why Leo did not respond favorably to his appeal that Leo halt the abuses of the indulgence preachers.[62] That appeal could not penetrate the shield of divine right which the laws of the church and the "flatterers" of the pope had constructed around the papal office.

Luther has still not attacked directly the reigning pope, Leo X. He has, however, rejected the claim of all popes, including Leo X, to rule by divine right in the church and consequently to expect the unequivocal acceptance of their pronouncements. Luther's intensive study of canon law has brought him a long way in a short time: from his refusal at Augsburg to accept specific decrees of past popes, to his rejection in January 1519 of the decree of a reigning pope (*Cum postquam*), to his categorical denial in May and June 1519 that all popes, past and present, rule by divine right. Inwardly, he has also come a long way from dependence on the papacy. At the conclusion of the *Explanation,* he confesses that he does not know whether Christian faith can suffer having on earth another head of the universal church besides Christ.[63]

THE LEIPZIG DEBATE

Although he did not receive personal permission to go to Leipzig for the debate, Luther included himself in the safe conduct which Duke George had granted to Karlstadt "and his party." Duke George did not oppose Luther's participation; in fact, he was anxious to see the debate take place. In allowing the debate, he had overruled both the university and the bishop of Merseburg in whose diocese Leipzig was located. As patron of the university, he rebuked the timidity of his theological faculty for not agreeing to host and judge a debate. As a layman, he was aware that the church could be pulling the wool over the eyes of the people and profiting from their ignorance about indulgences. When it was brought to his attention that the pope had ruled on indulgences,

Duke George replied that the pope had not forbidden debates; the pope could only be pleased to see the whole truth brought to light and the "poor laity" instructed.[64]

The prohibition Bishop Adolf posted just as the Wittenbergers arrived in Leipzig was not able to halt the debate, nor was the accident which befell Karlstadt's wagon as the Wittenberg party entered Leipzig, although some took it, after the fact, as an ill omen for the outcome.[65] Officially the debate was to take place between Eck and Karlstadt, and that is how it began and ended. The opening negotiations on June 26, however, provided time for Eck and Luther to confront each other. After Eck and Karlstadt had debated for the first week, Luther took Karlstadt's place at the rostrum opposite Eck in the great hall of the Pleissenburg.

Despite the notoriety it received, the Leipzig Debate between Luther and Eck (July 4–14) caused no decisive change in Luther's attitude toward the papacy. Although half of their time was spent on the subject of papal primacy, Luther did not advance beyond the arguments he had employed in his *Explanation of Proposition Thirteen.* The exegesis of Matthew 16 and John 21 was debated in detail. Additional historical arguments and citations of church fathers flew back and forth. When the dust had settled, however, Luther was just as adamantly opposed to the claims of papal rule by divine right as when he had mounted the podium.[66]

Luther did exploit the potential of some arguments which, up to now, he had mentioned only incidentally. For example, Eck opened the debate with the traditional argument for papal monarchy based on Dionysius the Pseudo-Areopagite. The congruence between the earthly and heavenly churches allowed the pope to serve as monarch of the militant church just as God ruled alone at the apex of the church triumphant. Whether or not Luther knew of Cajetan's sermon at the Fifth Lateran Council on this same theme is uncertain. But he was unusually well prepared to counter Eck's use of this argument at Leipzig. At the end of his *Explanation of Proposition Thirteen,* Luther had noted the danger of restricting Christ to the church triumphant so that the Roman pontiff could be established as head of the militant church. This restriction contradicted the words of Christ in Matt. 28:20: "Lo I am with you always, to the close of the age."[67] In response to Eck, Luther repeated his argument that an exclusive monarchy of the pope robbed Christ of his status as the invisible head of the earthly church. He added, however, a biblical text, which four years earlier he had cited as proof of the presence of Christ in the militant church. The church is a kingdom of faith, said Luther, where we do not see our head; but we have him present on the thrones of judgment (Ps. 122:5) as the invisible king behind every prelate who occupies a see of the church.[68] Luther was able to use the ecclesiological application of his earlier exegetical work to expose a dangerous weakness in Eck's argument.

Luther was no more impressed with Eck's other arguments for divine right. When Eck finally mentioned Christ's command to Peter in John 21:16, Luther said that he rejoiced after three days to hear an argument from divine right (namely, Scripture).[69] Luther, of course, was ready with his own interpretation of "feed my sheep." The debate had less impact on Luther's attitude toward the papacy than on his consensus of authorities. Eck forced Luther to realize how the rejection of the rule of the papacy by divine right affected the relative authority of Scripture, councils, and church fathers. Luther's already shaky consensus received another shock.

The story of how this happened is the most famous feature of the debate. On the second morning, Eck revived his old charge of Luther's affinity to Hus. This time Eck also named Wyclif and identified Luther's defense of papal primacy by human right alone with propositions of Hus and Wyclif already condemned by the church. Eck was aware that he was appealing to the German nationalist feeling and repugnance for heresy of his audience.[70] Luther protested as usual against this tactic of guilt by association, but during the noon break he must have consulted the decrees of the Council of Constance (1414–1418), which had condemned Wyclif and Hus.[71] When the debate resumed in the afternoon, Luther boldly affirmed that some of the articles of Hus and the Bohemians were plainly "most Christian and evangelical." The universal church could not condemn such articles as, for example, Hus's statement that there was only one universal church.[72]

This article naturally caught Luther's attention since he was trying to prove that Eastern Christians not subject to Rome could not be excluded from the universal church as if the universal church were identical with the Roman Church. Consequently, Luther also defended another statement of Wyclif that had been condemned at Constance: it is not necessary to salvation to believe that the Roman Church is superior to all other churches. This statement directly contradicted the decree of Boniface VIII (1302, *Unam sanctam*) which Eck had already cited.[73] Luther did not stop here, however. Since there was no scriptural basis for limiting the universal church of Christ to the particular church headed by Peter's successors, Luther objected that neither Roman pontiffs (such as Boniface VIII) nor inquisitors of heresy (such as Tetzel and Eck) had power to establish new articles of faith. "Nor could any faithful Christian be forced to go beyond holy Scripture, which is properly divine right, unless new and proven revelation had been received." To support this thesis Luther cited Gerson from among the "more recent" theologians, Augustine from the older church fathers, and his favorite authority from canon law, Panormitanus.[74]

Eck saw his opening and pressed the attack. He accused Luther of dishonoring the holy and revered Council of Constance. Luther protested that he had not meant to oppose the council and thought up several lame excuses for the council's action.[75] He had to admit, however, that a council was only the creature of the infallible word of God, the divine Scriptures, and it could err.[76] Although he later qualified his assertion by restricting the fallibility of councils chiefly to matters that did not concern faith, Eck retorted, "If you believe that a legitimately assembled council has erred or can err, then you are for me a pagan and a publican."[77]

Luther had previously appealed to the authority of Scripture over papal rulings which were not supported by Scripture, councils, church fathers, or other good arguments. Now, for the first time, he was forced to state in principle the authority of Scripture over church councils and to digest the fact that a highly respected council had committed an egregious error. Furthermore, Eck forced him time and again to place the clear meaning of Scripture as Luther perceived it over the opinion of a church father. For example, Luther opposed an argument of Jerome with the authority of Paul in 1 Corinthians 3, stating that he would not allow his greater authority to be taken away by the introduction of a lesser one. In cases where the fathers contradicted one another, one ought to accept the genuine and proper sense of Scripture which could stand up in battle.[78]

The weight within Luther's consensus of authorities had shifted heavily in favor of Scripture as the norm according to which other authorities must be judged. To name the result of this shift an "exclusive" Scripture principle or *sola scriptura* is misleading. Luther still appeals to church fathers and canon lawyers such as Panormitanus for support, and he has by no means denied that church councils can make valid judgments in matters of faith. Luther still wished for a consensus of the most authorities possible, but he now realized more astutely that Scripture in its clearest and most appropriate meaning had to govern that consensus. Eck's shrewdness brought Luther to this view of authority, which he now expressed as a principle: "The word of God is above all the words of men."[79] With Eck's help, Luther sought and found not the exclusiveness of Scripture, but the freedom of Scripture from false interpretations of human authorities: "I seek nothing except to shut up those who dare to hold captive in the interpretations and words of men and pontiffs the absolutely free understanding of Scripture given to us by Christ. They want to judge the words of God by the word of men, although the reverse is true: the words of men ought to be judged by the word of God, which judges all things" [1 Cor. 2:15].[80]

IMPACT

One day after the debate between Eck and Karlstadt began, Charles V was elected Holy Roman Emperor in Frankfurt. There was no longer any reason for the curia to court Frederick the Wise and to delay Luther's case; nevertheless, the trial was not resumed in Rome until 1520. In the meantime, the Leipzig Debate and Luther's *Explanation of Proposition Thirteen* cleared the air and had a decisive impact on both the participants and the witnesses to the debate. Luther's public challenge to the claim of the popes to rule by divine right called forth varied reactions. Such a highly charged issue as papal authority, like all controversial subjects, provoked some to an immediate response while others adopted a more cautious attitude.

For Eck the matter was clearer than ever: Luther was a heretic. Eck therefore touted himself as the victor at Leipzig and publicized his triumph at every opportunity. He wrote to the Elector Frederick and to Pope Leo in Rome. After the universities of Paris and Erfurt had been selected as judges for the debate, Eck asked the Dominican Jacob Hoogstraten in Cologne to use his influence to gain a favorable decision from the Paris faculty since he, Eck, had no connections there.[81] With Luther and the other Wittenbergers, Eck engaged in a battle of polemics. At least seventeen treatises written by Eck or against him appeared by early 1520, and most were in print by the end of 1519.[82] Eck not only provoked Luther to his first public challenge to papal authority; he also prolonged their encounter into an ongoing debate over authority in the church.

Eck did not stand alone. Future opponents of Luther began to turn against him in the aftermath of Leipzig. Duke George, who kept his part of Saxony subject to Rome until his death in 1539, was apparently swayed by Eck. Duke George was repelled by Luther's defense of Hus, as indicated by his notorious remark, "That's the plague." But he was equally disturbed by Luther's affront to papal authority. Looking back from 1545, Luther speculated that his own arguments had made some impact on Duke George when George admitted that "whether he be pope by human or divine right, yet he is pope."[83] More accurately, Eck recalled a similar remark in his own favor. According to Eck, Duke George warned them both not to treat the holy church or its councils with audacity and pointed out to Luther that the Roman pontiff would remain the highest pontiff.[84] Apparently, Duke George had decided that Luther's position was more dangerous than Eck's. Duke George took Luther aside and told him how his exposition of the Lord's Prayer had caused confusion of consciences in many people.[85]

The Leipzig Debate brought another opponent of Luther out into the open. Jerome Emser (1478–1527), secretary at the court of Duke George, had entertained Luther at his home in Dresden in July 1518.[86] Emser claimed that before the Leipzig Debate began he had asked Luther "for God's sake" to spare the poor souls who were so upset by the whole affair.[87] After witnessing Luther's defense of Hus during the debate itself, Emser wrote a letter on August 13, 1519, to the administrator of the Archdiocese of Prague, John Zack. With honorable intentions, as he later claimed, Emser attempted to free Luther from suspicion of harboring Hussite views and defended the divine right of papal rule. Luther, however, regarded the letter as a Judas kiss; it was a clever trick by Emser to force him to identify with Hus. In the exchange of acerbic treatises which followed, Luther's polemic made the most of the goat in Emser's coat of arms, and Eck seized the opportunity to intervene on behalf of Emser.[88]

The controversy between Emser and Luther rested at this point until late 1520 when it flared up again with renewed vigor. The combined attacks of Eck and Emser in 1519, however, seemed to strengthen Luther's resolve and to confirm his views on the papacy. He was beginning to acquire a historical perspective on the controversy and to appreciate the indispensable role of his opponents in helping him to clarify his views. In his *Addition to Goat Emser*, Luther wrote: "I am indebted to no one more, and should pray for no one more, than for John Tetzel, the author of this tragedy (may his soul rest in peace), and for you and Eck and for all my adversaries, so much do I think they have advanced and profited me."[89] Luther did not feel as bitter toward Tetzel as toward the others. Before Tetzel died in Leipzig during the debate, Luther sent him a comforting letter.

Luther suffered setbacks in the scholarly world as well. Although the official judges of the debate, Erfurt and Paris, refused to render a verdict, Luther was quickly condemned by the University of Cologne (August 30) and by the University of Louvain (November 7). In both cases the Dominicans, with the aid of Hoogstraten, played the key role.[90] Only in Wittenberg did Luther receive university support, and it was less than wholehearted. Karlstadt had already questioned the wisdom of Luther's Proposition Thirteen, and at Leipzig he and Eck did not deal with ecclesiological questions at all. Although Karlstadt had treated the issue of authority in his *Apologetic Conclusions* of 1518 and may have introduced Luther to Panormitanus, he was not yet willing to follow Luther in applying the argument of Panormitanus to papal authority. The first crack in Karlstadt's respect for the papacy became visible in August of 1520. The immediate impact on him of the Leipzig Debate is unknown.[91]

The first mention of the papacy by Philipp Melanchthon occurs in his report on the Leipzig Disputation, which he sent to his fellow humanist, Oecolampadius, the future reformer of Basel. Melanchthon praised Luther and criticized the theatrics of Eck; he recounted their arguments in detail but did not voice explicit support for Luther's point of view.[92] When Eck attacked his letter, however, Melanchthon defended Luther's appeal to the "simple sense" of Scripture over the divided opinions of the church fathers.[93] Luther would receive important support from his humanist colleague who was just beginning the formal study of theology. But the so-called "Wittenberg theology" was less united behind Luther's challenge to the papacy than it was united in the attack on scholastic theology. In his first public confrontation over papal authority, Luther was ahead of his Wittenberg colleagues. Even after the Leipzig Debate, it would take them a while to catch up.[94]

More immediate support came from two "Hussite" (Utraquist) pastors in Prague. By October 3 Luther had received their letters and a copy of Hus's treatise, *The Church*, which they enclosed. Luther's new respect for Hus may have caused him to read it immediately. By the beginning of November, Luther asserted that he now agreed with many more articles of Hus than he had at Leipzig.[95] This work would figure significantly in his relationship to the papacy in 1520.

The most critical support Luther received in 1519 was not theological but political. The Elector Frederick was still not willing to turn Luther over to Rome. How Luther's public defiance of divine right affected him is unknown. Frederick, however, had no obvious reasons for protecting Luther any longer. A new emperor had been elected, the academic debate which Luther had sought had been held, and his university was isolated in its support of Luther. In spite of all that, Frederick turned down a new invitation from Miltitz to escort Luther to a hearing before the archbishop of Trier. Miltitz and Luther had conferred at Liebenwerda on October 9–10, 1519. Luther remarked that instead of a tragedy, his conversation with Miltitz amounted to a comedy over the power of the pope.[96] In December, when Miltitz forwarded to Frederick a new warning of the curia, Frederick responded that he and the archbishop of Trier had agreed that Luther would receive a hearing at the next imperial diet and, accordingly, Luther's case was still pending.[97] Unquestionably, Spalatin played the key role in keeping Frederick on Luther's side during this vulnerable time.[98] But Frederick's own reasons remain as inscrutable as ever. More than likely, his main concern was to keep his territory and his university free from ecclesiastical, even papal, intervention. Luther's concern for the freedom of Scripture from burdensome ecclesiastical traditions meshed with Frederick's self-interest in maintaining territorial autonomy and dynastic prestige.[99]

For Luther himself, Leipzig was a "tragedy."[100] But he came out of it with new confidence in the necessity of the stands he had taken and in the arguments he had used. The right of Christians to adhere to the clear meaning of Scripture even against pope and councils is not just a principle, but a necessity that arises out of the tyranny and destruction to which the claims of the popes have led. These claims suppress the word, nullify its authority, exploit the people, and devastate the church. Therefore, not just laypeople, but all pastors and clergy should protest in the name of that word when they see monstrosities against the gospel of Christ committed in the name of the pope. The gospel takes precedence over all, and the pope should submit to the judgment of the gospel if he wants the church to be filled with Christians served by pastors instead of with pagans served by tyrants.[101]

In the aftermath of Leipzig, Luther appealed once again to the indispensability of the word for the people of the church and to the responsibility of its pastors at all levels to mediate that word faithfully. These persistent concerns are woven by Luther into an impassioned defense of his denial of divine right. He does not reject completely the papacy or publicly identify the pope with the Antichrist. He does, however, construct a positive criterion for the proper execution of papal and pastoral leadership. That criterion is service of the word, and only as that service is rendered does the papacy have a rightful place in the church. To be a servant of the word also means to be judged by that word, and that is what the claims to divine right do not permit.

Although this judgment is the right of individuals who possess the word, Luther does not play off individual rights against the church as a body. The corporate nature of the church prohibits any individual member from usurping power over the church and over the word which rules it. "The pope is not lord of the church, but its servant and steward; the church itself is lady and queen; Christ alone is Lord. Neither is the pope the bridegroom, as some prattle; but Christ is the bridegroom. Therefore the church, which is one body with its bridegroom, is lord over all its members and subject to no one except to the bridegroom alone. All the others have been subjected to it as the queen and bride."[102] The duty of laity and clergy alike to stand by the word is not derived from their status as individuals but from their subjection to Christ in his body, the church, which is ruled by that word.[103]

As Luther looked back on the year 1519, he described himself as a good example of how hard it was to break the habits of a lifetime. He had publicly defended the proposition that the pope was not head of the church by divine right. Nevertheless, he said, he did not draw the conclusion that the pope must be of the devil.

> So impressed was I, as I have said, by the example and title of holy church, as well as by my own habit, that I conceded human right to the pope, which nevertheless, unless it is founded on divine authority, is a diabolical lie . . . . For that reason I can bear with a less hateful spirit those who cling pertinaciously to the papacy, particularly those who have not read the sacred Scriptures, or even the profane, since I, who read the sacred Scriptures most diligently so many years, still clung to it so tenaciously.[104]

Although in retrospect his activity during 1519 looks overcautious, Luther had in reality come a long way since January. Emerging from the tension between his private reservations and public utterances on the papacy, he has issued a public challenge to papal authority and strengthened his own convictions in the controversies that followed. These open controversies of 1519 do not weaken his loyalty to the church, not even to the Roman Church. His primary goal is still reform of the church, not separation from it. Whereas Luther regards the yielding of divine right as the condition for this reform, his opponents are convinced that Luther's public challenge means an attack upon the structure of the church.[105]

Luther is aware of his opponents' increased activity, but in contrast to 1545 he does not know what will come next.[106] He enters the new year with a mixture of regret and confidence. On the one hand, everything is against him and he longs to be free of the obligation to lecture and teach. Spalatin has advised him that sacred theology can be taught without offending the prelates, but Luther maintains that "Scripture most powerfully attacks the abuse of holy things, which the prelates cannot bear to hear." On the other hand, Luther has accepted the tribulation which his teaching and his concern for the people have brought. The Lord has made him a doctor of theology and, if he is sorry, then the Lord should destroy his work. "This tribulation does not frighten me at all, but it blows up the sails of my heart with an incredible wind. . . . We are completely unaccustomed to suffering and evil, that is, to the Christian life. Therefore, let it be; the more powerfully they rise up, the more securely I laugh at them. I am determined to fear nothing and to scorn everything."[107]

5 | OPPOSITION
1520

But now [godless pontiffs] wish to ensnare the awareness of our liberty by making us believe that whatever is done by them is done well and by forbidding us to reprimand them. Although they are wolves, they wish to be regarded as shepherds, although they are Antichrists, they wish to be honored as Christ. For this liberty and awareness alone I cry out . . . .

—Luther, 1520
(WA 6, 537.8–12)

CHRONOLOGY

1520	January 9	Luther's case is reopened in Rome
	February 1	Leo X appoints the first commission to prepare a denunciation of Luther
	February 11	Leo X appoints a second commission
	After Mid-March	Eck arrives in Rome
	March 26	Luther responds to the condemnation of his teachings by the theological faculties of Louvain and Cologne
	End of April	Leo appoints a third commission to prepare a draft of the bull against Luther
	May 3	John Eck reports on Luther's case to a friend in Germany
	May 5	Luther has received the work of the Leipzig Franciscan Alfeld on the papacy
	May 20	The curia sends an ultimatum to Frederick the Wise
	May 21, 23, 25, June 1	In four consistories of cardinals the bull against Luther is discussed and finally passed
	June 7	Luther is planning the *Address to the Christian Nobility*

1520	June 13	Luther's preface to Prierias's *Epitome* is in press
	June 15	The bull *Exsurge Domine* is promulgated
	June 23	Luther dedicates the *Address to the Christian Nobility* to Nikolaus von Amsdorf
	June 26	*The Papacy at Rome* is in print
	July 17	In Rome Eck and Aleander are appointed to publish the bull in Germany
	August 5	Luther discloses his intention to write *The Babylonian Captivity of the Church*
	August 18	*Address to the Christian Nobility* appears
	August	*Exsurge Domine* is published in Germany by sympathizers of Luther
	September 1	Staupitz and Link arrive in Wittenberg to confer with Luther
	September 11	Ulrich von Hutten sends to Elector Frederick a summons to battle against the pope
	September 21–29	Eck publishes the bull in Meissen, Merseburg, Brandenburg; Aleander in Cologne, Antwerp
	October 3	From Leipzig Eck sends the bull to Wittenberg
	October 8	The bull is published in Louvain and Luther's works are burned there
	October 11	The bull has arrived in Wittenberg
	October 11–12	Luther confers with Miltitz in Lichtenberg
	October 31	Frederick the Wise and Charles V confer in the sacristy of Cologne cathedral
	November 4	Luther's open letter to Leo X and his response to the bull have appeared in print
	November 4–6	Frederick confers with papal nuncios Aleander and Carraciolo in Cologne and refuses to turn over Luther
	November 16	*The Freedom of a Christian* has appeared in German
	November 17	Luther appeals to a general council
	November 26	Luther attends the wedding of Melanchthon
	December 10	At 9:00 A.M. Luther burns the bull *Exsurge Domine* and other works in Wittenberg

1520   December 27   Luther publishes *Why the Books of the Pope and His Disciples Were Burned*

         December 29   Luther's defense of the articles condemned by *Exsurge Domine* is in press

TYRANNY LOOMS

Almost half a year passed between the resumption of Luther's case in Rome (January 9, 1520) and the execution of the papal bull, *Exsurge Domine* (June 15), which threatened Luther with excommunication. While his fate was being decided in Rome, Luther's own judgment of his case moved into a new stage. Revolt was not on his mind,[1] but he was beginning to place his struggle into a larger historical context. The conviction grew that he was caught in the perennial conflict between the truth of the gospel and the tyranny of the Antichrist. Luther had suspected as much for almost a year. By early 1520, he was ripe for the impact which the writings of others made upon him and he was discovering allies for his cause.

By mid-February, he had read John Hus's treatise on *The Church*, sent to him four months earlier by the Prague Utraquists. To Spalatin Luther confidently exclaimed:

> Up to now I have unwittingly taught and held all the teachings of John Hus. John Staupitz has taught them equally unawares. In short, we are all Hussites without knowing it. Even Paul and Augustine are in reality Hussites. See the monstrous things into which we fall, I ask you, without the Bohemian leader and teacher. I am so shocked that I do not know what to think when I see such terrible judgments of God over mankind: the most evident evangelical truth was burned in public and was already considered condemned more than one hundred years ago. Yet no one is allowed to admit this. Woe to this world![2]

Luther dropped all the reservations about being identified with Hus that he had harbored since before the Leipzig Disputation. The theological differences among Luther, Hus, and Staupitz, not to mention Paul and Augustine, which modern historians are able to spot, were ignored by Luther in his enthusiasm at discovering an ally of whom he no longer needed to be ashamed. Hus's concept of the church as the assembly of the predestined appeared to undergird the independence of the true church from the church of Rome. The taint of schism and heresy, which had thus far deterred Luther from a full endorsement of Hus, suddenly turned into a mark of distinction in the common struggle against papal tyranny. Aroused by this new perspective of the past, Luther reaffirmed his allegiance to Hus in his second lecture course on the Psalms:

> At Leipzig I was completely ignorant of the meaning of those articles, whose words I saw to be most Christian. Thus I was not able to refute the sense which that fan of the pope [Eck] gave to them. But now that I have at hand the book of John Hus, I see from the context of the articles that also their meaning is most Christian. What is the pope, what is the world, what is the prince of this world, that on his account I should deny the truth of the gospel for which Christ died? Let prevail who will, let perish who will, with God being merciful I shall always feel this way.[3]

The conviction that the pope and the "prince of this world" were on the same side in opposing evangelical truth received a decisive boost through another book Luther read during February of 1520. This book was an edition of Lorenzo Valla's (1407–1457) refutation of the authenticity of the *Donation of Constantine*; it was published by the German humanist, Ulrich von Hutten, in late 1519.[4] The *Donation*, a forgery which arose between 750 and 850 A.D., purported to be the account of Emperor Constantine's grant of imperial rule over the West to Pope Sylvester in the fourth century. It was incorporated into canon law, and it served as the main pillar of papal claims to temporal power. Valla's disclosure of the forgery jolted Luther: "I am so tormented, I scarcely doubt that the pope is properly that Antichrist which by common consent the world expects; everything which he lives, does, speaks and establishes fits so well."[5] In contrast to his utterance of a year earlier, Luther compared the pope directly with the Antichrist instead of with a disciple of the Antichrist, though not yet unequivocally and still in private correspondence.[6]

The convergence of the pope and the Antichrist was only part of Luther's tendency to see Satan at work wherever he perceived a threat to evangelical truth. In mid-July, when a melee erupted in Wittenberg between university students and apprentices of the painter Lucas Cranach, Luther condemned it as a tactic of Satan to discredit the word of God.[7] Local opposition to his own work was evaluated in a similar way. When rumors spread that Duke George and the bishop of Meissen might take action against him, Luther told Spalatin, "I am aware of Satan's fiendish plans for my ruin and the ruin of many others." Accordingly, he warned Spalatin that the word of God could never be handled without tumult.[8]

Luther's *Sermon on the Blessed Sacrament of the Holy and True Body of Christ* (1519) had caused a tumult of its own in Ducal Saxony, and on January 14, 1520, the bishop of Meissen ordered it confiscated. About the same time, Luther published an expanded German version of his *Sermon on the Power of Excommunication*. This new *Sermon on the Ban* (early 1520) sounds a new urgency. Repeated warnings against "tyrants" who "today" unjustly impose the ban punctuate the sermon. Since Christ instituted the ban as a mild and "motherly" punishment, the purpose of which is to aid souls, how can the "blind tyrants" who impose the ban boast that they have power to curse, damn, and destroy? They do not seek to improve the people, but only to arouse fear and unnecessary terror.[9] The ban had become an instrument of the ecclesiastical tyranny which Luther sees looming on the horizon of his age. Although there is no direct evidence that Luther applied this sermon to his own situation,[10] the tone and vocabulary betray the new perspective that has Luther in its grip.

The tyrannical conspiracy of ecclesiastical and satanic powers which loomed up before Luther added urgency to his concern for protecting the consciences of the faithful. During his lectures on the Psalms, Luther upbraided at length the "Roman and ecclesiastical tyrants who, without mentioning faith in Christ, multiply their laws into infinity and thus ensnare the wretched consciences of the Christian brethren." Whereas these tyrants execute their office by perplexing, confounding, and ensnaring consciences, the duty of good preachers (Luther is addressing himself as well as his students) is to soothe the perplexed, to straighten out the confused, and to calm the terrified. Still, it is useless to resist the tyranny of the prelates because the word of Sirach (34:28) will be fulfilled: "One builds and another destroys." "Whatever the inferior preachers of the word of God build up, the superior tyrants of the words of men tear down. Behold that for yourself, O Peter, your primacy and ecclesiastical monarchy!"[11]

Luther was more convinced than ever that the papacy was responsible for the tyranny that afflicted the faithful. Although he did not call for revolt, he did charge the people to dissociate themselves from the works and ceremonies which the hierarchy had imposed upon them. Luther admonished anyone who still put his trust in such works to abstain from them and not to seek papal or priestly dispensation from them. "For in those things which are of faith, every Christian is pope and church for himself; nor can anything be established or maintained which in any manner would endanger faith."[12] This affirmation of independence from the pope was not an abstract statement about papal authority, but a protest against the tyranny of the hierarchy, including the papacy, on behalf of the consciences of the people. In the eschatological urgency which beset Luther during the first half of 1520, he remained true to his original motivation.[13]

Luther protested against this tyranny not only in Latin lectures directed at theological students and the scholarly public; he also appealed directly to the people in German treatises which, like the *Sermon on the Ban*, occupied his special attention in early 1520. The excursus on ceremonies in his lectures on the Psalms is strikingly similar to the *Treatise on Good Works*, begun in March and published finally in late May or early June. In the dedicatory letter addressed to Duke John of Saxony, the brother of the Elector Frederick, Luther remarks that this work more than any other needed to be published. "Would to God that with all my ability my whole life long I had brought about the improvement of one lay person. I would let that suffice, thank God, and let all my other books go to ruin."[14] In contrast to all the spurious good works of satisfaction and ceremonies, Luther instructs the people that genuine good works are the commandments of God, which can only be kept when the greatest work of all, faith, is present.

Although Luther viewed this treatise as possibly his best work, the crowning effort of his writings for the laity also appeared in May of 1520: *A Short Form of the Ten Commandments, A Short Form of the Faith [Creed], A Short Form of the Lord's Prayer.* The pattern according to which Luther treated these primary documents of the faith would form the basis of the *Small Catechism* in 1529. The Ten Commandments supply the diagnosis of the human situation by exposing the illness of sin; the creed shows where the remedy is to be found; the Lord's Prayer instructs the Christian how to attain it. This work, like Luther's other writings for the people, enjoyed great success and went through several editions. Through the summer of 1520, Luther's writings for the laity averaged twelve editions and made him the most popular religious writer of his day.[15] Luther underestimated his impact in this role. While rejoicing at the success of Melanchthon's lectures on Romans, Luther bewailed the fact that he had lost his years in unhappy battles. He hoped at least that he would prove to be a David, spilling blood, while Melanchthon would be able, like Solomon, to reign in peace![16]

Luther's battles were fought with a two-edged sword: *against* the tyranny of the Antichrist and the Roman hierarchy and *for* the consciences of the faithful. The sword was sharpened on both edges during the first half of 1520. At the end of his long instruction of the laity in the *Treatise on Good Works*, Luther turned his exposition of the eighth commandment (against false witness) into a discussion of opposition to the gospel. This opposition comes from the great and the mighty; hence, most people are afraid to resist it. When the little people challenge the gospel, everybody is ready to rise up in its defense. But when the pope, bishops, princes, and kings oppose the truth, suddenly everyone flees, clams up, and pretends to see nothing, so afraid are they of losing their property, honor, favors, and even their lives. This desertion of the gospel betrays the absence of faith. When faith is present, however, it swells the heart with courage and defiance so that one can stand by the truth no matter what the cost, even against pope and kings.[17]

Luther's own resolve lay behind these words. To stand by the truth on behalf of the people now meant to stand, openly if need be, against the pope. In February, Bishop Adolf of Merseburg responded to Luther that he could not understand the reason for Luther's opposition to the pope. Many others, not least of all Erasmus, were able to endorse Luther's "spirit," his writings, or his theology, while advising moderation against the papacy.[18] Luther found it impossible to make this separation, however; the tyranny loomed too large, and the souls of too many people were at stake.

"ROMANISTS" AND "PAPISTS"

The only work Luther had devoted specifically to the papacy was the *Explanation of Proposition Thirteen*, published in June 1519, in preparation for the debate at Leipzig. The *Explanation* had not been intended for popular consumption. It was like a legal brief, containing the exegetical, legal, and historical arguments that Luther would use to challenge the papal claim to rule by divine right. By mid-1520 the conviction that the church was ruled by tyrants in the service of the Antichrist led Luther once more to write against the papacy, this time in German as well as in Latin, and with a broader public in view.

This fresh literary production took the form of three works which fully occupied him during the month of June and continued to demand his attention throughout the summer. The first, entitled *The Papacy at Rome,* was a reply in German to a treatise by the Leipzig Franciscan, Augustin Alfeld, who had defended the divine basis of papal rule. The second was Luther's reaction to a new work by an old opponent, Sylvester Prierias, who was still the only official at the Roman curia to have written against Luther. Prierias had composed a long refutation of Luther in two books and then summarized his arguments in a third book, an *Epitome*, which he published. Luther decided the best rebuttal of Prierias was Prierias himself, and he had the *Epitome* reprinted in Wittenberg with his own foreword, afterword, and marginal notes. Both *The Papacy* and Luther's edition of Prierias's *Epitome* appeared on June 26, 1520. The third work turned out to be Luther's most popular Reformation treatise: the *Address to the Christian Nobility of the German Nation on the Improvement of the Christian Estate*. Luther prepared this appeal at the urging of the elector's legal advisers. It was not published until August 18, but Luther was already at work on it during June. His dedication of the *Address* to Nikolaus von Amsdorf, jurist, official in the All Saints' Chapter, and close colleague of Luther, was dated June 23, 1520. June was a month of feverish literary activity for Luther, a sudden release of his dammed up apprehension about the nature of papal rule.

These works mark a new stage in his relationship to the papacy, an open opposition which Luther documents in a letter to Spalatin on June 7. Prierias's *Epitome* has convinced him that everybody at Rome has gone raging mad like fools, sticks and stones, hell and the devil. "Now see what can be expected from Rome, which permits this hell [the *Epitome*] to go out into the church." In responding to Alfeld, says Luther, "I will not be unmindful of the Roman pontiff. . . . The mysteries of the Antichrist should finally be brought out into the open since they push themselves forward and no longer wish to remain hidden." Finally, Luther announces that he will issue a public pamphlet to Emperor Charles and the nobility of Germany "against the tyranny and evil of the Roman curia."[19]

Luther regarded Alfeld's treatise as a ploy of his opponents, "Sylvester, Cajetan, Eck, Emser, and now Cologne and Louvain," to let Alfeld stick out his neck so that they would not be hurt if Luther chopped it off.[20] Luther first entrusted a rebuttal to his assistant, but he decided to respond himself after Alfeld's treatise appeared in German and after he heard that it pleased some people who, he thought, should have known better. Luther conceived of his reply as a summary statement of his stand on the papacy, which would answer the attacks of all his opponents up to that point. In addition, Luther was consciously setting forth his stand on the papacy for the first time in German. Although the writing of the treatise would keep him from better pursuits, he welcomed this opportunity "to explain something of Christianity for the laity and to counteract these seductive masters."[21] Luther not only expressed concern for the laity as he had done so often in the past; now he addressed to the laity a treatise on the papacy.

The decision to reprint Prierias's *Epitome* with comments was also a public challenge to the papacy even though the Latin text was intended for a different public. Perhaps for that reason it contained a stronger polemic, including the harsh words at the end:

> If we punish thieves with flogging, robbers with the sword, and heretics with fire, why should we not all the more attack with arms these teachers of perdition, these cardinals, these popes, all the dregs of the Roman Sodom, who have corrupted the church of God without ceasing, and wash our hands in their blood [Ps. 58:10] in order to free ourselves and those under our care from the conflagration that threatens to engulf all? O happy the Christians, wherever they are, if they are not under such a Roman Antichrist as we unlucky ones are![22]

The righteous anger expressed in these words was aroused by the same revulsion at papal tyranny that had been building up during the first half of 1520 and gushed forth here for the first time. The fact that Prierias was a member of the curia forced Luther to take his work as a portent that Rome had become the seat of the Antichrist. If the pope and cardinals agreed with Prierias, said Luther, then blessed be Greece, blessed be Bohemia, and blessed be all those who had cut their ties with Rome. Faith has been extinct in Rome for a long time, the gospel forbidden, Christ an exile, the city's morals worse than barbarian. Luther issued a ringing farewell to "unhappy, hopeless, blasphemous Rome. The wrath of God has come upon you as you have deserved. . . . We have cared for Babylon and she is not healed" (Jer. 51:9).[23]

What appears to be a complete break with the papacy in these highly charged comments is qualified by Luther's words in the afterword. There, he places respect for the pope on the same level with obedience to other human authorities, as the fourth commandment enjoins. Since the *Proceedings at Augsburg*, Luther conceded this human authority on the basis of Romans 13. Now he reduces the pope to the status of his other Christian brethren by subjecting him to the judgment of the church as Christ commands in Matt. 18:15–17.[24] Although the papacy is not denied in principle, its prerogatives are severely curtailed. The threat of papal tyranny has obviously diluted whatever hope Luther harbored for a reformed papacy ruling by human right.

The same kind of opposition to the papacy is evident in the less polemical treatise on *The Papacy at Rome*. Here, as well, Luther does not demand the abolition of the papacy. Instead, he disputes the claim of the papacy to be the head of the church by divine right[25] and reduces any hierarchy of bishops to the level of human right. This reduction is less than an enthusiastic endorsement of the papal hierarchy even at the human level. The power which the pope possesses over the other bishops must be the result of God's anger; he has permitted this plague to come upon the world. Therefore, Luther advises no one to resist the pope, but instead to endure God's counsel, to honor papal power, and to bear it with patience as if the Turk were ruling.[26] This concession explains why Luther's equation of the papacy with the Antichrist does not issue in an immediate call for revolt against the papacy. Even the Antichrist could not exercise his power except at God's behest. Papal and satanic tyranny must be first endured as an expression of God's anger.

But this endurance has its limits. Luther sets two conditions. First, he will not suffer the making of new articles of faith or the branding of Christians not under the pope as heretics. It is enough that the pope is allowed to be pope; it is not necessary that God and his holy ones on earth be blasphemed. Second, he will accept everything the pope does and establishes if he can subject it to the judgment of Scripture. If these conditions are met, says Luther, then he will let the pope be pope and exalt him as high as anyone wishes. If not, then the pope will be for Luther neither pope nor Christian.[27] These two conditions are in fact reducible to one. The "new article of faith" which Luther opposes is the claim of the pope to be by divine right head of the church and judge over Scripture. This claim contradicts the nature of faith because the object of faith is invisible, not a bodily, visible, and transitory institution such as the papacy.[28]

The vision of a reformed papacy also became dimmer in the third treatise, the *Address to the Christian Nobility*, which Luther devoted specifically to the subject of reform. Any reform of the church must first penetrate the three walls behind which the Romanists have ensconced themselves. When anyone has tried to attack them with force, they have claimed that spiritual power is over the secular arm. When Scripture has been used as a weapon, they claim that only the pope can interpret

Scripture. When they have been threatened with a council, they claim that only the pope can call a council. If the Romans do not give up these claims, they are the community of the Antichrist and of the devil. They have nothing in common with Christ but the name.[29] A radical reform of the papacy is therefore necessary. Topping the list of articles to be discussed at a future council is the worldly pomp of the pope. The proper office of the papacy is to weep and pray daily for all of Christendom and to set an example of humility. The pope is not a vicar of the glorified Christ, but of the crucified Christ.[30] This ideal picture pales, however, beside Luther's outburst of rage against the indulgence practice and the abuses connected with it. This practice is enough in itself to prove that the pope is the Antichrist: "Hear this, pope, not most holy, but most sinful: God will destroy your see straight from heaven and plunge it into the depths of hell!"[31]

Luther now speaks repeatedly of "Romanists" and, for the first time in the afterword to Prierias's *Epitome*, of "papists."[32] The use of both terms betrays how wide the gulf has become between the Roman curia and the papacy, on the one side, and Luther's conception of the church, on the other. Luther expresses this gulf pointedly in mid-June to Jerome Dungersheim: "When we ask for the church, you show us one man, the pope."[33] In *The Papacy at Rome* ("at Rome" should be underscored), Luther argues that the pope cannot be the head of Christendom because the church, properly understood, is a spiritual communion of the faithful bound together throughout the world in faith, hope, and love. Only this communion conforms to the concept of the church in Scripture; it alone is the true church and can be ruled by no earthly head but only by Christ himself.[34] Any attempt to restrict the church to Rome or to subject it to the headship of the pope contradicts the nature of the church. In fact, the Romanist Alfeld cannot deny that the majority of those who are under the pope, especially those in Rome itself, are outside this spiritual unity because of their unbelief and wicked living.[35] Luther finds here a specific application for his ecclesiology: the defense of the true church against what Luther regards as a Roman and papal usurpation of Christ's rule over his spiritual people.

The *Address to the Christian Nobility* was a transposition of this ecclesiology into a political and geographical key. Like his contemporaries, Luther conceived of Christendom as externally coextensive with the boundaries of the nation-states in Europe. In Luther's case, the boundary encircled the Holy Roman Empire of the German nation. Just as the Romanists had usurped power in the church at its genuine, spiritual level, so they had also usurped power in the church at the external, territorial level by demanding subjection to the Roman hierarchy. The protest against this subjection reinforced a dimension which was present in Luther's criticism of papal primacy from the beginning. The defense of true Christian existence outside the pope's hegemony over the Western Church had been a basic element in Luther's criticism since his *Explanations of the Ninety-five Theses*, and this very point had ignited the controversy with Eck.

In mid-1520, the occasion for protesting papal tyranny over the Christians in Germany came to Luther from the Saxon court, but it was not a foreign element in his ecclesiology. If the Christians in Greece and Bohemia were blessed because they had cut their ties with Rome, what could be a greater blessing for the Christians in Germany than to follow their lead? Germany will become "twice a Bohemia," wrote Luther on July 10, 1520, unless the Romans conquer Lutheran doctrine with Scripture and reason. The Germans have such a ferocious nature that, unless it be tamed by Scripture and reason, it is not safe to provoke it even with many popes, especially now, when good letters and languages reign in Germany and even the laity are becoming wise.[36] Although the patriotic tones of Luther's appeal were quite audible, the *Address* developed the fundamental geographical dimension of his ecclesiology more than it played on merely political and patriotic emotions. Electoral politics and Luther's ecclesiology meshed unusually well.

Luther's basic motivation for opposing papal tyranny remains unchanged as he moves into this new stage of public opposition. The *Address* contains familiar pleas for the poor, simple souls who have been deceived and exploited by the abuses of papal rule.[37] In *The Papacy at Rome*, Luther emphasizes the pastoral nature of the words of Christ which the popes have twisted into divine sanction for their control over the keys (Matt. 16:18–19; John 21:15–17). The keys are given to the church in common so that poor, sinful consciences can find consolation.[38] The duty of feeding the sheep of Christ is reserved for those who love him. If this word applies to the pope, then there are as many popes as there are those who love Christ and feed his sheep.[39] At Prierias's designation of the pope as pastor, Luther writes sarcastically in the margin: "To starve and destroy [the sheep]."[40]

The "battle trumpet," as John Lang in Erfurt dubbed Luther's *Address*, met with hefty criticism from both Lang and Spalatin. Soon after the *Address* appeared, Melanchthon wrote to Lang that he had not approved or disapproved of the *Address*; but he did not in any way want to impede the spirit of Luther in this matter, to which he seemed predestined.[41] As usual, Luther offered no apology. All things are permitted to us, he wrote on the same day to Lang, in opposing the deceit and trumpery of the Roman Antichrist for the sake of the salvation of souls.[42] He was no longer to be restrained. The eschatological urgency, the political promise, the pastoral necessity, the ecclesiological possibility of the moment—all of these converged to move Luther forward unrepentantly. A month earlier, while he was still writing, Luther reacted to a letter from Rome threatening the Elector Frederick: "If I am not permitted to be free from the office of teaching and from the ministry of the word, then I will certainly be free in performing that ministry. I am already burdened with enough sins; I will not add the unforgivable sin that I desert the ministry into which I have been placed and be found guilty of impious silence, truth neglected and [the ruin of] so many thousand souls."[43]

THE BULL

While Luther was beginning to envision the church apart from the papacy, the curia was taking decisive steps to sever Luther from the Roman Church. In the bull *Exsurge Domine*, executed on June 15, 1520, Luther was threatened with excommunication if he did not recant and seek pardon within sixty days of the bull's publication in Saxony. Hence, not one of Luther's three works against the papacy in the summer of 1520 appeared before the bull was issued. Although these could not serve as sources for the errors of Luther enumerated in the bull, Luther's previous challenges to papal authority played a key role in the curia's condemnation.

John Eck was primarily responsible for the inclusion of this subject matter and for the shape the bull assumed. This was evident to Luther and to his contemporaries.[44] Already in the fall of 1519 Eck composed a treatise on *The Primacy of Peter against Luther*, which was mainly a response to Luther's *Explanation of Proposition Thirteen* and to his stand at Leipzig.[45] Eck presented a copy of this work to Pope Leo upon his arrival in Rome during the second half of March 1520. By that time, two commissions had discussed the form a condemnation of Luther should take. The second commission, composed of theologians, recommended a mild document in which the works of Luther would be condemned but not Luther's person. After Eck's arrival, affairs took a radically different turn. It was a good thing, Eck himself remarked, that he arrived in Rome when he did because others knew little of the Lutheran errors.[46] Eck's arrival led to the appointment of a third commission, composed of himself, a Spanish theologian, and two cardinals, which produced the draft of a bull by early May and discussed it in person with Pope Leo. Afterwards the draft was presented to the cardinals and debated in four consistories in late May and early June. It was decided in these discussions to cite the errors of Luther verbatim from his works.

All forty-one condemned propositions of Luther except one can in fact be matched with a citation from Luther's works. The lone exception is article 25: "The Roman pontiff, the successor of Peter, was not instituted vicar of Christ over all the churches of the whole world by Christ himself in the blessed Peter."[47] Eck himself is probably responsible for the formulation of that article, since it is not found in the condemnations of Louvain or Cologne which the commission used as sources for some of the propositions. Indeed, neither of the condemnations contains an article corresponding to those which the bull cites from the Leipzig Disputation or from Luther's explanation of the propositions debated at Leipzig. The same is true for articles 26 through 30, which, together with article 25, specifically deal with Luther's challenge to papal and conciliar authority. Hence, it is difficult to resist the suspicion that Eck did have substantial influence on the shape of the bull and especially on the inclusion of those articles which condemn Luther's ecclesiology.

Luther was not condemned, however, only for challenging the authority of the papacy, and the bull was not a "papist" document directed only against an antipapal stance. Even though his treatise, *The Primacy of Peter*, revealed that Eck had moved closer to a papalist stance on church authority, he was no papist;[48] and Eck was clever enough to realize that some members of the curia harbored their own reservations about conceding absolute supremacy to the pope over a council of the church. The majority of the condemned articles were directed against Luther's views on the sacrament of penance and on indulgences. They betrayed some awareness of the subversive impact of Luther's views which Cajetan had discerned in 1518. The bull condemned the dependence of forgiveness on faith in the word of Christ and rejected Luther's declaration that indulgences were only pious frauds.[49] Cajetan's exclamation that such views amounted to building a new church found implicit endorsement in *Exsurge Domine*.

In its own way, the bull expresses that concern for the salvation of the faithful that Luther's opponents consistently made dependent on subjection to the Roman hierarchy and its system of salvation. Even the biblical images under which the bull introduces its condemnation, comparable to Luther's own colorful pictures, reflect the same concern. A general summons to defense of the church is issued to Christ himself, Peter, Paul, all the saints, and to the universal church to protect the vineyard of the Lord from the wild boar who has invaded it (Ps. 80:13–14). In particular, Peter is invoked to rise up and champion the cause of the holy Roman Church on the basis of the "pastoral care" that has been divinely entrusted to him by Christ.[50] *Exsurge Domine* portrays Luther's challenge as a usurpation of authority and devastation of the church just as Luther judged papal "tyranny" to be.

Still, Eck undeniably gave the condemnation of Luther a sharp ecclesiological edge, and this condemnation did ultimately rest on Luther's refusal to acknowledge the authority of the papacy. The errors of Luther were judged "pestiferous, pernicious, scandalous, seductive of pious and simple minds" because they offended reverence to the holy Roman Church and cut the "nerve of ecclesiastical discipline, obedience." *Exsurge Domine* offered no rebuttal to Luther beyond his refusal to submit to the judgment of Rome. Rome's judgment was infallible on the basis of Christ's promise to his disciples that he would be with them to the end of the world. That judgment rested, according to the bull, with the papacy because Christ had entrusted the care, rule, and administration of his vineyard to Peter as the head, the vicar of Christ, and to his successors "in the image of the triumphant church."[51] For Luther, faith had long since replaced the pope as the true vicar of Christ in the militant church. There was little chance that he would change his mind now.

For his part, Eck was promoted to papal nuncius and pronotary and, together with Jerome Aleander, entrusted with the publication of the bull in Germany. He was also given permission to attach the names of Luther's sympathizers to the condemnation. Five of the six names which Eck selected were agreed upon in Rome, and Eck wanted Leo to include them in the bull. In addition to prominent laypersons such as Lazarus Spengler in Nuremberg and Willibald Pirckheimer in Augsburg, Eck selected his originally intended opponent for the Leipzig Disputation, Karlstadt, and one other Wittenberger for specific mention.[52] This inclusion finally spurred Karlstadt to write against the papacy, a fact which Luther casually noted in October 1520 with a tinge of irony.[53] The inclusion of these names had the effect of solidifying Luther's support in

Wittenberg and caused Eck more difficulty in publishing the bull than he had expected.

Eck encountered stiff resistance in Leipzig, the site of his self-proclaimed victory a year earlier. The sixty-day grace period ordered by the bull began with Eck's publication of the bull in the dioceses of Meissen, Merseburg, and Brandenburg, and Eck accomplished this in late September. On September 29, placards were posted against Eck at various spots in Leipzig, and personal threats forced him to seek refuge in the monastery of St. Paul. Even then protestors, among them perhaps students from Wittenberg, made up satirical songs about him and harassed him with threatening letters sent to the monastery.[54] It was no wonder that Eck was glad to return safe and sound to Ingolstadt on October 14 and resolved to stay out of sight for a while.

While Eck was making his way north with the bull, Luther was gaining confidence. In August and September he worked hard on another treatise which reveals how far he had moved from Rome. The title, *A Prelude on the Babylonian Captivity of the Church,* betrayed the same attitude toward the papacy and the Roman Church he had adopted in May and June: the church is subjected to the tyranny of the Romanists and the papists and needs to be liberated. For the first time in public, Luther documents the progress of his opposition to the papacy and his indebtedness to his opponents. First, he regrets that he had published his *Explanations of the Ninety-five Theses,* for at that time he was still mired in the great superstition of Roman tyranny and had not rejected indulgences completely. Helped by Prierias and his brothers, however, he learned better, and now he desires all his books on indulgences to be burned and this proposition to be put in their place: "Indulgences are the useless trifles of the Roman flatterers." Unfortunately, he had also conceded the legitimacy of the papacy by divine right. But now, helped by Eck and Emser and their conspirators, he has learned better. He is certain that the papacy is the kingdom of Babylon, and he compares it to the dominion of Nimrod, the mighty hunter (Gen. 10:8–9).[55]

Luther says that he is still not aware of having fallen away from the Roman see, nor has anyone proved as much.[56] Nevertheless, the charge of tyranny resounds throughout the work, and the pope as well as his disciples are judged guilty. The entire sacramental system of the church is an instrument of this tyranny, but nowhere is it more conspicuous than in the sacrament of baptism. What is responsible for the fact that our glorious liberty and the proper understanding of baptism are today held captive if not the tyranny of the Roman pontiff? More than all others, the pope as chief pastor ought to preach this liberty and proclaim this understanding.[57] If the disciples of the pope and the defenders of papal tyranny were at least aware of the tyrannical nature of their action, then Christians could endure it as part of the suffering that belongs to the Christian life. Instead, the tyrants insist on immunity from criticism, "and although they are wolves, they wish to be regarded as shepherds; although they are Antichrists, they wish to be honored as Christ. For this liberty and awareness alone I cry out."[58]

Luther's concern for the consciences of the faithful comes to the fore in the form of an ultimatum to the papacy:

> Because few know this glory of baptism and joy of Christian liberty (nor can they know it owing to the tyranny of the pope), I here and now liberate myself and redeem my conscience, and I charge the pope and all papists that, unless they lift their own laws and traditions and restore to the churches of Christ the liberty which is theirs and see that this liberty is taught, they are guilty of all the souls which perish in this miserable captivity and the papacy is indeed nothing but the kingdom of Babylon and of the true Antichrist. For who else is the man of sin and the son of perdition [2 Thess. 2:3] than he who multiplies sin and the destruction of souls in the church with his own doctrines and statutes, sitting nevertheless in the church like God?[59]

Luther's justification of his own conscience on behalf of the consciences of all Christians strikes a cord already sounded in his *Proceedings at Augsburg.* He asserts anew his responsibility as a pastor of souls and teacher of Scripture. He does not threaten any schismatic action with his ultimatum, but he does declare that the pope and the "papists" lose their legitimacy as the church if they do not fulfill their pastoral responsibility. The church of Christ is less and less the Roman Church for Luther. His language gives him away. In protesting that he has not been able to condemn the Bohemians because they have the word and deed of Christ whereas "we" have neither, Luther immediately weakens the solidarity with Rome implied in that "we." He says, "We have only that inane commentary of men: 'The church has so ordered,' although not the church, but tyrants over the churches without the consent of the church (i.e., the people of God), have so ordered."[60]

The confident and even taunting tone of the *Babylonian Captivity* permeates Luther's letters while he awaits the arrival of the bull. Everything is in the hands of God, Luther says. Furthermore, he does not care if his books are destroyed since they are confused and unpolished anyway. He would much rather see living books, preachers, raised up, multiplied, and promoted.[61] The arrival of the bull in Wittenberg on October 10 is a relief for Luther. He feels much freer once he has become certain that the pope is the Antichrist and the seat of Satan. A tone of finality, however, accompanies the sense of relief. "I will forward a copy of the bull," Luther writes to Spalatin, "that you may see the Roman monsters; if they are master, then faith and the church are doomed."[62]

LEO

Two ultimatums now faced each other: Luther's in the *Babylonian Captivity* and Leo's in *Exsurge Domine*. Neither had any chance of success, but the indefatigable Karl von Miltitz was initiating a last effort at reconciliation. Although he was unable to hinder the publication of the *Address to the Christian Nobility*, he did persuade two of Luther's closest Augustinian brothers, Staupitz and Wenceslaus Link, to urge Luther to make a personal appeal to Pope Leo X. On September 11, 1520, Luther confirmed the success of their efforts. He promised to write to Leo that he had never intended to attack his person. "What more easily and accurately could I write? Moreover, I will forgo a more severe treatment of his see and of this affair; nevertheless, it will be seasoned with its own salt."[63] After Eck arrived in Leipzig with *Exsurge Domine*, Luther changed his mind. It took all the finesse which Miltitz could muster to persuade Luther to write the letter anyway. Miltitz only had the opportunity to practice his art because the Elector Frederick agreed to his request for a meeting with Luther. When the request reached Luther, he felt he had no choice but to do "just as the prince has ordered"—no comment, positive or negative.[64] It must have been an uncomfortable trip to Lichtenberg to meet Miltitz on October 11, 1520. One day after he had received *Exsurge Domine* and concluded for certain that the pope was the Antichrist, Luther had to reconsider writing directly to Leo himself.

We do not know exactly how Miltitz convinced Luther to change his mind. Presumably, Miltitz argued tenaciously a point of view which Luther had wanted to believe all along and could now indulge in for one last time. Leo himself was not an opponent of the gospel; he had been deceived by his advisers and his flatterers in the curia. Leo could still be persuaded to favor Luther if the guilt for the whole affair were placed on Eck. As incredible as this may sound in view of the bull, Miltitz was not the only one to press this argument on Luther in 1520. In March Conrad Pellican had written to Luther that, except for the influence of his courtiers, the pope did not think evilly of Luther.[65] Eck had already been made the butt of ridicule and was widely proclaimed to be the real perpetrator of the bull.

Furthermore, it was by no means inconceivable that Leo was better than his advisers. As the second son of Lorenzo the Magnificent in Florence, Giovanni de' Medici was early initiated into the turmoil of the age and acquired a political savvy of his own. After his warlike predecessor, Julius II, the Medici pope was greeted with joy by proponents of reform when he ascended the papal throne in 1512. Two Venetian monks presented him with a memorandum which in some respects anticipated both Luther and the reform proposals of the counterreformation. The guilt for the evil that beset the church was laid on the popes who had surrounded themselves with greedy flatterers. As the principle of positive reform, the pope was deemed responsible for seeing that the remainder of the hierarchy did its job. It cannot be said that Leo fulfilled that responsibility well. He devoted himself more to political maneuvering than to pastoral leadership. In Leo's manner of ruling the church, writes Hubert Jedin, there is "hardly a trace" of responsibility for the salvation of souls.[66] Despite the shortcomings that emerge when his papacy is judged by the strict standards of monastic spirituality or of a post-Reformation age, Leo certainly had a better reputation than his immediate predecessors. A modern Catholic historian even makes a distinction similar to that of Luther. The blame which Leo receives "does not belong to his person as much as to the system, taken over and expanded by him, which from a religious viewpoint cannot be justified."[67]

Luther betrayed some awareness of Leo's reputation in his *Explanations of the Ninety-five Theses* and in his letters to Leo. He is not adopting a new attitude toward Leo, therefore, when he tells him in the open letter that he has always spoken honorably about Leo whenever he has mentioned his person. Luther reminds Leo how he called him a Daniel in Babylon and appeals to the public way in which he defended Leo's innocence against his "slanderer," Sylvester (Prierias).[68] Nor does Luther deviate from that stance when he wishes Leo the best for his person and depicts him as a sheep among wolves, Daniel among lions, Ezekiel beside the scorpion (Ezek. 2:6).[69] Luther repeats his old warning that Leo should not let himself be deceived by flatterers; he should not believe those who elevate him, but instead those who humble him.[70] Leo deserves to be pope in better times; even though he has a few devoted cardinals on his side, they are not enough to counteract the crowd of knaves who control the curia.[71] Luther bases his right to counsel Leo on the example of St. Bernard and Pope Eugenius and, more significantly for Luther's new attitude, on the duty of brotherly love which every Christian is obligated to fulfill. I dare not flatter you, says Luther, in such a serious and dangerous matter. People can understand if they will that in this affair I am your friend more than your subject.[72]

Although Luther does not say anything positive about Leo which he has not said before, his stance has changed from submissive subject to responsible peer.[73] This confident equality is revealed in the remainder of his letter. Instead of apologizing for his polemic and for his harsh criticism of the papal see as the stool of the Antichrist, Luther defends the necessity of his sharp words. He also tells Leo that he should have done the job which Luther and other critics of the curia have done. All who desecrate the curia honor Christ; in short, all are good Christians who are bad Romans.[74] Furthermore, Luther addresses directly to Leo a point he had made earlier in the Leipzig Disputation, which leads back to the roots of his ecclesiological development: he denies that the pope is the vicar of Christ. The popes are all too truly the vicars of Christ because they rule the church in the absence of Christ. What is such a crowd, asks Luther, but an assembly without Christ? And what is such a pope but an Antichrist and an idol? How much better the apostles called themselves servants of a Christ dwelling in them instead of vicars of an absent Christ![75]

Luther could hardly have expressed himself more pointedly to Leo if he had called him the Antichrist outright without the use of irony. Whether Miltitz was able to arouse in Luther even the slightest hope for a change of heart in Leo is impossible to determine. From the letter itself there is little reason to assume that Luther truly expected Leo to change his mind. Why, then, did he write the letter?

External factors were more important than internal ones. Luther's awareness that the elector wanted him to meet with Miltitz and the public character of an open letter suggest that it was primarily a political document. It is the final public statement of his case directed to the pope. The intentional dating of the letter prior to Luther's reception of the bull supports this suggestion. It was not meant as a public reaction to *Exsurge Domine*, but as an appeal to Leo himself. Such an appeal would allow both Luther and the electoral court to claim that they had done all they could for the sake of peace. On November 4, 1520, Melanchthon wrote to Spalatin, who was with the Elector Frederick in Cologne for the coronation of Charles V: "A few days ago [Luther] wrote a letter to the Roman pope Leo. I believe you will approve of it; it is sufficiently modest and devoted."[76] Although the letter did not have the same legal status as Luther's renewed appeal to a general council on November 17, it served a similar political purpose of leaving no formal channels unused.

Another external stimulus for the letter was a treatise Eck published in September 1520 against a section of Luther's *Address to the Christian Nobility*. Eck wrote that Luther disgraced the pope with unheard-of blasphemies, whereas the pope personally was a pious man and led a better life than Luther. Moreover, Luther was guilty of elevating himself above all teachers and councils. By mid-October, Luther was at work on his reply, entitled *The New Bulls and Lies of Eck*. He makes a sharp distinction between life and doctrine, both in his own defense and in defense of his opposition to the papacy. He elevates Christ above all teachers and councils. He has never thought of the pope otherwise than with honor; he has only spoken in general of evil popes and of a harmful papacy.[77] The charge of Eck in all likelihood spurred Luther to construct his letter on the distinction between the person of Leo and the papal office. Eck was foremost on his mind when he justified his letter to Leo on the grounds that people accused him of not having spared Leo's name.[78]

Given the public, political character of his letter, is a charge of duplicity or dishonesty justified by this appeal of Luther to the person of Leo over the papal see?[79] The distinction which Luther makes between the person of Leo and the office of the papacy is indeed an artificial one when viewed from the angle of the papacy or even from the facts of Luther's case. In spite of Leo's reputation, no real evidence supports the argument of Miltitz that Leo was ever disposed more favorably to Luther than Eck or members of the curia. The distinction is a crucial one for Luther, however, and is consistent with his criticism of the papacy from the beginning. He has not attacked the morals or the reputation of the incumbent in the papal office. Rather he has criticized that office, and indeed all his opponents, only for the sake of the truth of the divine word. He will yield to everyone on everything else, says Luther, but he cannot and will not abandon or deny the word of God.[80]

Coupled with his defense of the word is the persistent concern for the people's access to that word. Accordingly, Luther argues that his attack on the papacy was necessary because under Leo's name and the name of the Roman Church people throughout the world have been deceived and damaged. He will protest against that as long as his Christian spirit lives. He is the indebted servant of all Christians to warn them against the Roman flatterers.[81] He refuses, therefore, to retract what he has written unless he is proven wrong on the basis of Scripture, and he will only be silent if his opponents are silent. Luther makes these two points in the form of a demand toward the end of his letter. If Leo will restrain the flatterers and will allow free course to the word of God, Luther will do everything for the sake of peace. The matter rests in Leo's hands.[82]

In the letter, Luther does not say anything he does not mean. That includes the distinction between the person of Leo and the office of the papacy. The distinction between person and office will remain a component of his criticism of the papacy. On the basis of this distinction he will claim that his rejection of the papacy is more radical than that of John Hus.[83] He will continue to apply the distinction to himself as well. His right to criticize the papacy is not based on his personal holiness, but on his office as preacher and teacher in the church and on the responsibility for the faithful which that office imposes.[84]

Whether or not Luther thinks Leo might change his mind, the uncompromising tone of the letter is genuine. This tone colors the description Luther gives of his prior relationship to the papacy. Even before Eck challenged him to debate, Luther says, he had already bid Rome farewell and decided to concentrate on his preaching and teaching. The attack on the papacy resulted solely from Eck's seizing upon a remark which Luther let slip concerning the papacy.[85] Although the seriousness which Luther attributes to the early opposition from Prierias and Cajetan is noteworthy, his farewell to Rome was more the desire to be left alone than a conscious leave-taking of the papacy. Luther does document the escalation of his criticism until it finally reached the papacy, and he is generous with the blame. Luther confirms, however, that Eck was the catalyst for his public challenge to papal authority. That decisive step in the progress of Luther's estrangement culminated in his opposition to papal tyranny in 1520 and in this pointed address to Leo.

Meanwhile, his confidence surged. Introducing the Latin text of his gift to Leo, the *Freedom of a Christian*, Luther stressed the impossibility of understanding faith unless one has experienced the courage it gives.[86]

Luther was certainly speaking for himself. And Melanchthon spoke for Luther when he noted, "To me Martin appears to be driven by some spirit!"[87]

THE BREAKS

That drive finally led to his break with the papacy. Older tendencies to date that break around the time of his *Address to the Christian Nobility* have receded in favor of some date after he had received *Exsurge Domine*. About the exact time there are as many theories as there are letters and treatises from Luther's hand after mid-October 1520.[88] Luther's response to the bull was swift and prolific. In November a preliminary rebuttal, *Against the Bull of the Antichrist*, was printed in Latin and in German. This was followed by a thorough Latin defense of the articles condemned in *Exsurge Domine*, which Luther himself translated into German and published after the turn of the year. On November 17 he appealed to a general council, and on December 10 he burned a copy of the bull along with other "papal" books. Almost immediately he issued a defense of this action in German, *Why the Books of the Pope and His Disciples Were Burned*. Only weeks later, on January 3, 1521. Leo X excommunicated him in the bull *Decet Romanum Pontificem*

Almost any of these works could be used to document Luther's break with the papacy. His immediate response to the bull, although formally maintaining uncertainty about its real author, contained a reverse denunciation of the papacy as the seat of the Antichrist.[89] The designation "papist" was sprinkled liberally throughout the work, now and then supplemented with "bullist." Luther's appeal to a council was a renewal of his appeal of 1518 with an antipapal edge.[90] The most dramatic documentation of the break was the burning of the papal bull on December 10, 1520. Luther was in effect carrying out the stipulations of the bull against its author, the "pope and his disciples," in return for the burning of his books. Melanchthon's invitation to students to appear at the bonfire summoned them to witness "a pious and religious spectacle, for perhaps now is the time when the Antichrist must be revealed."[91] On the same afternoon, Luther sent a justification of his act to Spalatin. He reported that the collections of decretals in canon law, the bull, a penitential handbook, and works of Eck and Emser were all set ablaze. Apparently, bystanders threw in their own favorites.[92] On the next afternoon Luther is supposed to have told his students that they could not be saved unless they opposed the papal kingdom with their whole heart.[93]

The treatise which justified the burning is, in its form, a "counter-bull." The body of the treatise contains thirty articles from canon law, the "pope's own books," which Luther judged to be worthy of condemnation. His comments on these articles and his introduction to them reflect his intensified opposition to the papacy. The seducers of the people have not only persisted in their seduction, wrote Luther; they have become so hardened that now they damn and burn evangelical teaching. As a baptized Christian, sworn doctor of Holy Scripture, and a daily preacher, it is his duty, said Luther, to ward off such false, seductive, unchristian doctrine. He does not think that the burners of his own books have acted at the behest of Leo, but even so he does not care. Concern for the people is his motive, and his opponent is false teaching.[94] Among the errors in canon law which justify their destruction, the chief article is the claim that the pope is above human judgment. If this article stands, says Luther, then Christ and his word are defeated. If it does not stand, then all of canon law with the pope and his see lies prostrate.[95] At the end, Luther serves notice that he is now very serious, whereas up to now he has only joked and dallied with the pope's affair.[96]

Taking Luther at his word, some historians have regarded this document as the seal on the break of Luther with the papacy.[97] Viewed from the legal perspective of Luther's trial, however, the break may have come not in Wittenberg, but in Cologne. There, on November 4–6, 1520, the Elector Frederick rejected the demand of the papal legate, Jerome Aleander, to enforce the bull *Exsurge Domine* against Luther. Frederick repeated his demands for a fair hearing and to some extent made himself responsible for the break of Luther with the papal church.[98] Actually, an earthshaking event such as Luther's break with the papacy results from the shifting of several layers at the same time. Instead of singling out one break, it is more accurate to speak of several "breaks" of Luther with the papacy within this one stage of definitive opposition that he reached in 1520. In terms of ecclesiastical politics, Luther's break was not final until his excommunication; at the level of imperial politics, it was not until much later.

At the level of his self-awareness and his personal opposition to the papacy, all the signs of separation are present in his preface to the German version, in press by the end of 1520, of his defense of the articles condemned by *Exsurge Domine*. The tendency, already evident in *The Papacy at Rome*, to treat the church of Rome as an alien institution has become stronger than ever. Luther no longer speaks of the church more or less properly defined but of true and false churches. Even the laity can unmask the false, disguised church in an age when God has opened the eyes of so many.[99] Moreover, Luther restricts the true church to a remnant, the minority of God's people who have remained faithful to the truth in every age. This image of a remnant church, an old rubric in ecclesiological thinking, is a sign that the Roman Church is no longer part of the true church for him.[100]

Joined with the conception of the true church as a remnant is a corresponding shift in Luther's attitude toward the laity. They are no longer only poor, deluded souls: they have become theologically astute. Even farmers and children understand Christ better than popes, bishops, and doctors of theology.[101] Luther entrusts to the laity the judgment between truth and falsehood, between the true and the false churches. That judgment must be based on the clarity and certainty of Scripture. *Exsurge Domine* had quoted a famous statement of Augustine against Luther; in return, Luther now cites Augustine in praise of the canonical books.[102]

Luther has attained a new level of self-awareness as well. Luther begins to conceive of himself as a prophet. He will not say it outright, of course, but the idea is not unwelcome to him. His opponents have all the more to fear that he might be a prophet the more they despise him. If he is not a prophet, then he is at least certain that God's word is on his side. God has always chosen to announce his message through a solitary and unlikely spokesman. In Balaam's day there were many asses in the world, but God chose to speak through the ass of Balaam.[103] A prophet leading a remnant church: this heightened ecclesiological self-awareness is the new plateau Luther has reached, and there is little room for the papacy at that altitude.

Even former allies have to step aside. John Hus, after a tenure of less than a year at Luther's side, is one of the first to go. Hus fell short because he argued that an evil pope, though not a member of the true church, should still be endured like any other tyrant. Luther had passed on the same admonition as recently as the *Babylonian Captivity of the Church*. Now he says that "even if St. Peter would preside at Rome today, I would deny that the Roman bishop is pope. The pope is a fictitious thing in this world; he never was, nor is, nor will be; he is only fabricated. Hence I deny the very seat of the beast and I care not at all whether he who occupies it is good or evil. In the church there is no seat which would be above the others by divine right. All are equal."[104]

In spite of his ringing identification with Hus as recently as February, Luther now claims that "they act wrongly who call me a Hussite."[105]

Luther's opposition at all levels seems to presuppose a rejection of the papacy under any condition, yet Luther refused, publicly at least, to go that far. Denying again that the pope is the vicar of Christ, he names this a chief point to be sure, and he recounts his exegesis of Matthew 16 and John 21 against this papal claim. Luther adds, however, that he does not deny that the pope is the vicar of Christ because he wants to reject the pope. The pope can have as much power as he wants, but he, Luther, will not ignore two things: that the popes abuse Scripture to support their claims, and that they treat those Christians who are not subject to Rome as if such subjection were a condition for being Christian.[106] Luther's opposition is adamant, but ultimately he wants it known that his opposition is not arbitrary. At all other levels, the breaks with the papacy have been made. The last official tie to mother Rome has to be cut by the church itself.

6 | CONVICTION
1521-1522

The experience and the complaints of all testify that
through the laws of the pope and the doctrines of men the
consciences of the faithful have been miserably ensnared,
vexed, and flayed. . . . If therefore I recant these [books],
I will in effect do nothing but add strength to tyranny and
open not just the windows but also the doors to this great
ungodliness.

—Luther, 1521
(WA 7, 833.10–13, 17–19)

CHRONOLOGY

1521	January 3	Luther's excommunication is formally pronounced in the bull *Decet Romanum Pontificem*
	January 20	Jerome Emser's response to Luther's *Address to the Christian Nobility* is published in Leipzig
	January 27	The Diet of Worms opens
	March 6	Luther is cited to Worms by Emperor Charles V
	April 1	Luther completes the manuscript of his reply to Ambrosius Catharinus
	April 2	Luther leaves Wittenberg for Worms
	April 7	Luther preaches in Erfurt
	April 15	The University of Paris issues its judgment on the works of Luther
	April 16	Luther arrives in Worms
	April 17	Luther appears for the first time before the diet
	April 18	Luther appears a second time and gives a speech before the diet
	April 24–25	Negotiations begin with Luther at the diet
	April 26	Luther leaves Worms
	May 4	Luther is "kidnapped" and taken to the Wartburg Castle, where he remains until March 1, 1522

1521	May 8	Emperor Charles places Luther under the imperial ban
	May 26	Emperor Charles publishes the Edict of Worms against Luther
	June	At the Wartburg Luther writes his reply to Latomus and an exposition of Psalm 37 for his congregation in Wittenberg
	September 29	Gabriel Zwilling and his followers in the Augustinian Cloister in Wittenberg decide no longer to celebrate mass
	November 1	Luther dedicates *The Misuse of the Mass* to the Augustinians in Wittenberg
	November 21	Luther dedicates his treatise *On Monastic Vows* to his father
	December 1	Pope Leo X dies in Rome Luther demands that Archbishop Albert of Mainz abolish the "idol at Halle"
	December 25	Karlstadt celebrates "evangelical" communion service in Wittenberg against the command of Elector Frederick
1522	January 9	Cardinal Adrian of Utrecht (Hadrian VI) is elected pope
	January 20	The Imperial Governing Council warns Elector Frederick not to condone innovations in his territory
	March 6	Luther returns to Wittenberg
	March 9–16	Luther gives his "Invocavit" sermons
	June 28	Emser publishes a German translation of the *Assertion of Seven Sacraments* by Henry VIII
	July 26	Luther: *Against the So-Called Spiritual Estate of the Pope and the Bishops*
	August 1	Luther: *German Response to the Book of King Henry*
	August 29	Pope Hadrian VI enters Rome for the first time
	September 21	Luther's translation of the New Testament is published
	November	Henry of Zütphen preaches in Bremen after his escape from Antwerp

1522 December 1   Pope Hadrian VI summons Eck and Erasmus to battle against Lutheranism

1523 January 3   The "Confession" of Hadrian VI is read to the Diet of Nuremberg

IRRECONCILABLE ALTERNATIVES

Luther's defiant burning of the "papal" books on December 10, 1520, was the unmistakable sign of his refusal to comply with the terms of *Exsurge Domine*. On that same day, his period of grace ran out and he was excommunicated from the Roman Church by Pope Leo X on January 3, 1521, in a new bull entitled *Decet Romanum Pontificem*. Appropriately, the bull began with an affirmation of papal power and responsibility. Power divinely committed to the pope made him the dispenser of spiritual and temporal punishments; as such, it behooved the pope to suppress the wicked endeavors of perverse men.[1] Luther's time "under the papacy," as he liked to describe his life to this point, was over. His relationship to the papacy entered a new stage; both outwardly and inwardly Luther stood no longer "under" but "over against" the papacy.

Only gradually did Luther realize what this new stance would mean for himself and for his followers. Besides formal freedom from the pope, it did not mean much in terms of his day-to-day existence. There was no overnight metamorphosis from monk to Protestant. In a letter to his fellow Augustinian, John Lang, in Erfurt, Luther exulted in his release from the laws of the Augustinian Order and of the pope; but, he said, he did not plan to pack away his habit or leave the monastery.[2] No immediate upheaval was called for as long as the Elector Frederick was supporting the presentation of Luther's case at the Imperial Diet of Worms, which finally opened on January 27, 1521.

Although the practical consequences of his excommunication remained unclear, the theoretical basis for his new life apart from the papacy congealed in his mind. The contrast between Christ and the pope, whose similarity to the Antichrist dominated his thought, hardened into irreconcilable alternatives. The celebration of Epiphany on January 6, 1521, offered Luther an opportunity to describe the alternatives. Instead of the traditional three kings, Luther took two other kings mentioned in the story, Christ and Herod, as his point of departure. Christ is the legitimate heir of Judah (Gen. 49:10) whereas Herod is the impostor. Herod's rule stands for the illegitimate kingdom of the pope and the Antichrist; it can never come to terms with the kingdom of Christ, because it is built upon works, whereas the kingdom of Christ is built upon firm faith. Therefore, Luther admonished his congregation, guard yourselves against the deceiving Herodian preachers![3]

Luther's warning was shriller and his description of the alternatives sharper in a letter which he wrote to Staupitz. The roaring of the "lion" (=Leo), said Staupitz, had reached him in his haven among the Benedictines in Salzburg. Pope Leo asked Cardinal Matthew Lang, who had been with Staupitz and Luther in Augsburg in 1518, to force Staupitz to recant the errors of Luther.[4] In February 1521, having heard of Leo's ultimatum and of Staupitz's reply, Luther warned his former superior against the slightest compromise with the pope's demands. In his bull, argued Luther, the pope damned everything which Staupitz had ever taught and understood about the mercy of God. Now is not the time to be afraid, argued Luther; instead, we should cry out in protest when our Lord Jesus Christ is damned, stripped, and blasphemed. Afraid that Staupitz would try to walk a middle road between Christ and the pope, Luther painted them as absolute antagonists.[5]

The sharpening of alternatives was not made by Luther alone, nor was it confined to the written word. As part of their pre-Lenten cavortings, Wittenberg students dressed up as the pope, cardinals, and bishops and marched through town mocking the hierarchy. Luther approved of their fun since the "enemy of Christ" deserved such ridicule.[6] About the same time, the artist Lucas Cranach was preparing woodcuts for his *Passional of Christ and the Antichrist*. In thirteen sets of two pictures each, Cranach cleverly illustrated contrasts between Christ and the pope.[7] The idea of such an antithesis was not new; but, although Luther himself probably did not compose the captions for the pictures,[8] his writings inspired Cranach to produce the *Passional*. In particular, Luther's citation of thirty articles from canon law in his "anti-bull," *Why the Books of the Pope and His Disciples Were Burned*, contributed both impetus to the idea and material to the captions. In May, Luther had already called the pictures a good book for the laity and, when he saw the finished product after his return from Worms, it pleased him greatly.[9]

The antithetical pictures in the *Passional* reflect traditional criticism of papal wealth and pomp in contrast to the poverty and simplicity of Christ. A particular source of Luther's satisfaction with the work, however, may have been pictures number thirteen and fourteen. Number thirteen shows Christ preaching outdoors to the gathered multitude, and number fourteen depicts the pope, well attended and musically entertained, enjoying a hearty meal with a bishop, a monk, and other companions. The caption for number thirteen cites the words of Jesus in Luke 4:43–44: "I must preach the good news of the kingdom of God to the other cities also; for I was sent for this purpose." The counter-caption for number fourteen begins, typically, with a quote from canon law, which excused the bishops from preaching if their dioceses were too large or if they were overburdened with administrative duties. Then follows the commentary: "Those bishops have forgotten their proper office and have become creatures of the belly, saying: 'Come . . . let us get wine, let us fill ourselves with strong drink; and tomorrow will be like this day, great beyond measure' (Isa. 56:12)."[10] Looking at these two pictures, Luther may well have felt that Cranach did justice to his complaint that the word of God had been silenced in the church.

Another pointed contrast depicted in the *Passional* is anticipated by Luther in his *Assertion of All the Articles,* which was published in January. The pictures in the second Wittenberg edition of the *Passional* depict, on the one side, Christ falling down under the weight of his cross on the way to Golgotha. On the other side, the pope is carried comfortably in a sedan chair on the shoulders of his bearers. The pictures display more than a contrasting lifestyle when they are viewed in light of Luther's *Assertion.* In that work, Luther argues that his denial of free will could not stand alongside the church of the pope any more than Belial could stand alongside Christ or darkness alongside light. He continues, "This theology, which condemns whatever the pope approves and makes martyrs, is of the cross . . . I have no stronger argument against the kingdom of the pope than that it rules without the cross."[11]

During the months prior to Worms, the sharpened alternatives did lead Luther to pursue more confidently and aggressively the care of his own people. Luther set to work on a task which the Elector Frederick had asked him to undertake more than a year earlier. That task was to write brief expositions of the lessons appointed for the Sundays and festivals of the church year. In his dedication of the first set to the elector, Luther wrote that he had now given up hope of peace and recognized that the duty of pastors and bishops was to withstand adversaries. He had decided to fulfill the elector's request, therefore, not in order to display elegance of language, but to expound the pure and simple sense of the gospel for the people.[12] It was time to sound out how Christians would receive the gospel "after this long and hard captivity of Babylon."[13]

When Nikolaus Hausmann asked Luther if he should accept a pastorate in Zwickau, Luther painted the situation in the darkest colors. Wolves have become pastors, and no one can be saved unless he fights against the statutes and mandates of the pope and the bishops. The pope is totally the adversary of Christ, and no one should dare preach unless he leads the sheep away from the pope and drives him away like a wolf. The choice is clear-cut: if Hausmann accepts the pastorate, then he must be an enemy of the pope and of the bishops and fight against their decrees. If he does not fight against them, then he is an enemy of Christ. The freest faith in Christ does not stand alongside their snares and traps.[14] The liberty which Luther had long sought for the people and had now experienced anew in his own excommunication could become a reality for the people through the resistance and resilience of their pastors.

OPPOSING CHURCHES

Opposition to Luther did not die down after his excommunication formally took effect. Some of the opponents were carryovers from the preceding three years while a few new faces appeared on the scene. In his exposition of Psalm 37 for "his congregation" in Wittenberg, written from exile at the Wartburg in the summer of 1521, Luther named most of them: first in order, Sylvester Prierias, then, John Eck, Thomas Rhadinus,[15] Ambrosius Catharinus Politus, the universities of Cologne and Louvain, the pope with his bulls, the theological faculty at Paris, James Latomus in Louvain, and, finally, Alfeld and Emser in Leipzig. In Luther's mind they all fit under the rubric of the "pope and his papists." They were incapable of understanding either Scripture or the arguments for their own case which, according to Luther, consisted of human teaching and their own dreams.[16] It was a clear case of "us and them": Luther and his people versus the pope and his papists, or, as Luther now labels his opponents, the pope's or "papist sects."[17] The irreconcilable alternatives had become opposing churches.

Luther disputed more intensely the claim of his opponents that the Roman Church was the only true church and reinforced his view that the church could exist apart from the hierarchy of the Romanists. In his controversy with Jerome Emser, which flared up again in early 1521, Luther accused the Roman Church of having stolen the priesthood just as it had stolen the church. Against Luther's defense of the priesthood of believers, Emser attempted to prove that 1 Pet. 2:9 referred to the sacerdotal priesthood. In his rebuttals, Luther argued that 1 Pet. 2:9 referred to a spiritual priesthood of all Christians and that the New Testament spoke only of a spiritual priesthood of Christians just as Scripture spoke only of a spiritual church. Luther's argument against Emser for a spiritual priesthood paralleled his argument against Alfeld for a spiritual church. A sacral priesthood like the one of which Emser dreamed and a church as the papists imagined it were as contrary to Scripture as life to death. Hence, claimed Luther in conscious opposition to Emser and the "papists," *we* have regained the names of priest and church which *they* have stolen, although we will leave them their tonsures in place of the word of God which they never wore.[18]

Luther himself has given up hope for reform of the papacy. In response to Emser, who accused him of decapitating the church and splitting the body in two, Luther argues that his previous books did not aim at abolishing the papacy but at reforming it. If the pope would become equal to the other bishops, the church would not be without a head, as Emser argues, since Christ is the head of the church. Luther definitely does not expect that to happen, however, at least not before the last judgment. Christ himself must depose this enemy who cannot be reformed; the pope is nothing but a heretic and a knave.[19]

Luther further intensified the debate by introducing a fresh point of controversy. He challenged the tradition, based in part on the church father Jerome, that Peter had lived in Rome for twenty-five years. The establishment of Peter's early residence in Rome was crucial for tying the words of Christ, on which the claims of Roman primacy were based, to Rome. In early 1521, Luther had become newly aware of the problem through the work of Ulrichus Velenus (Oldřich Velenský) published in late 1520. Velenus claimed to provide "various important and reliable arguments, based on Scripture, . . . showing that the Apostle Peter neither came to Rome nor suffered there, and that it is therefore quite useless and audacious for the Roman pontiff to suppose that he is, and to call himself, the successor of Peter."[20] When Luther received a copy of the work, he wrote to Spalatin that he was not convinced by it;[21] but that judgment did not prevent him from using one of Velenus's arguments against Emser.

That argument exposed the difficulty of adjusting the evidence of the New Testament and of tradition to support a twenty-five-year residence of Peter in Rome. The main problem was the testimony of Paul (Gal. 1:18 and 2:1,11) that he saw Peter in Jerusalem three years after his conversion and again fourteen years later. If Peter was martyred in Rome under Nero in 68 A.D., then he could not have lived in Rome for twenty-five years unless, of course, he traveled back to Jerusalem from Rome. John Eck had already argued for the latter possibility in his book on *The Primacy of Peter*. Luther did not deny that Peter was ever in Rome; he only expressed uncertainty on this point, and he continued to do so for the rest of his life.²² Still, for Luther, the chronological difficulties were enough to undermine the papal claims of primacy. The burden of proof was on the papal party since they were making the claim. Hence, says Luther, if they cannot prove that Peter was at Rome, then we must not believe that the pope sits on the throne of Peter or has inherited it. The journey of Paul to Rome, and not the journey of Peter, is recounted in Scripture because God knew that the papists would try to build their claim on Peter.²³

Luther's main argument against the papacy, however, is not his attack on patristic chronology but his own interpretation of just those words of Christ to Peter on which the claims of papal primacy were based: Matt. 16:18–19 and John 21:15–17. In his reply to Thomas Murner, a Strasbourg monk, Luther asserts he has found no stronger argument against the papacy in all of Scripture than Matt. 16:18, the text which Murner, true to form, held up to Luther as the strongest in its favor.²⁴ The thrust of Luther's argument lies in the words of Christ: "And the gates of hell shall not prevail against it." One look at the errors and evils of the pope and his party confirms, says Luther, that the gates of hell prevail daily over the Roman Church. Consequently, the rock and the church of which Christ speaks resemble the pope and his churches as closely as light resembles darkness or Christ resembles Belial.²⁵ The church of which Christ speaks cannot be tied to any one place or person. Such visible supports of the church will always be overcome by sin and hell. Instead, the holy Christian church can only be believed; it is spiritual, built invisibly in the spirit upon the rock which is Christ.²⁶ This church, the holy church of Christ, is categorically opposed to its counterpart, the "mad church of the pope."²⁷

Luther employed the same interpretation of Matt. 16:18 against a more formidable opponent, the Italian Dominican, Lancellotto de' Politi (1484–1553), who, after his entry into the Dominican cloister San Marco in Florence, assumed the names Ambrosius Catharinus. At the urging of his superior, Catharinus wrote in 1520 a *Defense of the Truth of Catholic and Apostolic Faith and Doctrine against the Impious and Exceedingly Pestiferous Dogmas of Martin Luther*.²⁸ It was directed primarily against Luther's *Explanation of Proposition Thirteen* and, consequently, the key text from Matthew 16 found a prominent place in his work.

For Luther, the papacy as an issue was settled. Making ironical use of scholastic logic, Luther says that the investigation into the existence and nature of the pope has been concluded. It has been established that the pope is the Antichrist and all that remains is to elaborate on that conclusion.[29] So that he would not appear at a loss for words, however, he would deal with Catharinus's interpretation of Matt. 16:18, "And the gates of hell will not prevail against it."[30] Luther's argumentation leads him once again to the affirmation of the true church as invisible and spiritual, built only upon Christ. But he is aware of the criticism of Catharinus that this church is too "spiritual," lacking a visible and tangible embodiment such as the pope by which people could always locate the church. Luther's response to this criticism is not new, but it now helps him to mark with finality his passage from the church of the pope to the church of the gospel.

In words reminiscent of his first lectures on the Psalms, Luther explains his understanding of the spiritual and invisible nature of the church. These terms mean that the church is not tied to any one place, person, time, or ceremonies, that is, "all things are indifferent and free." Though the church lives "in the flesh," it does not therefore live "according to the flesh," and hence it is spiritual.[31] The church must still have marks, however, by which "we are called together to hear the word of God." These marks are baptism, the bread, and, the most powerful sign of all, the gospel. Where these are present, no matter at what place or among which persons, you need not doubt that the church is present. But where you do not see the gospel (as in the synagogue of papists and Thomists), there you can be sure that, except in babies and simple folk, the church is absent. The gospel outranks even the sacraments as the most certain and noble mark of the church, since by the gospel alone the church is "conceived, formed, nourished, generated, raised up, fed, clothed, adorned, strengthened, armed and preserved." In short, as Luther said in his sermon for the prior at Leitzkau in 1515, "the whole life and substance of the church is in the word of God."[32]

In his strife with the papacy, Luther uses his early ecclesiology to arrive at a new understanding of the exegetical pillars of papal primacy: Matt. 16:18 and John 21:15–17. The invisible and spiritual church, founded upon faith, which emerged from his early occupation with the

Psalter, finds confirmation and a crucial application in the spiritual rock of Matt. 16:18. Likewise, the church which lives by the word of God also lives from the words of Christ in John 21:15–17: "Feed my sheep." In the charge of Christ to Peter, all pastors are required to feed their sheep, that is, to teach the gospel with a "living voice."[33] Hence, Luther cannot abide Catharinus's exposition of this verse. In place of the charge to preach, Catharinus interpreted the words of Christ as the conferral of authority and power which was the precondition for preaching. Furthermore, Catharinus refused to tie authority to preach to the love which Christ sought from Peter.[34] Luther responds decisively: this figment of the papists' imagination, that the office of jurisdiction and the office of brotherly love are two different things, must be scorned. "The gospel and the church know no jurisdictions, which are nothing but tyrannical human inventions. They only know love and servitude, not power and tyranny. Therefore, whoever teaches the gospel is pope, the successor of Peter; whoever does not teach it is Judas, the betrayer of Christ."[35] Once again, the alternatives are stated as strongly as possible.

By 1521 silence on the issue of the true church and the papacy was speaking as loud as words. The condemnation finally issued by the theological faculty of the University of Paris contained no mention of Luther's rejection of the papacy. This omission by the notorious bastion of conciliar views was an embarrassment to the papal side. It did not go unnoticed by Luther either; he prepared a German edition of the condemnation alongside Melanchthon's rebuttal and his own glosses and afterword. Luther pondered, partly in jest, why Paris omitted this article when almost all his other opponents made it the chief point of controversy.[36] In no way did Luther want this silence to be read as an endorsement of himself, because the silence of Paris did not stem from the "love of truth."[37] Since the papacy was the only issue besides indulgences well known to the common man,[38] Luther wanted to make sure that his motives were clear. The Diet of Worms gave him that opportunity.

THE CONSCIENCES OF THE FAITHFUL

Luther completed the manuscript of his response to Catharinus on the day before he left Wittenberg for Worms, and the condemnation of the University of Paris was issued on the day before he arrived in Worms. Emperor Charles V had cited Luther to Worms on March 6.

The citation was a victory for the Electoral Saxon court over the stiff resistance of the papal nuncio, Jerome Aleander, and a good part of the imperial court.[39] Ever since he arrived in Worms before Christmas of 1520, Aleander had opposed suggestions that Luther be summoned to appear before the diet or that Luther needed to recant only those heretical articles that had been condemned by past councils in the presence of the emperors. Aleander labeled the latter suggestion "absolute nonsense," since it completely ignored Luther's attacks on the reigning pope and his predecessors. Aleander argued that many heretics before Luther had been condemned by popes without a hearing before secular authorities; the princes were only executors of papal sentences. If Luther were refused a hearing, it would demonstrate again that the welfare and unity of the church depended on the unlimited and absolutely superior power of the pope.[40]

For Aleander, the major issue at stake in Luther's appearance at Worms was the authority of the papacy and Luther's chief error was in denying that authority. Luther viewed his upcoming appearance in the same light. For him Worms was not just the site of an imperial gathering, not a neutral site to be sure, but a "nest of papists" who had already swayed Emperor Charles in their favor.[41] If he is killed, Luther does not want Charles but only the papists to be guilty of his blood.[42] If a recantation is desired, then he will not go to Worms since he could deliver that from Wittenberg. His only revocation will be to make his judgment of the papacy even harsher. Whereas, before, he admitted that the pope was the vicar of Christ, he will now recant that and assert that the pope is the adversary of Christ and the apostle of the devil.[43] The real issue at Worms in April of 1521 was not Luther and the empire or Luther and secular authority, but the same issue which had dominated his case for three years: Luther and the papacy. In Luther's eyes, of course, it was now Christ versus the pope, a shorthand formula for the alternative views of Christian faith and life. Luther stated the alternatives transparently in a sermon delivered to a packed church in Erfurt on his way to Worms: "Christ has demolished death and our own will, so that we are saved not by our own works, but by his works which are alien to us. Papal power, however, handles us quite differently. Fasting is prescribed, praying, eating butter. If you keep the commands of the pope, then you are saved; if you don't, then you are given over to the devil."[44]

The alternatives did not shift after Luther's entry into Worms on

April 16, which he characterized as his "Palm Sunday."[45] Luther was ordered to appear before Emperor Charles and the estates at 4:00 P.M. on the next day, April 17, 1521. The Imperial Marshal and the Imperial Herald escorted him to the meeting by a back way in order to avoid the crowds waiting to catch a glimpse of the notorious monk. The meeting, held in a small room of the bishop's residence, consisted more of a special hearing than an official session of the diet. Luther had been instructed beforehand that he was allowed only to answer questions put to him by the official of the archbishop of Trier, John von der Ecken. There were two questions: Did Luther acknowledge the books which had been published under his name, and did he stand by their content or did he wish to recant anything in them?[46] After the Saxon lawyer, Jerome Schurf, demanded that the titles of the books be read aloud, Luther replied to the questions. He acknowledged the books as his own and then, surprisingly, asked for time to think over the second question so that he could answer it satisfactorily without injury to the divine word or danger to his own soul.[47] Although von der Ecken argued that Luther should already have prepared his answer, the delay was granted.

When Luther reappeared before the imperial gathering on the next day, April 18, around 6:00 P.M., he delivered no harangue, but a well-organized, ten-minute speech in both Latin and German on the subject of his authorship. Luther asserts that he has taught and written in simplicity of spirit with regard only for the glory of God and for the sincere instruction of the faithful of Christ.[48] Furthermore, claims Luther, his books fall into three distinct groups. First are those books in which he has treated Christian faith and life so simply and evangelically that even his opponents have admitted that these books are useful. In the second group of books he has inveighed against the "papacy and the affairs of the papists" because they have devastated the whole Christian world. In a third group, he has written against private individuals who have attempted to uphold Roman tyranny and to weaken the piety taught by Luther. He confesses that he has written more acerbically against these persons than behooves his monastic profession, but he has never made his own holiness or life a matter for debate, only the doctrine of Christ. In contrast to Jesus, Luther describes himself as one who is certainly able to err and repeats his offer to stand corrected if he is overcome with "prophetic and evangelical" Scriptures. Finally, he acknowledges that he did consider the warning that his teaching could cause popular unrest. Instead of apologizing, however, Luther rejoices that dissension has arisen for the sake of the word and warns that one should consider what God might stir up in addition if peace is sought by condemning the word.

In reply, von der Ecken offered his own categorization of Luther's books: those which Luther published prior to the judgment of the pope, that is, before *Exsurge Domine*, and the much more reprehensible works which he published thereafter.[49] Indeed, Luther had not adequately answered his question, since no distinction among his works would remove the errors contained in them and since heretics had always appealed to the inability of their accusers to prove they were wrong. In vain could Luther expect a debate; hence, von der Ecken demanded a direct reply with no strings attached. Luther then delivered the forceful conclusion of his speech: "Unless I am overcome by the testimony of Scripture or by clear reason (for I believe neither the pope nor councils by themselves), I remain conquered by the Scriptures which I have adduced. As long as my conscience is captive to the words of God, I neither can nor will recant, since it is neither safe nor right to act against conscience. God help me, Amen."[50]

The moving appeal of Luther to conscience has led to the view that in Worms Luther was standing on the threshold of the modern era, heralding its principles of political and religious freedom.[51] Whatever truth may lie hidden in this romantic view of Luther's stand, such an interpretation fails to appreciate the conviction behind Luther's reforming efforts. Luther was appealing not only to his own conscience or to an abstract principle of freedom but also to the consciences of all faithful Christians in whose name he had begun and now upheld his opposition to the papacy. The body of Luther's speech, and not the famous conclusion, best illustrates his conviction:

> . . . the experience and the complaints of all testify that through the laws of the pope and the doctrines of men the consciences of the faithful have been miserably ensnared, vexed, and flayed. . . . If therefore I recant these [books], I will in effect do nothing but add strength to tyranny and open not just the windows but also the doors to this great ungodliness. . . .[52]

Luther's protest against papal tyranny on behalf of the people was behind his stand at Worms. His refusal to recant was pastoral and not political. The issue was obedience to the pope and not to the emperor. The conscience captive to the word of God was not just his own, but the consciences of the faithful. From Luther's perspective, he was protesting against the usurpation of the church by an unfaithful hierarchy on behalf of the faithful people, not against the church on behalf of the individual.

Political, personal, and theological factors that played a role in Luther's stand are not excluded by the foregoing sharp contrasts. Luther was aware of the political implications of his stand and acknowledged the debt of obedience that he owed to "my Germany."[53] He realized the threat of revolution but refused to be swayed by it. He also included himself in the crowd whom he saw as having long been victimized by the papacy. His personal experience was part of the collective experience to which he appealed as the witness to papal tyranny. And he did mistrust ecclesiastical authority; neither popes nor councils sufficed any longer, only the promises of God in Scripture and evident arguments.[54] As a doctor of that Scripture in the church he was at the moment of his reply one man alone against the combined forces of church and empire. The most striking feature of his appearance at Worms, however, and hence the epitome of his reforming work, was not his isolated courage, but his sense of solidarity with the people.

That solidarity must have looked more like stubbornness to those who attempted to persuade Luther to soften his conviction. On the morning of April 19, Emperor Charles summoned the estates of the empire and read to them the "confession" of his orthodoxy and the declaration of his intention to proceed against Luther as a notorious heretic.[55] In reply, the estates asked for time to negotiate and, during the next week, Luther met with the archbishop of Trier, who was in charge of the negotiations, Jerome Vehus, the chancellor of Baden, and John Cochlaeus, the Frankfurt theologian who became an avid opponent of Luther. The negotiations concentrated on the question of authority and on the dangerous consequences of Luther's refusal to recant. Luther did not budge. He refused to allow his alleged errors to be submitted to a council if these errors contained his endorsement of the teachings of John Hus condemned at the Council of Constance.[56] At one point, when Luther claimed that he had called no names, Cochlaeus reminded Luther that he had labeled Pope Leo a heretic, an apostate, an unbeliever, and a tyrant. Maybe so, answered Luther, but it was justified because Leo was a public and not a private person.[57] As the long arm of this public person, Emperor Charles placed Luther under the imperial ban with the Edict of Worms. It was composed primarily by

Aleander on the basis of earlier drafts and publicly declared to the estates and signed by the emperor on Trinity Sunday, May 26, 1521.[58]

The question of authority dominated Luther's reflection on Worms after his departure on April 26, 1521. Reporting to Charles on the negotiations, Luther made the whole controversy hinge on the fact that the word of God could not remain free. Luther reached back to a favorite verse from Romans 3 and Psalm 116 to stress once again that "every man is a liar" and that God alone is the truth. God does not risk submitting to one person judgment over his word and over eternal matters.[59] Hence, the pope cannot judge matters that pertain to faith and God's word; these belong to everyone in the community. Luther reports that during the negotiations he based this position on 1 Cor. 14:30: "If a revelation is made to another sitting by, let the first be silent." Luther interpreted the text to mean that a teacher has to listen to a pupil whenever the pupil has a better opinion based on the word of God.[60] The citation of such a text understandably did little to allay fear of Luther's radicalism, although Luther claims that the text stood unassailed and brought the discussion to an end.

Luther's resistance to the papacy made him indeed an ecclesiastical radical. His uncompromising stand for the word of God on behalf of the people possessed the characteristics of radicalism: absolute dedication to the abolition of tyranny, allegiance to a superior authority, and the belief that refusal to compromise would benefit the people. Worms impressed upon his mind both the limit and the extent of his radicalism. The limit was that Luther resisted authority only for the sake of the word and, as a result, reserved his harshest opposition for ecclesiastical and not secular superiors. But precisely because his radicalism was so concentrated, it cut much more deeply. Luther attacked pope and council only because of false teaching, but false teaching was exactly the point at which the power of pope and councils ceased and obedience to them was no longer required.[61] When Latomus offered Luther the advice of a "wise old man" to hope and pray patiently for improvement, Luther asked scornfully what would happen if he followed this advice in regard to the pope who did not care about the gospel. Such advice only made the pope into an idol and left the sheep to feed themselves and to make their own way, while supplying food to the pastors and making a trail for the leaders.[62] If we are to endure the evil of a magistrate, then let it be at most the evil of a secular magistrate, not of an ecclesiastical superior. The evil of a secular ruler does not harm the soul, whereas "a bishop who neglects the word, even though holy, is a wolf and an apostle of Satan. Whoever does not guard the sheep against the wolf is no different from the wolf."[63]

Against the moderate advice of Latomus, Luther unleashes the pent-up frustration of his hopes for reform and reveals how deeply his opposition to the papacy is embedded in his outrage at the perversion of the pastoral office:

> But although we know that the devil does not sleep, we stroke sleeping bishops; we protect those cooperating with the devil while we kill and damn those who stir up the bishops and admonish them to do their duty. What, I ask, is more outrageous than this? Thrice accursed be anyone who in this respect does the work of the Lord fraudulently and flatters the pope, who himself conspires and connives with the infernal wolf and has no pity on the miserably perishing souls of so many of his brethren which have been bought with the blood of Christ. If Latomus had written nothing else, this one hellish piece of advice suffices to show that he is filled with the spirit of Satan. And what hope is there that these sophists will read, understand, and teach the Scripture with zeal and devotion? How will they pass judgment on Christian teaching? Finally, what salutary thing can you expect from these people, to whom this advice, fit to pass for the words of Satan, appears wise, who think so lightly of the church, the evils of pastors and the salvation of souls as if it were only the guilt of secular tyranny which destroys bodies and goods? I, poor wretch, am very afraid that I have been much too lenient and modest toward the pope and the pontiffs, those collaborators and associates of the devil, and that I myself have taken too lightly the thousands of souls who are killed without ceasing by that Antichrist with his priests and sophists, those last plagues of the earth.[64]

THE "FIRST FRUITS OF VICTORY"

Luther wrote this indictment from his "Patmos," the Wartburg Castle near Eisenach, to which he had been spirited after his "kidnapping" on the evening of May 4, 1521. His communiques from exile, like the letter to Melanchthon quoted at the beginning of this book, reveal his preoccupation with the papal Antichrist and its ravage of the church. Initial uncertainty about the future, exacerbated by physical irregularities, caused periods of gloom alternating with bursts of renewed determination. "I will continue," insists Luther, "to polish the truth and make it shine, and the more my unmerciful lords scorn me, the less I will fear them. Neither of us is over the mountain yet, but I have the advantage that I am travelling unburdened. God grant that truth keep the victory."[65] Luther could probably envision the other side of the mountain, but it was still defined in terms of the old alternatives. "We want Christ and not the pope; they can keep the pope, but not Christ, since the teaching of Christ cannot and will not rule alongside the teaching of the pope. Christ will be master by himself. . . ."[66] Whoever wants to keep his soul must protect himself against pope, cardinal, bishop, priests, monks, and the universities.[67]

But how? A separation from the papacy had occurred, but not yet a reformation of the church. Changes had taken place in Wittenberg, of course. The theological curriculum had been revised and, at least in some confessionals, the interrogation of parishioners must have eased. The task of rescuing worship and piety from "the teaching of the pope" and making them conform to the "teaching of Christ" still lay ahead. As concrete changes were introduced under the leadership of Melanchthon, Karlstadt, and Gabriel Zwilling, it became clear how much Luther's own attitude toward constructive reform was indebted to his struggle with the papacy. Luther's positive conception of what was "Protestant" was born in that struggle; it was not merely a reaction to the different views of the Wittenbergers.

Several aspects of his conflict with the papacy contributed to that positive conception. The most obvious contribution concerned the legitimacy of change. Sensitive to the careless use of Scripture to support practices under the papacy, Luther sought Scriptural justification for the superior interpretation of his followers and their right to apply it. After dismissing the use of Matt. 8:4 ("go, show yourself to the priest") by the papists as a proof text for private confession, Luther said it was no wonder that the sheep must teach their shepherds and the blind show their leaders where to walk. This reversal of roles, far from unexpected, was foreseen in Scripture itself (Ps. 119:98–100): "Thy commandment makes me wiser than my enemies, for it is ever with me; I have more understanding than all my teachers, for thy testimonies are my meditation. I understand more than the aged, for I keep thy precepts."[68] These were, not by chance, the same verses Luther had used to demonstrate the inferiority of human traditions in his first Psalms lectures of 1515. Luther was more certain than ever of the superior judgment which he had postulated on the basis of Ps. 119:98–100 and 1 Cor. 2:15: "We are not the pope's; the papacy is ours!"[69] This exclamation, made in response to Henry VIII in 1522 and followed by the quotation of 1 Cor. 2:15, marks the culmination of Luther's claim to a superior interpretation of Scripture.

As certain as he was of the superiority of his interpretation, the carelessness of his predecessors reminded him to be careful in the application of Scripture to Christian life. The danger was in substituting a new set of external regulations for the papal rules, or, as Luther put it more graphically, "Previously, Satan wanted to make us too papal; now he wants to make us too evangelical."[70] Specifically, Luther was referring to reforms in Wittenberg instituted by Karlstadt and Zwilling and to the more radical challenges of the "Zwickau prophets." The major issues were monastic vows, priestly celibacy, the form of communion, and the presence of statues, paintings, and carvings in the churches.[71] As Karlstadt and Zwilling proceeded with changes, Luther at the Wartburg struggled with his own positions. Early he became convinced that it was better to claim too little for Scripture than too much when it came to practice. If there was not "evident Scripture for us," then practices which might pose a stumbling block should be avoided even if they were permissible.[72] For example, Luther rejected Karlstadt's use of the warning in 1 Tim. 5:11 against young widows as an argument against the celibacy of young priests and monks. This passage was an "elusive authority" and could not serve as a "reliable rock for consciences."[73] Luther saw Karlstadt's goal, the strict conformity of Christian life and worship to biblical precepts, as running the danger of setting up a new biblical and Protestant tyranny.[74]

Luther's goal was different: not practice modeled strictly on biblical precedent, but practice which guaranteed "spiritual freedom," and such freedom existed "when consciences remained free."[75] Consciences could not remain free if they were forced to conform to Protestant practices when even the slightest compunction remained. For example, it was true that the papacy had held the Lord's Supper captive by depriving the laity of the cup. But the consciences of the laity had been ensnared so long that they should not be expected suddenly to believe that taking both bread and wine in their hands was right whereas having the bread alone placed in their mouth was wrong. If they were compelled to receive both elements in their hands before they were ready, they would regret it afterwards and run to confess it to the priest. Luther drew on his own experience as a guide. It had taken him three years of preaching, reading, wrestling, debating, writing, and listening to free his conscience. How could the laity be expected to attain such freedom in any less time?[76]

Luther's goal and strategy of reform were shaped predominantly by his life under the papacy. The most striking documentation of that influence was the dedication of his treatise, *The Misuse of the Mass*, to his fellow Augustinians in Wittenberg on November 1, 1521. Luther was afraid that not all of the monks would be able to accept with good conscience the abolition of the mass. The ridicule that they would receive from outside would be enough to shake them. And,

> in addition to these things comes that which I daily experience in myself, how difficult it is to recall a conscience vexed by long acquaintance with impiety to the wholesome knowledge of piety. With how many remedies, what strong balm of Gilead, with what powerful and evident Scriptures did I scarcely brace my conscience so that I, only one, could dare contradict the pope and believe him to be the Antichrist, the bishops to be his apostles and the universities his brothels. How often did my anxious heart flutter and reproach me with their strongest, in fact, their only argument: "Are you alone wise? Are so many others mistaken? Suppose you are wrong and drag so many with you into eternal damnation?" Finally, Christ strengthened me with his certain and faithful words, so that now my heart neither trembles nor flutters, but scorns these papistic arguments like a sheltered shoreline laughs at storms which swell up and threaten it. Moved by this experience and meditation, I thought it good to send this letter to you to strengthen and console whoever among you is still weak and not able to withstand the onslaught of a terrifying, hostile and intimidating conscience.[77]

Since the danger of introducing a new tyranny of conscience was so great, the safest strategy was not to make any more changes than necessary at first, but to instruct the people through preaching until their consciences were adequately braced to accept changes without fear and compunction. "I condemn the laws of the pope on confession, communion, prayer, and fasting, but I do it by the word, so that I might free consciences from them."[78] Luther's strategy to prepare the people for practical changes was the same strategy he had used to resist the papacy. According to the colorful description in his Invocavit sermons of 1522, the word alone toppled the papacy while he drank Wittenberg beer with his friends Philipp and Amsdorf.[79] What had looked like boldness and daring in opposition to the papacy, however, now looked to Karlstadt and Zwilling like foot-dragging. In reality, the notorious "conservatism" of Luther stemmed from his fear of imposing a new tyranny on those consciences that he had just fought so hard to liberate.

If the heart of Luther's reform strategy was preaching, the key to its success was the supply of preachers. This, too, Luther had learned from his experience "under" the papacy. The message of freedom which had been muffled now had to be broadcast. One of Luther's first concerns at the Wartburg was to receive news of the preaching schedule in Wittenberg.[80] In his own absence Luther admonished Melanchthon, a layman, to be diligent in the ministry of the word and commented on Melanchthon's complaint that they were without a pastor in Wittenberg: "That would be the saddest and bitterest news of all!"[81] Justus Jonas, who moved from Erfurt to Wittenberg as provost of the All Saints' Chapter, was challenged by Luther to take his ministry seriously, especially the lectures on canon law which he was obliged to give. He should teach the decretals of the Antichrist armed with Scripture in order to expose their lethal nature and to give the youth an antidote against them.[82] Already from the Wartburg, Luther envisioned the spread of the reform movement through the sending out of preachers. Half seriously, Luther teased Melanchthon about the oversupply of preachers in Wittenberg:

> You lecture, Amsdorf lectures, Jonas will lecture. For goodness' sake, do you want the kingdom of God to be proclaimed only in your town? Don't others also need the gospel? Will your Antioch not release a Silas or a Paul or a Barnabas for some other work of the Spirit? I tell you: although I would be very happy to be with you all, yet I would not be disturbed if the Lord deigned to open to me a door for the word either at Erfurt or Cologne or anywhere else, since you already have a surplus [of preachers and teachers]. Look how big a harvest there is everywhere—and how few are the harvesters! You are all harvesters. Certainly we have to consider not ourselves but our brethren who are spread out all over the country, lest we live for ourselves, that is, for the devil and not for Christ.[83]

The problem, as the city council of Altenburg described it to Luther, was that they had too many clergy, namely the priests, but no preachers.[84] The need was indeed there. "Everywhere people thirst for the gospel! From every direction people seek evangelists from us."[85] Luther's reformation spread by preaching as well as by the printed word, and it survived in opposition to the papacy by carving out a space in which, as Luther would have put it, consciences could breathe freely again.

In spite of the territory still to be conquered, shortly after his return from the Wartburg Luther talked as if the decisive battle had been won: "Certainly Satan has been conquered; the pope with his abominations has been conquered. . . . We believe that Christ, the Son of God, is Lord over life and death. Whom, therefore, should we fear? We have the first fruits of victory and we celebrate our triumph over papal tyranny. . . ."[86] There was still plenty of resistance, however, from secular as well as ecclesiastical authorities. The bishops posed the biggest obstacle because of their jurisdiction over the preachers and the life of the laity in their dioceses. Ironically, it was Archbishop Albert of Mainz who incited Luther to a scathing attack on the bishops and brought Luther's struggle with the papacy, as it were, full circle.

While Luther was at the Wartburg, Albert opened a relic exhibition, accompanied by the offer of generous indulgences, in connection with the new collegiate chapter established in his favorite residence of Halle. Angered by this new flaunting of old papal practice, Luther sent Albert an ultimatum: he was to abolish this "idol at Halle," which was depriving poor, simple Christians of their money and of their souls. Albert should leave the people unseduced and unshorn and himself be a bishop instead of a wolf. Indulgences were obviously nothing but foolishness and deceit, and only Christ should be preached to the people.[87] Luther reminded Albert how such tiny sparks had once ignited a horrendous blaze. No one took the matter seriously then, because no one thought the little monk was a match for the pope. But God gave the pope more than he could handle, so much, in fact, that the situation of the pope was daily growing worse.[88] Four years and one month after his first letter to Albert on November 1, 1517, Luther unmistakably betrayed the tone of victor. Even though the issue had moved from indulgences to the papacy and back once more to indulgences, Luther's conviction remained firm—against the seduction of the people and for their nourishment with the word.

The treatise that Luther wrote *Against the Idol at Halle* was held back from publication by Spalatin for obvious political reasons. Frederick had his hands full with imperial pressure during Luther's stay at the Wartburg. Part of this treatise, which is no longer extant, may have been included in Luther's general attack on the Roman hierarchy which appeared in July 1522, after his return to Wittenberg: *Against the So-called Spiritual Estate of the Pope and of the Bishops*.[89] Luther took the offensive, relishing the first fruits of his "victory." The attack of Christ on the chief priests and the scribes entitles all preachers to attack the hierarchy, an attack which is all the more necessary "since the ruin or the recovery of the people depends most of all on their leaders."[90] They have completely neglected their responsibility to feed the people. What is a waterless spring and a cloud without rain (2 Pet. 2:17) but a bishop without preaching?[91] The bishops who now rule are not Christian bishops instituted by divine order, but wolves, tyrants, murderers of souls, and apostles of the Antichrist.[92] By issuing indulgences alone, they have deserved a much stronger assault than Luther has so far delivered. "Everything which I do is a thousand times too little."[93] From Constance, Ambrose Blaurer wrote to his brother Thomas in Wittenberg: "We have read the book of Luther against the bishops. They should perhaps not read it lest they be forced to bewail their own misery."[94]

On the same day on which Luther sent his ultimatum to Albert of Mainz, December 1, 1521, Leo X died in Rome. For Luther's relationship to the papacy, it was an event of no consequence. Luther's opposition to the papacy had long since outrun his attitude toward any individual pope. Still, he remained to the end uncertain about Leo. In his attack on Luther's treatise, *The Babylonian Captivity*, Henry VIII had argued that indulgences could not be bad if Leo, as even Luther confessed, was good. In an incisive reversal of Luther's favorite imagery, Henry asked, "Is it not more probable to believe that this one little brother is a sick sheep than that so many former popes were unfaithful pastors?"[95] Luther responded that the argument was absurd. Indulgences were a matter of doctrine, in which anyone, even a good person, could err, although only the openly godless would persist in their error. Still, today (August 1522), said Luther, he was uncertain what Leo really thought and whether he remained pertinaciously in error.[96]

By the time Luther wrote these words, it was immaterial what Leo had thought. When Hadrian VI arrived in Rome on August 29, 1522, he was presented a copy of John Fabri's *Treatise Against Certain New Dogmas of Luther*. In the dedication to Hadrian, Fabri exhorted the new pope to preach the gospel to his flock.[97] Hadrian was not insensitive to the abuses of the past or to the need for reform. He composed a famous "confession" of the past sins of the hierarchy and had it read by his legate, Chieregati, to the Imperial Diet at Nuremberg on January 3, 1523. Nevertheless, Hadrian had no intention of compromising with Luther. Instead, he was seeking the favor of the German estates for a renewed campaign against the German heretic. On December 1, 1522, he wrote letters to both Eck and Erasmus, summoning them to battle against Lutheranism.[98]

Although Luther's case was by no means settled, seen in retrospect Luther's feeling of victory was justified. A new church, free of the papacy, was succeeding in taking root. As the separation became more entrenched, it became increasingly difficult to sympathize with Luther without taking a stand against the papacy. Some were still able to distinguish, as Ulrich Zasius did, between the "abuses of Leo and the Romanists" on the one side and the apostolic see on the other.[99] Most, however, were like Luther's former Augustinian brother, Henry of Zütphen, preacher in Bremen and soon to be martyred, or Urbanus Rhegius, the recently converted preacher in Augsburg. These early preachers who formed the nucleus of Protestantism interpreted their new allegiance as freedom from the papacy. In spite of the differences that then sprouted within the Protestant camp, this experience of liberation from the "laws of the pope" was the common denominator of these early Protestant "freedom fighters."[100] In this sense, Protestantism owed its common identity to Luther's conflict with the papacy and to his persistent struggle to free the consciences of the faithful. Perhaps because he had felt the burden of papal tyranny so heavily, he exulted all the more in his freedom and guarded it more jealously and stubbornly than many could comprehend and approve. "My conscience has been freed, and that is the most complete liberation. Therefore, I am still a monk and yet not a monk. I am a new creature, not of the pope but of Christ."[101]

7 | PERSISTENCE
1522–1546

What kind of church is the pope's church? It is an uncertain, vacillating, and tottering church. Indeed, it is a deceitful, lying church, doubting and unbelieving, without God's Word. For the pope with his false keys teaches his church to doubt and to be uncertain. . . . It is difficult enough for a wretched conscience to believe. How can one believe at all if, to begin with, doubt is cast upon the object of one's belief? Thereby doubt and despair are only strengthened and confirmed.

—Luther, 1530
(WA 30/II, 483.36—484.2; 484.12–14)

CHRONOLOGY

1522		Hadrian VI (Adrian of Utrecht) becomes pope
1523		Clement VII (Giulio de' Medici) becomes pope
1525	May 5	Elector Frederick of Saxony dies; his brother John becomes elector
	May 27	Thomas Müntzer, leader of the peasants in central Germany, is executed
	June 13	Luther marries Katharina von Bora
1525		Luther publishes his treatise *Against the Heavenly Prophets* against Karlstadt
1525		The Anabaptist movement begins in Switzerland and south Germany
1526		The organization of a Protestant church in Saxony formally begins
1529	April 19	The protest of the Protestant princes occurs at the second Diet of Speyer
	October 1–4	The Marburg Colloquy between Luther and Zwingli takes place

1529		Luther's catechisms are published
1530		The Diet of Augsburg; Luther remains at the Coburg
	June 25	The *Augsburg Confession* is read before Emperor Charles V
1530		Luther: *The Keys*
1531		Luther: *Warning to His Dear Germans*
	October 11	Zwingli is killed in Switzerland
1532	August 16	Elector John of Saxony dies; his son John Frederick becomes elector
1533		Luther: *The Private Mass and the Consecration of Priests*
1534		Paul III (Alessandro Farnese) becomes pope
1534–1535		The Kingdom of the Anabaptists at Münster
1536		Pope Paul III calls a council to meet at Mantua in 1537
1536		A commission of cardinals presents to Pope Paul III proposals for reforming the church
1536	December	Luther composes the *Smalcald Articles*
1537		The Protestants meet at Smalcald; Melanchthon composes the *Treatise on the Power and Primacy of the Pope*
1540–1541		Religious colloquys take place at Worms, Hagenau, and Regensburg
1541		Albert of Mainz has to cede Halle to the Protestants
1541		Luther writes *Against Hanswurst* against Duke Henry of Brunswick-Wolfenbüttel
1542		The Smalcald League drives Henry out of Brunswick-Wolfenbüttel
1545		Luther writes *Against the Roman Papacy, An Institution of the Devil*
1545–1547		First session of the Council of Trent is held
1546–1547		The Smalcald War is fought between the Protestants and Emperor Charles V

1546 February 18   Luther dies in Eisleben

1547 April 24   The Protestants are defeated at Mühlberg

1548   The *Augsburg Interim*

1550   Julius III (Giovanni Maria del Monte) becomes pope

1555   The Peace of Augsburg

OBSTINACY

Luther's rejection of the papacy persisted to the end of his life. The prayer he uttered on the night of his death apparently testifies to that rejection.[1] Such persistence was not inevitable. Although the upheaval of 1517 to 1522 was dramatic enough to harden any person's attitudes for a lifetime, the remaining twenty-four years of Luther's life spanned an entire generation and offered numerous reasons for softening his attitude toward the papacy.

For one thing, Luther's opponents became diversified. The 1520s were dominated by his conflict with Karlstadt, Zwingli, and the other "sacramentarians," and in the 1530s the Anabaptists challenged radically his concept of reformation. As Luther put it, these were the "sacramentarian and Anabaptist affairs," which followed the "indulgence affair" after 1522.[2] In addition, Luther had to cope with other "false brethren,"[3] former allies in the struggle against Rome who turned against him, such as the revolutionary leader, Thomas Müntzer, or John Agricola, the "antinomian." No sooner was Luther ousted from the Roman Church for his unyielding resistance to the papacy than he came under repeated attack for remaining too papal. Such pressure from the left might have nudged Luther back toward the Roman Church, but that did not happen. The emergence of diverse opponents did not diminish the threat he continued to see in the papacy.

Other matters as well could have distracted Luther from his opposition to the papacy: the task of organizing a Protestant church in place of the Roman episcopal system; the constant pressure of advising princes how to deal with the uncertain political situation after Worms; the radical reorientation of his personal life, breaking the monastic habit, taking a wife and raising six children, two of whom predeceased him. His academic responsibilities continued as well; lecturing and administrative duties, preaching, and translating the Bible still preoccupied him. Even the apathy of the papacy itself could have lulled Luther into tak-

146

ing a more conciliatory stance. Popes Clement VII and Paul III failed to push the religious question,[4] and Emperor Charles V, although loyal to the Catholic cause, refrained from attacking the Protestant estates in order to gain their help in staving off the Turkish threat to the empire.

In spite of the distractions, Luther thrice summed up his lifework as a battle against the papacy, and he bequeathed this struggle to his heirs.[5] In the epitaph which he composed prematurely for himself in 1537, Luther addressed himself to the pope as "alive, your plague, dead . . . your death."[6] Luther refused to give an inch. At critical junctures such as the Diet of Augsburg in 1530 and at Smalcald in 1537 he cautioned against concessions. And in his last sermon, preached in Wittenberg on January 17, 1546, Luther warned against the false security that failed to recognize how the "God of this world" would ambush "us" through the pope, the emperor, and even through the experts on "our" side who said it did no harm to let up a bit. Luther's response was unequivocal: we should not give in a hair's breadth.[7]

This unyielding opposition of the older Luther could be read as an attempt to display consistency with the cause of his youth. Already in the sixteenth century this unbending attitude was viewed as appropriate Protestant vigilance. In contrast, Melanchthon's willingness to negotiate and to make concessions might appear as a deviation from the norm of what a good Protestant should have done. Melanchthon's attitude appeared to some of his contemporaries to deviate from Luther, at least. If Luther's adamant opposition is taken for granted, then the coarseness of his polemic against the papacy is difficult to explain except through conjectures about the ravages of age upon his personality or reference to the vulgarity of the era. Such conjectures and references have been adopted by Luther apologists to hide their embarrassment.

It is misleading, however, to designate any one Protestant reaction to the papacy as normative. The historical picture is more complex. Protestants adopted different attitudes toward the papacy and toward possible reconciliation with the Roman Church. Melanchthon's inclination to negotiate and Luther's obstinacy illustrate the main alternatives. If anything, Melanchthon's flexibility is more understandable than Luther's rigidity, given the consequences of Luther's separation from the papacy mentioned earlier and the constant political threat which haunted Protestants until 1555. The mere persistence of Luther's opposition to the papacy, and not foremost the polemical nature of that opposition, begs for historical explanation. Historians have frequently noted that by 1522 Luther had taken the stand on the papacy which he would hold for the remainder of his life, but they have seldom explored why Luther remained so adamant.[8]

REMEMBERING

It was impossible for Luther to consider returning to the Roman Church. Luther's personal experience under the papacy saturated his life apart from the papacy, and his life apart from the papacy reinforced the feelings that hardened in him between 1518 and 1522. In the *Warning to His Dear Germans* issued in 1531 after the Diet of Augsburg, Luther deplored in impassioned detail the ignorance of the Christian life which prevailed under the papacy and praised the enlightenment the reformers had brought. To sum it up, he says, we did not know anything that a Christian ought to know. Everything was suppressed and obscured by the pope.[9] Luther himself would like to have known just one item from the catalogue of ignorance which he gives.[10] Under no condition was Luther willing to advise compliance with Emperor Charles's rejection of the *Augsburg Confession* and thereby risk destroying "all the good which has been restored and established through the gospel."[11] In a sixteenth-century version of the "forget, hell" attitude, Luther never tired of reminding his readers what an abomination the papacy was and how horrible it had been to live under it. As more years passed and a new generation grew up which was only barely acquainted with that life, Luther became more and more afraid that his followers would forget what it had been like. He frequently used this concern to justify the sharpness of his polemic against the papacy.[12] Certainly no reformer took more seriously the task of reminding the young of the cause for the Reformation; but, then, no other reformer documents so dramatically the experience of being wrenched from the papacy.

The years following 1522 confirmed what Luther's memory would not let him forget: the papacy did not wish to reform itself or the church at large. Of this Luther was already convinced before 1530, and the Diet of Augsburg did nothing to change his mind.[13] The continued practice of private masses and of indulgences hardened Luther's conviction of the irreformability of the papacy. The reason in both cases was the same. Through these practices the papacy was guilty of the murder of innocent, pious Christians and the destruction of thousands of souls. "These souls shout eternal accusation of the papacy, which is obligated to bring them back to God."[14]

This conviction prevented Luther from taking seriously the evidence for papal reform which was initiated by Pope Paul III (1534–1549). Luther favored Protestant attendance at the papal council called by Paul III to meet in 1537 at Mantua, but Luther's position paper for this eventuality, the *Smalcald Articles* of December 1536, lists the papacy, along with the mass and monastic vows, as the institutions that Protestants had to oppose without fail. Luther proclaimed these items nondiscussible because they contradicted the doctrine of justification, but they were not just doctrinally objectionable. Luther's disagreement with the papacy was never an abstract doctrinal matter. It remained grounded in his concern for the destructive effect that papal sovereignty had upon the people of the church. These three institutions of the Roman Church—the papacy, the mass, and monastic vows—were the main obstacles to achieving the practical effects of the doctrine of justification: protecting the honor of Christ as the sole mediator and providing consolation for burdened consciences. Theologians could discuss whatever theoretical topics they wished; Luther sketched some of these, including justification, in Part III of the *Smalcald Articles*.[15] When it came to the application of justification to the lives of the people, however, there could be no concessions in Luther's mind because the Christian freedom of the people was at stake. Hence, Luther continued to oppose those practices which restricted this freedom just as he had done from the beginning. Along with the mass and monasticism, the papacy remained a chief obstacle to that freedom.

Luther did not expect that to change. Even the pope's own people, charged Luther, recognized that the pope would rather see the whole of Christendom lost and all souls perish than reform himself and put limits on his tyranny.[16] Nor was Luther impressed by the *Counsel* drawn up by several eminent cardinals at the order of Paul III to be used as a guide for reform. After the *Counsel* was printed prematurely and a copy found its way to Wittenberg, Luther published a German translation with his own preface, marginal notes, and on the title page a picture of three cardinals cleaning the church with foxtails.[17] When the cardinals traced ecclesiastical abuses back to the papacy and its claim that the will of the pope was the guide for all actions, Luther jokingly called for fire to burn those cardinals as heretics.[18] By his own admission, Luther had lived too long and seen too little evidence of reform to take the memorandum seriously.

The passage of years convinced Luther that the papacy was not just irreformable, but indeed unnecessary. Luther enjoyed living apart from the papacy since the thesis which he had earlier proposed proved true for him: Christian life was only possible if one abolished the laws of the pope altogether. The pope was useless because he exercised no Christian office, said Luther in the *Smalcald Articles*. Christ himself sufficed as the head of the church, and under him all bishops should be equal.[19] Since 1519, Luther had challenged consistently the argument that the church needed a single visible head. The organization of Protestant churches did not give him any reason to change his mind, even though he was not always in agreement with the way that organization proceeded. For Luther, the danger of tyranny always outweighed the advantage of one visible symbol of unity, and he stuck by that position even after witnessing the breakup of Protestantism. Furthermore, in Luther's opinion, God provided enough guides for Christian life. Scripture and reason adequately taught what impeded the salvation of souls and what could be altered without sin.[20] The government of the pope only led the faithful astray from the three orders through which God governs his creation: civil regimes, the home, and the church.[21] Simple as it may sound, Luther continued to oppose the papacy because he discovered, as he had predicted, that the church could well survive without it.

ANTICIPATING

In the years following 1522 Luther looked ahead as well as behind. What he saw was mounting evidence for the truth of another old conviction: the pope was indeed the Antichrist, and the time was drawing near for the final confrontation between Christ and his antagonist. In the church postil of 1522, commenting on the traditional apocalyptic lesson for the second Sunday in Advent (Luke 21:15–36), Luther asserted that this conviction more than anything else forced him to believe that Christ would soon come again.[22] At the end of the 1545 preface to the first edition of his collected Latin works, Luther bade the reader pray for the increase of the word against Satan, who was now raging more than ever, since he knew that only a brief time was left and the kingdom of his pope was endangered.[23] Although Luther never speculated on the date of a second coming of Christ, he did share the apocalyptic view of history that was characteristic of his age, down to the detail of identifying the pope with the Antichrist. Luther found comfort in the fact that others had made the identification before him. In 1528, John Briessmann, Protestant preacher in Königsberg, sent Luther a late medieval commentary on the book of Revelation. Luther published it, with his own preface, so that the public would know that he and his followers were not the first to equate the papacy with the kingdom of the Antichrist.[24]

Indeed, Luther was drawing on a wide layer of popular belief in stressing this equation. Rather than giving him "courage for a revolution,"[25] however, this identification was one of the factors that lent staying power to his rejection of the papacy. The designation of the papacy as the Antichrist resulted from Luther's suspicion that the papacy had usurped the headship of Christ and was guilty of that tyranny over consciences which nullified the freedom of the Christian. That suspicion persisted, as Luther illustrated in 1531 while reiterating a favorite Protestant theme: the torturing of consciences in the confessional. Everything the papists have done and taught, said Luther, has been aimed at leading us away from Christ and back toward our own works. That matched exactly what the Antichrist was supposed to do: teach in opposition to Christ and elevate himself over Christ. All that has been fulfilled in the papacy more vividly than anyone had imagined.[26]

The designation of the papacy as the Antichrist fit neatly into Luther's theological worldview. The pope's seduction of souls was only a special case of the seduction of the world by the devil. "This life is not a life, but a den of murderers subject to the devil," wrote Luther in 1527.[27] The devil has demonstrated his mastery over the world in the prevalence of so much error, false faith, and so many sects and heresies.[28] Already in 1527 he identified the papacy as one guise of Satan, who was restless and angry at the impending end of the world.[29] By 1537 the satanic ambition of the papacy had become more pronounced in Luther's eyes. That ambition exceeded the swindle of the world's material goods through indulgences, purgatory, and adoration of the saints. The spiritual seduction of souls through the pope's lies was really the devil himself at work to lead souls to hellfire and eternal death.[30]

The origin of the papacy in the devil, depicted outrageously in a series of cartoons from 1545, is a theme that belongs to the essence of Luther's rejection of the papacy. It should not be dismissed merely on psychological or historical grounds,[31] but understood as expressing the peculiar menace of the papacy as the Antichrist. The papacy is illegitimate because it works under the aegis of the devil to seduce souls and to bring them under the devil's sway. It has infiltrated the heart of the church and attacked the kingdom of God from within. As the agent of satanic power, the papacy qualifies better than the Turk for the label of Antichrist.[32] At least the Turk, along with other wordly rulers, could claim some legitimacy as part of the order of creation through which God rules the world. However threatening or tyrannical, they could expect obedience from their subjects in civil affairs. The pope, however, springs from none of God's hierarchies of civil government, the home, or the church. His origin is the devil and, therefore, he cannot claim rights to obedience which one concedes even to worldly tyrants. In this political and theological no-man's-land, the main charge against him remains the intention of destroying souls.[33]

THE "STERN PHYSICIAN"

In his funeral oration for Luther, Melanchthon conceded that Luther was too coarse; in these last days, however, when frailty and feebleness had become so prevalent, God had sent a tough and stern physician to treat the malady. Anyone who was horrified at Luther's writings would have to take God to task and could scarcely expect to succeed.[34] Luther's provocativeness was the subject of some of the earliest reactions to him. Spalatin counseled moderation every time he expected a new blast from Luther. From Wittenberg, in February 1521, Thomas Blaurer argued that Luther's acerbity was for the good of the people. According to Blaurer, Luther had to counteract the bad example set by the prelates and to jolt the people into new patterns of conduct.[35] Luther himself provided a similar explanation early in his career. Appealing to Isa. 58:1 ("Cry aloud, spare not. . . ."), he argued that although everyone should suffer injustice, it was the special duty of the preacher not to remain silent. In the spirit of the prophetic tradition, Luther saw a big difference between having patience and remaining silent about the evil of the prelates.[36] Already by mid-1522, Luther announced that he would give up restraint and concessions (which hardly anyone had noticed) and meet the toughness of his opponents head-on. Too optimistically he announced, "Whoever would accept my teaching with the right spirit would not be offended at my scolding."[37]

Luther kept his promise and made no attempt to moderate the tone of his subsequent works. The polemic which became a mark of his later writings is vivid evidence of the relentless way in which he pursued the papacy to the end. However, he misjudged the impact of his polemic even on those who accepted his teaching; his contemporaries and modern readers have been offended by the coarseness of his metaphors. Both have accused him of being motivated by hatred, a view to which Luther himself contributed. In his brush with death at Smalcald, Luther is supposed to have bequeathed hatred of the pope to his followers. The *Table Talk* and Luther's first biographer, John Mathesius (1504–1565), use the word "hatred" in recounting this incident.[38] Some historians have modulated this odium into the higher key of "abysmal hatred"[39] and parlayed Luther's remark into evidence for discrediting his whole battle against the papacy. Remigius Bäumer has argued that Luther cut his ties with the Roman Church because of this hatred.[40] Although one can separate the nonpolemical arguments against the papacy from their polemical wrappings,[41] that separation distorts the historical picture. As Karl Holl observed, to remove the passion from Luther is to cut the nerve of his piety.[42]

Luther considered his polemic to be an appropriate vehicle of his indictment of the papacy. That appropriateness was grounded not so much in Luther's passion as in his purpose. This purpose was to make as vivid as possible the sabotage of the church by papal tyranny. Protesting against the compulsory laws and practices introduced under the papacy, Luther was reminded of a picture of the Last Judgment in which hell was portrayed as the gaping jaws of a dragon devouring both secular and ecclesiastical magnates, among them the pope. Certainly, interpreted Luther, hell was where the pope and all the world were devoured by the devil's jaws, that is, by devil-like preaching and teaching. Luther speculated on Isa. 5:14 as the basis for the picture; but even if it originated as a joke or without a particular text in mind, Luther regarded it as a useful way of introducing the unlearned to the threat posed by the papal church. Right away they could arm themselves against it.[43]

In the same vein, Luther described the Roman Church as every kind of whore which he could name (and the list is impressive). That church was originally the bride of Christ; but when she introduced her new regulations, she became the devil's whore and corrupted the young people who had once received the purifying waters of baptism in her. She made virgins of Christ into arch-whores! The course and consequences of this infidelity, said Luther, were described sufficiently in Hosea and more coarsely in the twenty-third chapter of Ezekiel. The Bible spared no feelings on the matter of unfaithfulness; and, added Luther, he had spoken German so that everyone would understand the import of his remarks.[44] Luther believed that he saw biblical precedent for his blunt portrayals of the papacy and that the situation warranted such metaphors. The danger had to be dramatized so that no one would underestimate the deception fostered by the papacy or accept its claim to be the true church.

This claim illustrates how much was at stake in the historical situation that led both sides to make use of hefty polemic. In Germany, the monopoly of the Roman Church was not replaced by confessional plurality until 1555. The so-called "later Luther" was still standing in the midst of a political and ecclesiastical situation which, despite its ambiguity, allowed only one "true" church and forced each side into denunciations.[45] Attempts to discredit the Lutherans as "church" were answered by Luther with the argument that the papal church had forfeited its claim to this distinction through the betrayal of the souls given into its charge. The subject of the debate was not an irrelevant ecclesiological issue. The salvation of the people depended, in Luther's mind, on the correct location of the true church. He was solidifying, as it were, his Protestant constituency by stating the alternatives as sharply as possible, and in the sixteenth century the two churches were still alternatives, not options. In this respect, Luther's polemic and satire had an objectifying effect on the social and ecclesiastical process, even though it was not objective by nature.[46]

Luther did not lose sight of this purpose even in the most vehement of his antipapal works: *Against the Roman Papacy, An Institution of the Devil (1545)*. A specific occasion prompted this last broadside against the papacy. Emperor Charles V had conceded that the religious question might be handled at the next diet of the empire in a format similar to that of a free German council which Luther had always endorsed. Pope Paul III, still planning to convene his own assembly, protested in a letter to Emperor Charles that the religious controversy could only be settled in a general council under the pope. Luther's denunciation was written in reply to this brief and was published on March 25, 1545, the day on which the Council of Trent was supposed to open.[47] It was praised by Protestant leaders and denounced by papal legates. Some of the outrage, and the praise as well, was aroused by a series of cartoons created by Lucas Cranach, which probably were intended to serve as illustrations for the treatise.[48]

Luther acknowledged both the treatise and the cartoons as his own and was aware of their offensive nature. As for the cartoons, though he approved them, Luther agreed to a request made by Nikolaus von Amsdorf that another cartoon be modified to spare the feelings of female viewers.[49] Despite their earthiness, the cartoons were not lewd; they vividly ridiculed papal bulls and mocked the pope's claim to be the sole interpreter of Scripture. In keeping with the occasion, a prominent theme was the duping of Germany by the popes. The birth of the papacy from the devil, an illustration of the title, strikes one as more ludicrous than vulgar. According to Mathesius, the "sharp pictures" were to illustrate Luther's rejection of the papacy for persons who could not read his treatises.[50] Such illustrations certainly gave his views wider exposure, and many literate persons may have enjoyed looking at the pictures more than reading the book.

In the treatise itself, Luther acknowledged that he was using "scornful, wounding, stinging" words to the pope. He felt, however, that such words were necessary because "no one can believe what an abomination the papacy is." Therefore, "those who now live and those who will come after us should know what I have thought of the pope, the damned Antichrist, so that whoever wishes to be Christian may be warned against such an abomination."[51] As he did four years earlier in *Against Hanswurst*, Luther repeatedly voiced his commitment to the freedom of all Christian consciences that were being held bound by the laws of the papacy.[52] People were still being made uncertain, although the "pope should show himself a willing servant for the consolation and benefit of the unfortunate people."[53] Whereas Luther had earlier expressed his concern for the survival of the faithful politely and with caution, he was now conveying his great anguish with clumsy words in the confidence that Christ would pardon it.[54] "Do not I as a Christian," wrote Luther, "and as a lover of our Lord Christ, have a right to be impatient, angry and intolerant, to curse the accursed papacy and to call it the most shameful names, when it is not ashamed to blaspheme our Lord in the most shameful fashion and to turn his promise into a lie?"[55]

Luther took great pains to demonstrate that anger at specific persons was not the motive behind his attacks.[56] His emotions were strong, but they never obliterated his arguments even if his language may have offended sensibilities. The anger which his language conveyed was an anger that grew out of his abhorrence of the papal institution. That institution was still threatening to destroy the church, to betray its head, and to seduce its people. To describe the motive behind Luther's polemic as "abysmal hatred" is therefore both insufficient and misleading. Underneath Luther's abhorrence and angry words lay not the bottomless pit of irrational hatred but the core of conviction. Luther's polemic was radical evidence of the persistence of that conviction which preoccupation with his polemic has all too often obscured.

THE "DUTY OF A GOOD PASTOR"

The motivation which inspired Luther's rejection of the papacy from beginning to end was summed up by Philipp Melanchthon in 1521, when he attributed the *Ninety-five Theses* to Luther's intention to "exercise the duty of a good pastor."[57] That duty was to protect the people from the deception fostered by the indulgence practice and, later, by the accumulated traditions of the papacy. The devotion to that duty caused Luther to persist in his rejection of the papacy to the end of his life and accounted for his amazing single-mindedness in other matters as well. What appears as inconsistency or stubbornness often falls into a sensible pattern if one views it from the angle of what Luther regarded as necessary for the people's instruction. Even Luther's political advice to Protestant leaders seems to have been guided by his intention to provide a firm foundation for Christian consciences rather than by abstract theories of justice.[58]

Recognition of this motivation lends a unity to Luther's work which is not otherwise always apparent. For example, in his later works against the papacy, Luther does not replace theological arguments with irresponsible polemic. Instead, he combines theological argumentation and polemical expression in order to fulfill the duty of a pastor who believes he must warn his people against an insidious enemy. That combination is evident in some of Luther's most serious charges against the papacy, such as the accusation of lying and inconstancy. The papacy is built on lies, says Luther, clothed in lies and teaches lies.[59] Its satanic character derives from the satanic lies with which it deceives souls and draws them away from Christ.[60] In contrast, the true church cannot lie; it must serve as the pillar of truth (1 Tim. 3:15), so that the people have a reliable basis for their faith. In this matter the papacy has utterly failed. It teaches people to doubt God's grace, and even if they had won in everything else this fault alone would have toppled the papists.[61] Luther makes clear why deceit is such a serious charge against a church. It undercuts the very reason for the church's existence, the exercise of the pastoral office:

> What kind of a church is the pope's church? It is an uncertain, vacillating and tottering church. Indeed, it is a deceitful, lying church, doubting and unbelieving, without God's word. For the pope with his wrong keys teaches his church to doubt and to be uncertain. . . . It is difficult enough for a wretched conscience to believe. How can one believe at all if, to begin with, doubt is cast upon the object of one's belief? Thereby doubt and despair are only strengthened and confirmed.[62]

Did Luther fulfill his duty too well? Did his devotion to the duty of freeing Christian consciences cause him to persist in his rejection of the papacy beyond the point where it was necessary? Was he too zealous for the house of the Lord as he conceived it?

These are fair questions, but more susceptible to theological judgments than to historical ones. Historical judgments have to take into account the fact that, soon after Luther's death, Protestantism as he knew it in Germany was threatened with extinction. Protestant forces were defeated in the Smalcald War; Wittenberg was taken by Emperor Charles; the Protestant leaders, Elector John Frederick and Landgrave Philipp of Hesse, were taken captive. The *Augsburg Interim* (1548), a religious compromise abhorrent to many Protestants, threatened to undermine Protestant identity, and only a fortunate turn of events secured the survival of Protestant territories after 1555. In all probability, Luther would have been most unhappy with the compromises of 1548, and that realization led to the open break in Lutheran ranks. In one sense, therefore, Luther's persistence was justified by the events which followed his death insofar as he regarded salvation as dependent on the ability of Protestant structures to protect the people from papal tyranny.

In Luther's own eyes, the events that preceded his death also justified his persistence. The continuation of papal practices aggravated him. In 1537, he claimed no one took the coercion of the papacy seriously any longer, especially in contrast to 1517 when everyone was compelled to believe in indulgences, purgatory, and the adoration of saints. Be thankful to the grace of God, he admonished, and pray that you do not again fall into temptation and be deceived.[63] Luther never stopped warning the people against these practices. In 1531 he inveighed against the deception of indulgences and purgatory. Indulgences alone were enough to draw all souls down to hell,[64] and the invocation of saints was nothing but tyranny for miserable consciences. Confession, the ban, and the mass completed the catalogue of papal practices that still needed to be exposed.

Indulgences remained a serious issue to the end. One incident involving them must have been an uncanny reminder of the beginnings of the Reformation. In 1541, Cardinal Albert of Mainz had to give up his residence in Halle to the Protestants. Albert arranged for the relics that had been in Halle to be displayed once a year in St. Martin's Church in Mainz. Indulgences were promised to those who visited the relics and contributed toward their upkeep. When he heard about this, Luther published a short, satirical piece in which he exposed not just the deception involved in indulgences, but also the fraud of relics themselves. According to Luther, Albert had added some remarkable new items to his relic collection, such as three flames from the burning bush on Mt. Sinai and half a wing from the archangel Gabriel. Luther also made fun of the indulgence through which Pope Paul was supposed to grant forgiveness of all sin in exchange for an offering.[65]

Such chicanery must have made Luther feel vindicated for continuing his struggle against the papacy for so long. His lifelong protest against the deception of the people by indulgences demonstrates how the same concern for the freedom of the faithful could brace his lifelong opposition to the institution of the papacy and its "human traditions." That persistent protest also indicates that the *Ninety-five Theses* were more than merely a catalyst in the beginning of the Reformation. Luther's criticism of the indulgence practice in the *Smalcald Articles* of 1537 is the same as in the *Ninety-five Theses* of 1517. The merits of Christ are not applied to the faithful by money and papal power but by faith and the preaching of God's word.[66]

As he looked back from 1541 on the beginning of the "Lutheran ruckus," the figure whom Luther deemed most responsible, besides Tetzel, was the most holy father, Pope Leo X, with his ill-timed ban.[67] In other accounts of the past Luther saw Cajetan and Albert of Mainz as responsible for the outbreak of the Reformation. As the years passed, however, responsibility for the enduring rupture shifted in Luther's eyes to the papacy. Regardless of how Luther assigned the responsibility, the

Reformation was not consummated in the *Ninety-five Theses* or, for that matter, at the Diet of Worms in 1521. The formation and establishment of Protestantism was a long process, and a driving force behind that establishment was Luther's unyielding resistance to the papacy. That resistance gave continuity and unity both to the Protestant cause and to Luther's own reforming career. It found expression in the irony of the *Ninety-five Theses* as well as in the blatant satire of *Against the Roman Papacy*.

Despite the marked differences in tone, the motivation behind that resistance was to protect the people from coercion and from the undermining of their faith. As long as the papacy persisted in that deception, Luther persisted in opposing the papacy. As long as the pope did not allow the faithful to believe,[68] Luther would not allow the people to believe the pope. As long as the Antichrist under the guise of the papacy was still seducing the people, he would continue to expose that abomination and to denounce the popes as archliars.[69] Because the responsibility lay so heavily with the papacy in Luther's eyes, his reform was much more distinctively antipapal than that of urban reformers such as Zwingli, Bucer, and Calvin.[70] At the same time, the criterion that Luther urged every true Christian to apply to the pope could be applied to the bishops as well. That criterion was their faithfulness to the commission of Christ to feed the people with the word of God, without which the church could not survive.[71] Luther himself applied this criterion with provocative zeal. If he became convinced of anything new during his last years, it was that the starvation of the flock of Christ was owing not merely to the negligence of the papacy but also to its malicious intention to suffocate the people of God. Disappointment and anger at that perversion of the pastoral office spurred Luther to exercise "the duty of a good pastor" to the end of his life.

NOTES

INTRODUCTION

1. *Papal Primacy and the Universal Church*, ed. P. C. Empie and T. A. Murphy. Lutherans and Catholics in Dialogue V (Minneapolis, 1974), pp. 21, 25–27.

2. G. R. Elton, "Thomas Cromwell Redivivus," ARG 68 (1977): 206.

3. E. Bizer, *Luther und der Papst* (Munich, 1958).

4. R. Bäumer, *Martin Luther und der Papst*, 2d ed. (Münster, 1971).

CHAPTER 1—AMBIVALENCE, 1505–1517

1. WABr 2, 332.10—333.17 (May 12, 1521). LW 48, 215.

2. WA 8, 45.17–25. LW 32, 140–141.

3. WA 54, 179.22–33. LW 34, 328.

4. WA 38, 267.23–27 (1534). *Dokumente zu Luthers Entwicklung*, 2d ed., ed. O. Scheel (Tübingen, 1929), no. 299.

5. WA 40/I, 134.2–4 (1531 [1535]). Scheel, *Dokumente*, no. 162.

6. WA 41, 713.34–37 (1536). Scheel, *Dokumente*, no. 340.

7. WATR 4, 25.13–15, no. 3944 (1538). Scheel, *Dokumente*, no. 402. Just prior to this remark, Luther said he was such a papist that he even wrote against Erasmus, who was criticizing the papacy.

8. WA 54, 179.34—180.4.

9. Scheel, *Dokumente*, no. 535.

10. WA 39/I, 7.36–40.

11. Ibid., 7.6–8.

12. WATR 3, 438.21—439.2, no. 3593. The text reads: "After the pope, with force and cunning, usurped all power and authority, so that he could not be humiliated by either emperor or king, then it was fitting that by the power of the word the son of perdition should be revealed [2 Thess. 2:3]. However, I came upon it quite innocently; for I never would have dreamed this twenty years prior to that day. Rather, if someone else had taught such a thing, I would have damned and burned him. But God is the cause, because he did such things miraculously." The meaning of the key phrase *"nam hoc ante viginti annos ab illo die nunquam cogitassem"* is ambiguous. "Twenty years prior to that day" might mean simply "twenty years ago" (from 1537) and refer to the beginning of the indulgence controversy in 1517. K. Aland has deciphered the phrase in that way: *Der Weg zur Reformation* (Munich, 1965), p. 71. However, "that day" seems to have a more specific referent, since it is part of the verse in 2 Thessalonians 2.

This would be the "day" on which the pope was revealed to be the son of perdition, i.e., the time when Luther came to believe he might be the Anti-christ and opposed him as such (1519–1520). Twenty years prior to this would take Luther back to the beginning of his university studies. Although this predates his theological study proper and his entry into the monastery (1505), it does embrace in round figures Luther's early days of involvement with the life and teaching of the church. That is apparently what Luther intended. Better justice to the context is done with this interpretation, since Luther subsequently refers to his time as a master in Erfurt and the development of his attitude toward the pope. The major theme of the excerpt is the way in which God miraculously revealed to Luther the true nature of the papacy and drew him gradually into opposition to it before 1520. "Twenty years prior to that day" best fits the early period and not the twenty-year span from 1517 to 1537.

13. WATR 3, 439.2–12.

14. WATR 2, 164.32—165.2, no. 1653. Cf. WATR 3, 211.5–8, no. 3176.

15. WA 38, 143.25–29 (1533). Luther is defending himself against a charge by Cochlaeus that he had violated his monastic vows. See J. Köstlin and G. Kawerau, *Martin Luther: Sein Leben und seine Schriften*, 5th ed. (Berlin, 1903), I, 55.

16. *Constitutiones Fratrum Heremitarum sancti Augustini ad apostolicorum privilegiorum formam pro Reformatione Alemanie* (n.d., n.p.), chs. 4, 8, 17.

17. Ibid., chs. 47–50.

18. WA 40/II, 15.15–20. Cf. WATR 1, 200.26—201.1, no. 461 (1533).

19. J. Köstlin, *Martin Luther: Sein Leben und seine Schriften* (Elberfeld, 1875), I, 68.

20. Köstlin and Kawerau, *Martin Luther*, I, 58.

21. WATR 5, 654.1–12, no. 6420.

22. G. Biel, *Canonis misse expositio*, ed. H. A. Oberman and W. J. Courtenay (Wiesbaden, 1963), I, Lectio 23 I–K, pp. 215–217.

23. Ibid., Lectio 22 D, p. 199; 23 L, pp. 217–218.

24. Ibid., Lectio 23 M–O, pp. 218–221.

25. O. Scheel, *Martin Luther: Vom Katholizismus zur Reformation* (Tübingen, 1917), II, 44.

26. WATR 5, 213.15–29, no. 5523 (1542–1543). Cf. WATR 5, 327.13–17, no. 5711. Deliberate consent to a sinful act was the most widely applied criterion in determining if the guilt incurred made the sin mortal. Gerson was no exception here. See T. Tentler, *Sin and Confession on the Eve of the Reformation* (Princeton, 1977), pp. 148–153.

27. WATR 5, 440.8–14, no. 6017. Cf. WATR 1, 496.7–9, no. 979. The description of Gerson as *doctor consolatorius* (WATR 5, 213.22–23) was not original with Luther, but had been applied to Gerson as early as 1520 by Jacob Wimpfeling. See E. Wolf, *Staupitz und Luther* (1927; reprinted in New York and London, 1971), p. 148, n. 1. Among the medieval

writers on the practice of penance and confession, Gerson was especially sensitive to the danger of scrupulosity, quoting the common saying: "God does not want to demand anything beyond man's power" (cf. 1 Cor. 10:13). Gerson's works were among the most popular and widely used resources for confessors, and it is not surprising that his works would have a great impact on Luther. See Tentler, *Sin and Confession*, pp. 76–78, 45–46. In his 1520 treatise, *How Confession Should Be Made*, Luther refers to Gerson's advice that one should at times go to the altar or to the sacrament of penance *with a scruple of conscience* so that one learns to trust more in God's mercy than in one's own confession: WA 6, 166.2–7.

28. WATR 5, 213.27–29, no. 5523.

29. *Canonis misse expositio*, I, Lectio 7, pp. 51–57.

30. Ibid., I, Lectio 8 A, p. 58.

31. J. Altenstaig, *Vocabularius theologiae* (Hagenau, 1517), fol. XLVI^v.

32. WA 31/I, 226.9–17 (1530).

33. WATR 3, 345.9–11, no. 3478 (1536).

34. Ibid., 348.18–27, no. 3479 (1536).

35. Scheel, *Martin Luther*, II, 309–318.

36. WA 30/III, 386.30—387.15 (1531): "However, I, Dr. Martin, have been called to this work and was compelled to become a doctor, without any initiative of my own, but out of pure obedience. Then I had to accept the office of doctor and swear a vow to my most beloved Holy Scriptures that I would preach and teach them faithfully and purely. While engaged in this kind of teaching, the papacy crossed my path and wanted to hinder me in it. How it has fared is obvious to all, and it will fare still worse." LW 34, 103. See Siegfried Freiherr von Scheurl, "Martin Luthers Doktoreid," *Zeitschrift für bayerische Kirchengeschichte* 32 (1963): 46–52; W. Borth, *Die Luthersache (Causa Lutheri) 1517–1524* (Lübeck and Hamburg, 1970), pp. 23–25, 94–97.

37. WA 30/III, 522.2–8 (1532). LW 40, 387–388.

38. WABr 1, 72.6–13 (October 26, 1516). LW 48, 27–28.

39. WA 4, 26.4–6.

40. Ibid., 26.14–15.

41. WA 1, 69.11–13.

42. See J. Vercruysse, *Fidelis populus* (Mainz, 1969), pp. 153, 164; R. Bäumer, *Martin Luther und der Papst*, 2d ed. (Münster, 1971), pp. 11–13.

43. H. Preuss, *Die Vorstellungen vom Antichrist im späteren Mittelalter, bei Luther und in der konfessionellen Polemik* (Leipzig, 1906), pp. 101–102. F. Rickers takes a stronger position. He believes that Luther's handling of passages such as Matt. 16:18–19 and his treatment of Peter prior to 1517 give good reason for doubting that Luther would have agreed with the official interpretation of papal primacy and authority if he had been confronted with that interpretation: *Das Petrusbild Luthers*, Diss. (Heidelberg, 1967), pp. 44–47, 264–265, n. 32. In the fifteenth century, the exegesis of the rock as Christ could appear in works by authors with monarchical views of church authority (such as Antonio Roselli, *d.* 1466) as well as in the

works of conciliarists such as Pierre d'Ailly. See K. Eckermann, *Studien zur Geschichte des monarchischen Gedankens im 15. Jahrhundert* (Berlin-Grunewald, 1933), pp. 115–117.

44. WA 4, 657.13–19; 657.31—658.1.

45. Ibid., 658.2–18. In his *Explanations of the Ninety-five Theses* (1518) Luther writes: "Why therefore do we magnify the pope on account of them [the keys] and make him out to be a terrible man? The keys are not his, but mine, given to me and granted for my salvation, my consolation, peace and rest." WA 1, 596.29–33. He accuses flatterers of the pope and not the pope himself of this abuse of the keys.

46. WA 56, 252.7–8; 8.17–18.

47. WA 4, 403.31–35; 404.33–40; 407.5–8. For the importance and authority of the pastoral office, especially of the office of preaching, in Luther's early lectures, see J. Aarts, *Die Lehre Martin Luthers über das Amt in der Kirche* (Helsinki, 1972), pp. 57–76; D. Hinrichs, *Die Kirche in Luthers Vorlesung über den Römerbrief,* Mag. diss. (Hamburg, 1967), pp. 32–42.

48. WA 3, 424.17–20.

49. WA 56, 417.20–32.

50. WA 56, 454.18–23.

51. E.g., WA 3, 417.1–9; 433.14–18. See Vercruysse, *Fidelis populus,* pp. 121–124, 129–133. Luther's view of the bishops of his day, compared with the bishops of the early church, was so negative that he strongly opposed the Elector Frederick's wish to see Staupitz made Bishop of Chiemsee: WABr 1, 45.34–43 (June 8, 1516).

52. WA 1, 10–17. A German translation has been made by J. Haar, "Das Wort der Wahrheit," *Luther* 47 (1976): 5–22. Haar, following Knaake (WA 1, 9), dates the sermon at 1512, while Köstlin and Kawerau (I, 124–125) and Clemen (WABr 1, 59) set the date at 1515 or later. R. Fife, *The Revolt of Martin Luther* (New York, 1957), p. 189, n. 44, follows Clemen. H. A. Oberman and L. Grane disagree on the significance of this sermon in ARG 68 (1977): 107–109 and 312. See below, n. 64.

53. WA 1, 12.11–20.

54. Ibid., 12.29—13.13. The failure of the clergy to preach the word is the main theme of Luther's criticism in his *Lectures on Romans.* See Hinrichs, *Die Kirche,* p. 52.

55. WA 1, 13.15—14.3.

56. Ibid., 17.2–6.

57. WA 4, 353.5–29.

58. Luther expresses this discovery most forcefully in the famous account in his preface to the Latin edition of his works: WA 54, 185.21—186.20.

59. See the collection of essays: *Der Durchbruch der reformatorischen Erkenntnis bei Luther,* ed. B. Lohse (Darmstadt, 1968). See also L. Grane, *Modus loquendi theologicus* (Copenhagen, 1975), pp. 147–151, 197–198.

60. WA 57/III, 108.17 ff.

61. See S. H. Hendrix, *Ecclesia in via* (Leiden, 1974), pp. 160–169.

62. WA 4, 376.10–20.

63. WA 1, 100.30–33.

64. This is the crucial point on which Oberman and Grane disagree in their assessment of the sermon written for the prior at Leitzkau. Oberman believes that the sermon reveals the *modus praedicandi* as the hinge (*Angelpunkt*) of the reformation of the church. No gap exists, therefore, between Luther the reformer of theology before 1518 and Luther the reformer of the church afterwards. (H. A. Oberman, "Reformation: Epoche oder Episode," ARG 68 (1977): 107–109.) Although Grane acknowledges the innovations in Luther's theology, especially in the Romans lectures (see his *Modus loquendi theologicus*), he regards the sermon as a typical late-medieval call for reform and says Luther first became a reformer of the church after the open controversy with Rome erupted. (L. Grane, "Lutherforschung und Geistesgeschichte: Auseinandersetzung mit Heiko A. Oberman," ARG 68 (1977): 312.) The disagreement hinges on the definition of "reformer." Prior to 1517 Luther was not a reformer in the sense of one who leads intentional, public opposition to the church hierarchy. Textual evidence demonstrates, however, that Luther's new theology of word and faith and his practical concern that the word be preached to the people remained the same both before and after 1517. Furthermore, before 1517 Luther publicly voiced this new theology and specific criticism of church practices in sermons and lectures. The official controversy which began in 1518 did not make Luther a reformer, but it did change his public protest into intentional opposition to the church hierarchy and the papacy. Grane's assertion that Luther did not intend to become a reformer of the church by willfully opposing the papacy is supported both by Luther's many testimonies and by the assessments of his reforming self-consciousness by modern scholars. See H. von Campenhausen, "Reformatorisches Selbstbewusstsein und reformatorisches Geschichtsbewusstsein bei Luther 1517–1522," *Tradition und Leben* (Tübingen, 1960), p. 322. The awareness of not having sought the conflict with Rome is the key element in Luther's later assessment of his role as an instrument of God in the preservation of his church. See W. Günter, "Die geschichtstheologischen Voraussetzungen von Luthers Selbstverständnis," *Von Konstanz nach Trient*, ed. R. Bäumer (Munich, Paderborn, Vienna, 1972), pp. 379–394.

65. For a helpful definition of terms, see U. Bubenheimer's review of *Nachwirkungen des konziliaren Gedankens in der Theologie und Kanonistik des frühen 16. Jahrhunderts* by R. Bäumer, in ZSSR 90 [kan. Abt. 59] (1973): 455–465.

66. Bäumer, *Martin Luther und der Papst*, p. 7.

67. Ibid., p. 14. Bäumer supports his view primarily with the work of Vercruysse, *Fidelis populus*, p. 149, who, like Preuss (above, n. 43), says only that Luther's silence concerning the papacy shows where his interest did not lie. Bäumer does not consider the conclusion reached by G. Müller in his detailed treatment: "Ekklesiologie und Kirchenkritik beim jungen Luther," *NZSTh* 7 (1965): 128 and 112, n. 76. Müller notes that the sub-

jection of the church to the word is parallel to Luther's later criticism of the papacy. In his article, "Der junge Luther und der Papst," *Catholica* 23 (1969): 402, Bäumer cites only Müller's remark that Luther's specific criticism of the papacy began in late 1518.

68. WA 4, 403.29—404.10. Long ago A. W. Dieckhoff called attention to the surprising absence of any mention of the pope in this text: *Die Stellung Luthers zur Kirche und ihrer Reformation in der Zeit vor dem Ablassstreit* (Rostock, 1883), p. 24. In reference to the *Dictata*, David Steinmetz stresses Luther's regard for obedience to the ecclesiastical magisterium: "Hermeneutic and Old Testament Interpretation in Staupitz and the Young Martin Luther," *ARG* 70 (1979): 42–43 and 42, n. 86. Although it supports the hierarchical structure of the church in the *Dictata*, the hidden presence of Christ in his vicars can upset that structure as well, as Luther later shows. See Hendrix, *Ecclesia in via*, pp. 228–232.

69. *Der authentische Text der Leipziger Disputation 1519*, ed. O. Seitz (Berlin, 1903), pp. 58–59.

70. WA 7, 48.11–18. LW 48, 342.

71. See above, n. 36.

CHAPTER 2—PROTEST, OCTOBER 1517 TO JUNE 1518

1. The summary of the indulgence practice presented here is based on the article "Ablass" by G. A. Benrath in *TRE* I, 347–364, esp. 347–355. For a thorough description of the penitential practice of the late medieval church, see T. Tentler, *Sin and Confession on the Eve of the Reformation* (Princeton, 1977).

2. *ST* III, suppl. q. 26 a. 3. See *TRE* I, 349.

3. See Luther's comments in his 1545 *Preface*: WA 54, 180.12–20; and in *Against Hanswurst*: WA 51, 539.32—540.14.

4. Printed in *Dokumente zum Ablassstreit von 1517*, 2d. ed., ed. W. Köhler (Tübingen, 1934), pp. 104–124.

5. Ibid., 110.24–30.

6. Ibid., 113.21—114.18.

7. Ibid., 115.20–32.

8. Ibid., 116.16–32.

9. See N. Paulus, *Johann Tetzel der Ablassprediger* (Mainz, 1899), pp. 32–34. On the basis of Tetzel's oath, which he discovered in the Würzburg archives, F. Herrmann suggested January 22, 1517, as the date on which Tetzel entered the service of Albert. See "Miscellen zur Reformationsgeschichte. Aus Mainzer Akten," *ZKG* 23 (1902): 263–265.

10. WA 51, 539.4–8. Cf. WA 54, 180.5–11.

11. WA 51, 539.8–10.

12. WA 1, 98. 14–22; WA 1, 141. 22–38.

13. WABr 1, 111.15–24 (October 31, 1517).

14. Ibid., 111.24–25.

15. Ibid., 111.10–12; 111.25–27.

16. As Luther himself recognized: ibid., 110.6—111.9.

17. WA 39/I, 6.16–17.

18. WABr 1, 111.27–36.

19. Ibid., 111.37–45.

20. Ibid., 112.53–60.

21. Ibid., 112.66–68. W. Köhler has shown how the *Theses* were directed in part against Albert's *Instruction* and that some theses cannot be understood without reference to the *Instruction: Luther und die Kirchengeschichte* (Erlangen, 1900), pp. 7–21.

22. For a summary of the debate and a commentary on the most significant publications, see H. Bornkamm, *Thesen und Thesenanschlag Luthers: Geschehen und Bedeutung* (Berlin, 1967); H. Volz, "Um Martin Luthers Thesenanschlag," *Luther* 38 (1967): 125–138.

23. In his letter to Leo accompanying the *Explanations of the Ninety-five Theses*, 1518: WA 1, 528.39—529.2. This was the main point of the letter to his bishop, Jerome Scultetus, in February 1518. Luther deplores the way in which his *Theses* were interpreted as assertions whereas in reality, he says, "some are dubious to me, some I do not know about at all, some I even deny, and I assert none of them with pertinacity." WABr 1, 135–141, esp. 139.46–54.

24. Thesis 38: WA 1, 596.38–39.

25. E. Kähler, "Die 95 Thesen: Inhalt und Bedeutung," *Luther* 38 (1967): 114–124.

26. Tetzel did preach this, but he interpreted "fly out" to mean that the soul was capable of seeing God immediately without any spatial interruption, thus emphasizing the velocity with which the freed soul flies into God's presence. See Köhler, *Dokumente*, 132.25–28; see also Paulus, *Johann Tetzel*, pp. 138–149.

27. Köhler, *Dokumente*, 107.25–27.

28. WA 6, 593.7–10 (*Von den neuen Eckischen Bullen und Lügen,* 1520). Köhler believed it likely that Luther had a copy of the bull before him when he wrote the *Theses* and the letter to Albert: *Luther und die Kirchengeschichte*, pp. 26–27.

29. Kähler, "Die 95 Thesen," 121.

30. Luther could know this either from Leo's bull itself (1515) or, more likely, from the *Instruction* where reference is made to the censures "thundered forth" (*fulminatis:* literally "lightened"—the same word which Luther uses) in the papal bull. Köhler, *Dokumente*, 105.5–6, 19–20; 106.7–8.

31. In a letter sent with the *Explanations* to Staupitz (May 30, 1518): WA 1, 526.30–32.

32. See above, n. 12.

33. Köhler, *Dokumente*, 110.18–19.

34. WA 6, 593.7–13.

35. Kähler, "Die 95 Thesen," 123.

36. Reproduced in E. G. Schwiebert, *Luther and His Times* (St. Louis, 1950), p. 319.

37. See Adolf Hauffen, "Husz eine Gans—Luther ein Schwan," in *Untersuchungen und Quellen zur Germanistischen und Romanischen Philologie. Johann von Keller dargebracht von seinen Kollegen und Schülern*, Zweiter Teil (Prag, 1908), pp. 21–22. Luther's application of the saying to himself is found in WA 30/III, 387.18–22 (*Glosse auf das vermeinte kaiserliche Edikt*, 1531).

38. WA 1, 302.16 (*Asterisci Lutheri adversus obeliscos Eckii*, 1518).

39. See above, n. 30.

40. See Herrmann, "Miscellen," 267. See also I. Lange, "Die kurfürstliche Universität Mainz und der Beginn der Reformation," *Blätter für pfälzische Kirchengeschichte und religiöse Volkskunde* 44 (1977): 149.

41. P. Kalkoff, *Zu Luthers römischem Prozess: Der Prozess des Jahres 1518* (Gotha, 1912), pp. 1–2. See R. Bäumer, "Der Lutherprozess," in *Lutherprozess und Lutherbann: Vorgeschichte, Ergebnis, Nachwirkung*, ed. R. Bäumer (Münster, 1972), pp. 18–48. Bäumer questions some assumptions about Luther's case made by Kalkoff and by W. Borth, in *Die Luthersache*, who depends to a large extent on Kalkoff. According to Bäumer, there is no solid evidence to support: (1) Kalkoff's view that the pope had already received Albert's denunciation of Luther by early December 1517, or (2) the widespread view that the Dominicans at their gathering at Frankfurt on the Oder in January 1518 forwarded a denunciation of Luther to Rome. Bäumer, "Der Lutherprozess," 22–24.

42. Bornkamm, *Thesen und Thesenanschlag Luthers*, p. 17, n. 49.

43. See Paulus, *Johann Tetzel*, pp. 48–52.

44. The Tetzel-Wimpina theses are printed in Paulus, *Johann Tetzel*, pp. 170–180, and in *Luthers 95 Thesen samt seinen Resolutionen sowie den Gegenschriften von Wimpina-Tetzel, Eck und Prierias und den Antworten Luthers darauf*, ed. W. Köhler (Leipzig, 1903). The theses referred to here are nos. 26–28 and 33 (Paulus, *Johann Tetzel*, p. 174).

45. Tetzel-Wimpina, no. 62 (Paulus, *Johann Tetzel*, p. 176).

46. Ibid., no. 76 (Paulus, *Johann Tetzel*, p. 177).

47. WA 1, 246.27–30.

48. Ibid., 246.21–26.

49. Köhler, *Dokumente*, 156.36—157.13.

50. Paulus, *Johann Tetzel*, p. 53.

51. Printed in E *var* 1, 306–312.

52. WA 1, 246.31–37.

53. Ibid., 390.1–2 and 390.12–15.

54. Ibid., 390.15–17.

55. See above, n. 50.

56. WA 1, 392.21–24 and 392.32–37.

57. Ibid., 393.8–15.

58. Ibid., 393.16–20.

59. See Luther's letter to John Lang (May 18, 1517): WABr 1, 99.8–13. The development of the Wittenberg theology was Luther's primary academic concern in 1517 and 1518. Leif Grane emphasizes that Luther's

opponent during this period was scholastic theology and not the pope: *Modus loquendi theologicus*, pp. 178–179. Grane views the indulgence controversy as the point where Luther recognized the fatal consequences of the scholastic theology he had opposed (ibid., p. 190). With revisions, Grane adopts the approach to Luther's reforming activity that Karl Bauer followed in his important work, *Die Wittenberger Universitätstheologie und die Anfänge der deutschen Reformation* (Tübingen, 1928). Bauer likewise viewed the indulgence controversy as a case of "applied theology" (ibid., pp. 63–80). A key text for both Bauer and Grane is Luther's letter to his old Erfurt teacher, Trutvetter, in which Luther asserts that it is impossible to reform the church unless canon law, scholastic theology, philosophy, and logic are displaced in the curriculum by the Bible and the church fathers: WABr 1, 170.33–38 (May 9, 1518). In the same letter, Luther reveals the motivation behind the *Theses* when he asks Trutvetter whether he is not also displeased that the poor people of Christ have been vexed and deceived by indulgences for so long. (Luther had referred to Trutvetter's displeasure with his own *Sermon on Indulgence and Grace*.) WABr 1, 170.44–47.

60. See above, n. 31, and WA 1, 527.19–27 (the dedicatory letter Luther sent to Leo with the *Explanations*).

61. For a summary of the events and specific sources, see K.-V. Selge, "Der Weg zur Leipziger Disputation zwischen Luther und Eck im Jahr 1519," in *Bleibendes im Wandel der Kirchengeschichte: Kirchenhistorische Studien*, ed. B. Moeller and G. Ruhbach (Tübingen, 1973), pp. 172–177.

62. See Köhler, *Luthers 95 Thesen*, where the *Obelisci* are keyed to the corresponding theses of Luther; in WA 1, 281 ff., they are given without context. On the association with Hus, see S. H. Hendrix, "'We Are All Hussites?' Hus and Luther Revisited," ARG 65 (1974): 138–141.

63. The following new interpretation of Karlstadt's theses is convincingly and thoroughly presented by U. Bubenheimer, *Consonantia Theologiae et Iurisprudentiae* (Tübingen, 1977), pp. 109–118.

64. Ibid., pp. 55–58.

65. In February Luther himself comments that Karlstadt does not agree that indulgences are merely a snare for souls and useful only to lazy Christians: WABr 1, 146.52–58. See R. Sider, *Andreas Bodenstein von Karlstadt* (Leiden, 1974), pp. 57–59.

66. WA 1, 582.14–26.

67. The statement of Luther that it makes no difference to him what pleases or displeases the pope is viewed by Bäumer as contradictory to Luther's submission to the pope in the dedicatory letter to Leo. However, Bäumer does not attempt to interpret the statement in context: *Martin Luther und der Papst*, p. 22.

68. WA 1, 582.34–36. See the text and corresponding note in *Cl.* 1, 89.23–25. For the bulls of Sixtus IV, see Köhler, *Dokumente*, 37–40.

69. K.-V. Selge, *Normen der Christenheit im Streit um Ablass und Kirchenautorität 1518 bis 1521. Erster Teil: Das Jahr 1518*. Habil. (Heidelberg, 1968), p. 34.

70. WA 1, 529.33—530.1.

71. Ibid., 611.9–20.

72. Köhler, *Luthers 95 Thesen,* 172.7–9; 173.16–18 and 21–26. The same principle applies to the statement in Luther's June *Defense,* which is sometimes cited as a contradiction to his letter to Leo: "On the fourth point, that Saint Thomas is recognized as an authority, I will let that go. It is generally known in all universities how far that recognition applies! Therefore, whatever the holy father proves with Scripture or reason, I will accept, but the rest I will leave to his own imagination!" WA 1, 390.29–32. Luther's principle of consensus also governs his acceptance of the scholastics.

73. WA 1, 527.2–5.

74. Ibid., 529.22–25. A first draft of this letter was discovered and published in WA 9, 173–175. H. A. Oberman judges this draft to mark the decisive break in Luther's confidence in the pope: *Werden und Wertung der Reformation* (Tübingen, 1977), p. 192, n. 90. Although this first draft states more emphatically that the Lord Jesus will teach the pope what to decide (WA 9, 174.22—175.10), it does not differ substantially in content from the letter in its final form, in which Luther acknowledges the voice of Christ residing and speaking in the pope.

75. As maintained, for example, by Th. Kolde, *Luther's Stellung zu Concil und Kirche bis zum Wormser Reichstag, 1521* (Gütersloh, 1876), p. 19. Kolde found an explanation for this contradiction in the "peculiar combination of trust in God and self-awareness" which had become characteristic of Luther (ibid., p. 20). Cf. K. Meissinger, *Der katholische Luther* (Munich, 1952), p. 167; Bäumer, *Martin Luther und der Papst,* p. 26.

76. WA 1, 573.16–25.

77. Ibid., 627.23–27.

78. Ibid., 619.28–31. See Köhler, *Dokumente,* 33–34.

79. WA 1, 387.14–18. In his letter to Leo, Luther says that the indulgence preachers conduct themselves as if the decretal *Abusionibus* did not pertain to them: WA 1, 527.30—528.1. That makes four references by Luther to this decree during the controversy.

80. Ibid., 528.7–10 (cf. Mic. 3:2).

81. Ibid., 628.1–8.

82. Ibid., 625.25–28.

CHAPTER 3—RESISTANCE, JUNE TO DECEMBER 1518

1. This has been the prevailing view, but it is questioned by R. Bäumer, "Der Lutherprozess," in *Lutherprozess und Lutherbann: Vorgeschichte, Ergebnis, Nachwirkung,* ed. R. Bäumer (Münster, 1972), pp. 24–25.

2. WA 1, 530.10–12. Cf. WA 1, 527.22–23; 528.39—529.1. Luther's controversial statement in his letter to Leo, *"revocare non possum,"* should not be translated "I cannot recant," i.e., interpreted as a refusal to go back on his position in the face of a charge of heresy. Instead, the context clearly dictates the translation "I cannot recall," namely, the *Theses* from circulation: WA 1, 528.36—529.9 and specifically 529.3. R. Bäumer lines up the

different sides on this translation and decides correctly: *Martin Luther und der Papst*, 2d ed. (Münster, 1971), p. 23.

3. Printed in *E var* I, 341–377.

4. See T. Tentler, *Sin and Confession on the Eve of the Reformation* (Princeton, 1977), pp. 35–37. For a summary of biographical details (not completely accurate) and of the works involved in the controversy with Luther, see F. Lauchert, *Die italienischen literarischen Gegner Luthers* (1912; reprinted in Nieuwkoop, 1972), pp. 7–30. Other treatments of Prierias are sketched by C. Lindberg, "Prierias and His Significance for Luther's Development," *SCJ* 3 (1972): 45–64.

5. *WABr* 1, 188.9–10 (August 8, 1518); *WABr* 12, 14.13–15 (October 4, 1518).

6. See U. Bubenheimer, *Consonantia Theologiae et Iurisprudentiae* (Tübingen, 1977), p. 63, n. 231.

7. Ibid., pp. 60–62.

8. Prierias, *Dialogus*, in *E var* 1, 345.

9. Ibid., 345–346.

10. Ibid., 346–347.

11. Ibid., 349–350.

12. In response to Luther's Thesis 82: ibid., 374.

13. Ibid., 367.

14. Ibid., 365.

15. Ibid., 377.

16. Probably a double entendre, too, since the Latin *incultus* means both uncultivated and uncultured. Luther also says that Prierias acts as both his accusor and his judge, in reference to the office of Prierias and to the summons that Luther received at the same time: *WABr* 1, 188.21–23 (August 8, 1518).

17. *WA* 1, 686.28–30.

18. *WATR* 1, 216.1–6, no. 491; *LW* 54, 83.

19. *WA* 1, 647.19–28. On *Abusionibus* see above, Chapter 2, n. 79. See the use of *Abusionibus* against Prierias at *WA* 1, 655.30–36.

20. Prierias, *Dialogus*, in *E var* 1, 349–350.

21. *WA* 1, 655.37—656.7. Cf. *WA* 1, 655.27–29.

22. Ibid., 656.26—657.8. As in the *Explanations*, Luther counts the campaigns of Julius II (1503–1513) among such monstrosities and adds to them the tyrannical actions of Boniface VIII (1294–1303).

23. Ibid., 655.23–36.

24. Ibid., 662.31–38.

25. H. A. Oberman argues that it was Prierias and not Eck who first forced Luther to reflect on the ecclesiological components of his call to reformation: "Wittenbergs Zweifrontenkrieg gegen Prierias und Eck," *ZKG* 80 (1969): 339. Even before Prierias, Tetzel forced Luther to do this rethinking, although Prierias certainly contributed to further reflection. C. Lindberg argues that Prierias forced Luther to recognize that "a particular 'abuse' (indulgences) could not be 'reformed' without a change in the entire context

of that issue. Historically speaking, the original issue of the Reformation was papal authority and not justification": "Prierias and His Significance," p. 58. Papal authority became an issue, however, because the components of justification, word and faith, were stifled by the papal hierarchy.

26. Bäumer applies the description of a modern interpreter of Panormitanus, K. W. Nörr, to Luther's own assertion of papal and conciliar fallibility: it is still a "foreign element in his position": *Martin Luther und der Papst*, p. 25.

27. WA 1, 678.40—679.12.

28. Ibid., 670.3–4.

29. Ibid., 683.16–23 and 29–30.

30. Oberman believes that Luther's encounter with Prierias led to a growing conviction that the pope, through his claim to infallibility, was stifling rather than amplifying the voice of Christ in the church: "Wittenbergs Zweifrontenkrieg," p. 340. Bäumer questions the evidence for this suspicion, but he exaggerates the papalistic cast of Luther's statement that the Roman Church cannot err: *Martin Luther und der Papst*, p. 24.

31. In his 1520 preface to Prierias's *Epitome*, which was Prierias's answer to Luther's *Response*: "If one thinks and teaches like this in Rome with the knowledge of the pope and cardinals (and I hope not), then I freely declare in these writings that the true Antichrist sits in the temple of God and reigns in Babylon, that Rome is clothed in purple, and that the Roman curia is the synagogue of Satan": WA 6, 328.12–15.

32. WA 1, 680.9–12.

33. WABr 1, 188.4–16 (August 8, 1518). On Spalatin's activity in Frederick's service during these crucial years, see I. Höss, *Georg Spalatin 1484–1545* (Weimar, 1956), pp. 78–96, 124–155. Over 400 letters of Luther to Spalatin are extant: ibid., p. 79.

34. P. Kalkoff, *Forschungen zu Luthers römischem Prozess* (Rome, 1905), pp. 135–150.

35. *Sermon on the Power of Excommunication*: WA 1, 638–643. The traditional date for the delivery of this sermon is May 16, 1518 (see WA 1, 634–636). But O. Clemen, in his preface to the German edition of the *Sermon* published in 1520, justifiably doubts that it could have been delivered so early: *Cl.* 1, 213.

36. In a letter to Staupitz: WABr 1, 194.29–37 (September 1, 1518).

37. Ibid., 194.29–31.

38. WABr 1, 191.4—192.10; 192.31–35.

39. WA 1, 639.1–17; 639.33–36; 642.15–21; 642.29–39.

40. Published by Luther as part of his *Proceedings at Augsburg* (*Acta Augustana*: WA 2. 23–25).

41. WA 2, 23.17–22.

42. See W. Borth, *Die Luthersache (Causa Lutheri) 1517–1524* (Lübeck and Hamburg, 1970), pp. 48–50; P. Kalkoff, *Zu Luthers römischem Prozess: Der Prozess des Jahres 1518* (Gotha, 1912), pp. 164–177.

43. Kalkoff, *Forschungen*, p. 153. Kalkoff also reports that the pope was

favorably disposed toward Frederick because he alone, of all the German princes, supported the papal proposal for a tax on the German estates to finance a campaign against the Turks: *Zu Luthers römischem Prozess*, pp. 184–185. Ironically, Luther was sarcastically criticizing such a levy about the same time in a letter to Spalatin: *WABr* 1, 196.33–39. The extent and timing of the influence of these political factors on Leo and Cajetan are difficult to determine with precision, as the varying historical accounts make all too clear.

44. Kalkoff, *Zu Luthers römischem Prozess*, p. 183.

45. *WABr* 1, 192.11–21.

46. Ibid., 193.4–8.

47. Ibid., 194.20–28.

48. WA 54, 181.13.

49. This account of his first days in Augsburg is contained in a letter to Spalatin: *WABr* 1, 209.5—210.45 (October 10, 1518).

50. WA 54, 181.20–29.

51. *WABr* 1, 210.44–45.

52. Cited by G. Hennig, *Cajetan und Luther* (Stuttgart, 1966), p. 11. Hennig (p. 11, n. 5) surveys the older biographical treatments, including the chapter in Lauchert, *Gegner*, pp. 133–177. For more precise details, see Angelus Walz, "Von Cajetans Gedanken über Kirche und Papst," in *Volk Gottes: Festgabe für Josef Höfer*, ed. R. Bäumer and H. Dolch (Freiburg, 1967), pp. 336–360.

53. Kalkoff, *Forschungen*, p. 94.

54. Hennig, *Cajetan und Luther*, pp. 13–29, summarizes the main points of the treatise.

55. Ibid., p. 25.

56. Ibid., pp. 30–41; Walz, "Von Cajetans," p. 337. The man finally chosen to respond to Cajetan was the young French conciliarist, Jacques Almain, who had just received his doctorate but had already established his competence in ecclesiological matters. His *Tractatus de auctoritate ecclesiae et conciliorum generalium* appeared in the spring of 1512. Francis Oakley has shown that Almain's thought did not represent a watered-down conciliarism on the eve of the Reformation but continued the mainstream of conciliarist thought, which affirmed the superiority in principle of a council over the pope in jurisdictional matters: "Conciliarism in the Sixteenth Century: Jacques Almain Again," ARG 68 (1977): 111–132. Almain died prematurely, in his thirties, in 1515. For an account of the events surrounding the controversy between Cajetan and Almain and an extensive analysis of their works, see O. de la Brosse, *Le pape et le concile* (Paris, 1965), pp. 70–78, 185–335.

57. See S. H. Hendrix, *Ecclesia in via* (Leiden, 1974), pp. 80–82.

58. Hennig, *Cajetan und Luther*, pp. 33–34.

59. Mirbt-Aland, I, 498, no. 785.

60. J. Wicks, "Thomism Between Renaissance and Reformation: The Case of Cajetan," ARG 68 (1977): 12.

61. Hennig, *Cajetan und Luther*, pp. 27–28.
62. Walz, "Von Cajetans," p. 341.
63. WA 2, 7.19–26.
64. Ibid., 7.26–40.
65. Luther referred twice to Cajetan's *fiducia*: ibid., 7. 32 and 39. By the the same token, Cajetan was dumbfounded that Luther refused to concede and wondered in what Luther was placing his *fiducia*: WABr 1, 234.69 (October 25, 1518). For the dates of Cajetan's treatises, see Hennig, *Cajetan und Luther*, pp. 46–47.
66. WA 2, 7.32–34; 8.1–7. Luther apparently does not have in mind a specific biblical text but, as he says later, the lack of proper biblical support for the idea that the merits of Christ constitute a treasure from which indulgences can be granted. Cf. WA 2, 12.23–30.
67. WA 2, 8.10–15.
68. Thus K.-V. Selge, "Die Augsburger Begegnung von Luther und Kardinal Cajetan im Oktober 1518," *Jahrbuch der hessischen kirchengeschichtlichen Vereinigung* 20 (1969): 46. Otto Pesch has cautioned that Cajetan's papalism should not be understood as an appeal to papal power apart from Scripture. Rather, Cajetan was assuming that a "pre-established harmony" existed between the decrees of the pope and the correct interpretation of Scripture. The guidance of the Spirit would preserve the church in truth through the authoritative pronouncements of its highest officials: " 'Das heisst eine neue Kirche bauen': Luther und Cajetan in Augsburg," in *Begegnung: Beiträge zu einer Hermeneutik des theologischen Gesprächs*, ed. M. Seckler et al. (Graz, 1972), pp. 645–661; esp. pp. 651–652.
69. WA 1, 608.22–35.
70. See Luther's letter to Spalatin: WABr 1, 214.14–18 (October 14, 1518); to Karlstadt: WABr 1, 216.16–19 (October 14, 1518). Cajetan's account of his meeting with Luther to Frederick: WABr 1, 233.19–21 (October 25, 1518). See also the letter of Christoph Scheurl to Otto Beckmann in Wittenberg, October 21, 1518, in *Christoph Scheurl's Briefbuch*, ed. F. von Soden and J. K. F. Knaake (reprinted Aalen, 1962), II, 51–52.
71. WA 2, 9.28–34. Luther said that *Unigenitus* lacked a "solid demonstration" of its position: WA 2, 10.5.
72. Ibid., 10.7–11.
73. Ibid., 10.18–25.
74. See the detailed analysis of pertinent texts by Hennig, *Cajetan und Luther*, pp. 49–61. Cajetan's comment that Luther's position amounts to building a new church is found in Cajetan's *Opuscula Omnia* (Lyon, 1562), I, 111.8. Cf. WA 2, 7.37; 13.10. In a postscript to his letter to Beckmann on October 21, 1518 (see above, n. 70), Scheurl quotes almost verbatim Luther's description of Cajetan's second objection in WA 2, 13.6–10. Scheurl's remark that "this theology appears new and erroneous" seems to be a restatement of Luther's account of Cajetan's reaction in line 10 instead of the opinion of Scheurl himself.
75. WA 2, 14.14–19. See Hennig, *Cajetan und Luther*, p. 50.

76. Pointed out by both Selge, "Die Augsburger Begegnung," p. 42, and Pesch, " 'Das heisst eine neue Kirche bauen,' " pp. 655–657, against Hennig, *Cajetan und Luther*, p. 78, who believes that Luther and Cajetan understood each other all too well.

77. Emphasized by Selge, "Die Augsburger Begegnung," p. 43.

78. WA 2, 8.16–18.

79. WABr 1, 217.60–63.

80. WA 2, 18.14–16.

81. Ibid., 14.5–8.

82. Ibid., 16.6–21.

83. See the helpful discussion by M. Baylor, *Action and Person* (Leiden, 1977), pp. 254–273.

84. WA 2, 17.9–20.

85. Ibid., 17.37—18.6. Selge contends that the Augsburg encounter made Luther "a different person" in relation to the Roman Church and the authority of the pope: "Die Augsburger Begegnung," p. 54. By this, Selge means that at Augsburg a new perspective, similar to the one outlined here, appeared for the first time. The encounter alone did not generate this new perspective, however. It must be seen together with the developments during the next two months.

86. WA 2, 29.11–25.

87. Ibid., 32.24—33.5.

88. As maintained by Kolde, *Luther's Stellung*, p. 34; and, following him, by Bäumer, *Martin Luther und der Papst*, p. 34.

89. WABr 1, 225.21–30 (October 31, 1518). Cf. WA 2, 22.29—26.2.

90. WA 2, 25.25–29.

91. WABr 1, 233.42—234.48; 234.70–82 (October 25, 1518).

92. Ibid., 245.373–382.

93. Ibid., 242.264–270.

94. WA 2, 18.34—19.27.

95. Ibid., 19.28—20.6.

96. Ibid., 20.6–8. Luther had made a similar observation in his explanation of Thesis 22 to support his argument that, if canonical penalties and indulgences issued by the Roman pope have not applied to all Christians who are living, then they are not valid for the dead who are not under the jurisdiction of any church: WA 1, 571.16–22.

97. WA 2, 20.18–32.

98. Ibid., 21.5–6. Luther's assertion that "divine truth is lord even of the pope" implies the same categorical priority. See above, n. 85.

99. WA 2, 22.11–22.

100. Although he does not label Luther a "scripturalist," E. Bizer describes Luther's stance after Augsburg as one of deciding "for Scripture and against the pope." On the basis of his interpretation of Luther's Reformation discovery, Bizer argues that Luther's attitude toward Scripture must have undergone a complete shift between October 1517 and October 1518: *Luther und der Papst*, pp. 9–10. In his rush to show that Luther's opposition

to the papacy grew out of his new theology and not out of conciliar influences, Bizer dismisses Luther's reference to conciliar authority.

101. WA 2, 39.40; 40.10. The motive behind Luther's appeal has been the subject of much discussion. Did Luther understand himself to be appealing to a higher authority now that his appeal to the pope had met with no success? Or was the appeal a propagandistic maneuver through which the Wittenberg jurists hoped to influence public opinion and put pressure on the pope? For the first alternative, see Christa T. Johns, *Luthers Konzilsidee* (Berlin, 1966), pp. 135–143; K.-V. Selge, *Normen der Christenheit im Streit um Ablass und Kirchenautorität 1518 bis 1521* (Heidelberg, 1968), p. 189. For the second alternative, see H. Jedin, *A History of the Council of Trent*, I, trans. E. Graf (London, 1957), p. 173; Bäumer, *Martin Luther und der Papst*, pp. 38–39. The answer to both questions is a qualified yes. The appeal was not entirely propaganda since Luther did not intend for the printed copies of the appeal to be distributed publicly. They were to be delivered to him and only then made public in case he was excommunicated and forced to flee. The printer Grunenberg thwarted Luther's intention by selling the copies instead of delivering them to Luther: WABr 1, 280.5—281.17 (December 20, 1518). Bäumer argues that the formal notarizing and witnessing of the appeal already constituted a public act: *Martin Luther und der Papst*, p. 36. Bäumer also agrees with E. Iserloh that Luther really desired the printed copies to be sold and used the precipitous action of Grunenberg as a pretense that he intended otherwise: ibid., p. 39. Cf. *HKG*, IV, 61–62.

The public act of notarizing and witnessing the appeal is not, however, the same as encouraging the sale of copies, and there is no evidence that Luther did the latter. The supposition of Bäumer and Iserloh that Luther allowed the sale in order to arouse popular support and to present the elector and his advisers with a fait accompli remains hypothetical and not even very probable. In his letter to Spalatin, Luther regrets that he allowed the appeal (and the *Proceedings*) to be printed now that Frederick has denied the extradition request of Cajetan: WABr 1, 281.18–20. The form of the appeal did recall the appeal to a council by the University of Paris in March 1518, as well as earlier appeals from the fifteenth century which may have been known in Wittenberg. Nevertheless, the similarities between the Paris appeal and Luther's appeal are not as strong as many have asserted. See Bäumer, *Martin Luther und der Papst*, pp. 36–42; and Bäumer, *Nachwirkungen des konziliaren Gedankens in der Theologie und Kanonistik des frühen 16. Jahrhunderts* (Münster, 1971), pp. 148–149. See also the review of the latter work by U. Bubenheimer, p. 464. There is no reason why Luther could not have combined his awareness of the possible political impact of such an appeal with genuine respect for the authority of a council.

102. Bäumer wants to make a conciliarist out of Luther during this period. He maintains that in 1518–1519 Luther adopted markedly conciliaristic views after having harbored papalistic tendencies prior to 1518: *Martin Luther und der Papst*, p. 45. Bäumer bases his argument on the passage in Luther's appeal which indicated it is generally accepted that in matters con-

cerning faith a council stands above the pope and the pope cannot forbid an appeal to a council: WA 2, 36.26–32. According to Bäumer, the legitimacy of an appeal to a council over the head of the pope constitutes one of the clearest differences between conciliarists and papalists in the late Middle Ages: *Nachwirkungen*, pp. 121–162. Another interpretation of the appeal is offered by C. T. Johns, *Luthers Konzilsidee* (Berlin, 1966), p. 139, with whom Bäumer fervidly takes issue. Johns maintains that Luther's appeal is based on his "Reformation view of the church and of councils" and not on traditional conciliar theory. Although Bäumer is able to point to certain weaknesses in the argumentation of Johns, he does not demonstrate that the traditional conciliar theory underlies Luther's appeal. For example, he cannot refute Johns's argument that Luther omits from his appeal any reference to the historical high points of the conciliar position, the decrees *Haec sancta* and *Frequens* of the reform council at Constance. Bäumer can only claim that Luther's assertion of conciliar superiority amounts to the same thing: *Martin Luther und der Papst*, p. 41. In his review of Johns's book, Bäumer couples his occasionally justifiable criticism (e.g., of John's reliance on Heckel) with ungrounded conclusions, e.g., that Luther's references to Panormitanus demonstrate how strongly Luther was attached to conciliar ideas: *Theologische Revue* 25 (1969): 198–202. In his book, Bäumer tries to take advantage of some disagreement between Johns and Selge, but the discussion of Luther's appeal by Selge is closer to the position of Johns than that of Bäumer. See Selge, *Normen der Christenheit*, pp. 185–189; Bäumer, *Martin Luther und der Papst*, pp. 43–45.

103. WA 2, 22.11–22. These jurists and prelates now become a specific example of those "enemies, teachers and elders" who, according to Luther's exegesis of Ps. 119:98–100 in the *Dictata* (1515), exercise human traditions against spiritual Christians and are thus less wise than those who are anointed by the Spirit: WA 4, 353.15–22.

104. WA 2, 22.22–27. Grane argues that it is of secondary importance theologically whether Luther here understood himself to be combating only a party within the church, e.g., the juristic flatterers, or already clearly understood that the pope belonged to this party. According to Grane, Luther was using the term "church" or "Roman Church" in two senses, which laid the groundwork for his explicit dissociation of the true church from the papacy in 1520: *Modus loquendi theologicus*, pp. 188–189. Grane appears to mean that Luther's theological definition of the church as the place where the word of God is proclaimed remained unchanged regardless of who belonged to that church. That is true, but *historically and theologically* whether Luther included the pope among his opponents in the church was of primary importance. The pope was not just another indulgence preacher or curial official. Luther's reluctant abandonment of hope in the papacy in late 1518 was a momentous historical step in his gradual move away from Rome as well as a serious test of his ecclesiology. Luther was indeed drawing the consequences of his theology and realizing the limits of his Roman ecclesiastical loyalty, as Grane says (ibid., pp. 185–186), but the process was theologically more com-

plex, as we have tried to demonstrate, and personally more painful than Grane implies. See Luther's own words after he arrives back in Wittenberg from Augsburg: "I do not know how long I shall remain [at Wittenberg], for my situation is such that I am both afraid and hopeful": WABr 1, 224.7–8 (October 31, 1518).

105. WA 2, 37.8–12; author's translation from the Vulgate (=Ps. 115:11).
106. Ibid., 39.32–39.
107. Mirbt-Aland, I, 503, no. 788.
108. WABr 1, 253.8–11.

CHAPTER 4—CHALLENGE, 1519

1. WABr 1, 267.5–10 (December 1518).
2. The letters are lost, but the account of the farewell meal has usually been accepted as authentic although it was recorded much later. See I. Höss, *Georg Spalatin 1484–1545* (Weimar, 1956), p. 141, n. 51.
3. See K. Müller, "Luthers römischer Prozess," ZKG 24 (1903): 76–77; P. Kalkoff, "Zu Luthers römischem Prozess," ZKG 25 (1904): 286. In a letter to Duke George of Saxony dated the day after Miltitz's arrival, Frederick acknowledged that he would be unlikely to get the Rose unless he banished Luther and declared him a heretic: *Akten und Briefe zur Kirchenpolitik Herzog Georgs von Sachsen*, ed. F. Gess (Leipzig, 1905), I, 51–52, no. 64.
4. The evaluations of Miltitz and his missions vary widely. For a balanced account which takes into consideration the pronounced views of Kalkoff and of Miltitz's biographer, Creutzberg, see R. Fife, *The Revolt of Martin Luther* (New York, 1957), pp. 307–326. See also the discussion by H.-G. Leder, *Ausgleich mit dem Papst?* (Stuttgart, 1969), pp. 9–16.
5. The letters from Scheurl to Luther are in *Christoph Scheurl's Briefbuch*, II, no. 182, pp. 70–73; no. 186, pp. 75–76; no. 190, p. 81; and in WABr 1, 272–280, 287–289. See esp. WABr 1, 275.91–101 (December 19 or 20, 1518).
6. Höss, *Spalatin*, p. 144. Luther also speaks of seventy briefs: WABr 1, 344.13–15 (February 20, 1519).
7. Höss, *Spalatin*, p. 144.
8. Since Miltitz was acting under Cajetan's orders, an appearance before the archbishop, with Cajetan perhaps present, did not promise to be the impartial hearing to which Luther and Frederick had agreed. See W. Borth, *Die Luthersache (Causa Lutheri) 1517–1524* (Lübeck and Hamburg, 1970), pp. 63–65. Against the traditional view that Miltitz should not be taken too seriously, represented by Kalkoff, Borth emphasizes that Miltitz understood his mission and tried diligently to accomplish it.
9. WABr 1, 270.11–14 (December 18, 1518).
10. Ibid., 286.82–86.
11. Ibid., 289–291 (January 5 or 6, 1519).
12. Ibid., 290.20–25.
13. Ibid., 292.24–30 (January 5 or 6, 1519).

14. Ibid., 293.45–48.

15. Ibid., 292.31—293.36.

16. This question was raised by N. Paulus, "Luther's Stellung zum Papst-thum in den ersten Monaten des Jahres 1519," *Der Katholik* 79 (1899): I, 476–480.

17. *WABr* 1, 348.14–17 and 20–22.

18. Ibid., 359.29–31 (March 13, 1519); *LW* 48, 114.

19. H. Preuss stresses this difference between speculating on the activity of the Antichrist in the curia and identifying the pope as the Antichrist. It would be yet another step to a public denunciation of the papacy as the Antichrist. *Die Vorstellungen vom Antichrist im späteren Mittelalter, bei Luther und in der konfessionellen Polemik* (Leipzig, 1906), pp. 105–106.

20. *WABr* 1, 307.37–47.

21. Ibid., 307.48—308.53.

22. Borth, *Die Luthersache*, pp. 62–63.

23. *WABr* 1, 308.54–59.

24. Ibid., 306.6–10.

25. *Unterricht auf etliche Artikel: WA* 2, 66–73; cf. *WABr* 1, 209.26–33.

26. *WA* 2, 73.6–16. Compare similar remarks in reference to the Hussites in Luther's Galatians commentary written about this time (though not published until the fall): *WA* 2, 605.12–22. In the dedication, Luther also affirmed his allegiance to the pope and the Roman Church, although he distinguished it from the Roman curia and reserved the right to prefer the words of Christ over those of his vicar: *WA* 2, 446.38—447.3; 448.37—449.2. R. Bäumer dismisses these statements as further evidence of the "surprising wavering, if not contradictions" in Luther's view of the papacy in 1519: *Martin Luther und der Papst*, 2d ed. (Münster, 1971), p. 53. The statements fit better into our picture of the tension in Luther's interim solution.

27. *WABr* 1, 307.23–28.

28. J. Eck, *Epistola de ratione studiorum suorum (1538)*, ed. J. Metzler, *CCath* 2, 46; cf. J. Schlecht, "Dr. Johann Ecks Anfänge," *HJ* 36 (1915): 5.

29. See Schlecht, "Anfänge," pp. 10–11; H. A. Oberman, *Werden und Wertung der Reformation* (Tübingen, 1977), p. 176.

30. Schlecht, "Anfänge," pp. 13–15; J. Greving, *Johann Eck als junger Gelehrter* (Münster, 1906), pp. 19–65.

31. Rhegius's remarks concerning Luther were contained in letters that he wrote to friends in south Germany after he had left Augsburg to organize the Reformation in the territory of Lüneburg. His accounts of the one-day meeting with Luther at the Coburg in 1530 were printed as independent excerpts at the end of Rhegius's *Loci theologici* under the title: *Iudicium D. Urbani Rhegii de D. Martino Luthero* (Frankfurt, 1545), 251ᵛ—252ʳ. The excerpts obviously circulated independently of their original epistolary context and may have enjoyed considerable popularity. They are found, for example, handwritten inside the front cover of Volume I of the Jena Edition

(1556) of Luther's works, owned by the library of Lutheran Theological Southern Seminary, Columbia, South Carolina.

32. Oberman, *Werden und Wertung*, pp. 174–195, esp. pp. 187–195.

33. Eck's *Chrysopassus* indicates that he was not a papalist to the extent of Prierias or Cajetan. He may have harbored a strong appreciation for conciliar authority: H. A. Oberman, "Luthers Zweifrontenkrieg gegen Prierias und Eck," *ZKG* 80 (1969): 344–346. Bubenheimer classifies him between curialist and conciliar types: review of *Nachwirkungen* by Bäumer, pp. 460, 463.

34. WABr 1, 322.89–111 (March 14, 1519).

35. WA 1, 571.16–18.

36. Luther wanted to prove that the penitential rules in canon law do not bind those Christians who are not subject to the pope just as they would not have bound the Eastern churches before the time of Gregory I (600): WA 1, 571.10–22.

37. WA 2, 185.3–6.

38. WABr 1, 322.112–116.

39. Ibid., 316.14–19 (open letter to Karlstadt on February 4 or 5, 1519, accompanying the first set of twelve countertheses).

40. Ibid., 346.16–18.

41. See above, n. 18. Luther had probably consulted canon law for his *Ninety-five Theses*, and he certainly studied it in early 1518 as preparation for his *Explanations*. His letter to Spalatin on February 24, 1519, reveals to what extent he intensified that study in preparation for Leipzig: WABr 1, 352-355. See S. Mühlmann, *Luther und das Corpus Iuris Canonici bis zum Jahre 1530*, I: *Prolegomena*, Diss. (Leipzig, 1972), pp. 301–319, 105.

42. WABr 1, 359.32—360.35.

43. Ibid., 359.31–32.

44. Ibid. 360.35–36; LW 48, 114.

45. Luther may have referred to this new resolve in an undated excerpt from his *Table Talk*: WATR 5, 686.22–23, no. 6480. He recalls specifically that reading the commentary of Dinus Mugellanus (*d.* 1304) on the *Decretum* of Gratian confirmed his intention to write "*contra papam.*" See Mühlmann, *Luther und das Corpus Iuris Canonici*, p. 69, n. 8. See also K. Bauer, *Die Wittenberger Universitätstheologie und die Anfänge der deutschen Reformation* (Tübingen, 1928), p. 89.

46. In response to Luther's not wholly accurate charge that Eck aimed the twelve theses against him alone, Eck inserted a new thesis against Karlstadt in a revised list, which he issued on March 14. Thus Eck's twelfth thesis on papal primacy, and Luther's counterthesis, became number thirteen.

47. WA 2, 161.35–38. In the heading to his explanation of the thesis published in June, Luther altered the thesis somewhat, but its original form remained the basis for debate. See K.-V. Selge, "Der Weg zur Leipziger Disputation zwischen Luther und Eck im Jahr 1519," in *Bleibendes im Wandel der Kirchengeschichte: Kirchenhistorische Studien*, ed. B. Moeller and G.

Ruhbach (Tübingen, 1973), pp. 197–198. Luther knew, of course, that papal decrees much older than four hundred years and contained in Gratian's *Decretum* (*c.* 1140) were used to support papal primacy. Apparently, though, he did not consider the *Decretum* legally binding on the church in the same way as the later collections of the popes: Gregory IX (*Liber extra.* 1234), Boniface VIII (*Liber sextus*, 1298), and Clement V (*Clementinae*, 1317). Luther tells Spalatin, therefore, that his thesis is a trap for Eck. When Eck cites the older decrees from the *Decretum*, he will argue that they have not been officially "received" by the church and will refer to the collections of the popes that are less than four hundred years old: *WABr* 1, 353.20–35 (February 24?, 1519). See Mühlmann, *Luther und das Corpus Iuris Canonici*, pp. 303–308.

48. WA 2, 159.32—160.2.

49. Ibid., 160.8–11; LW 31, 316.

50. WA 2, 160.11–18; LW 31, 316; cf. Luther's remark in a letter dated May 30, 1519: "Rome is burning to destroy me, but I coolly laugh at her." *WABr* 1, 408.12–13; LW 48, 125.

51. WA 2, 186.38—187.7; cf. WA 2, 20.27–32.

52. Ibid., 187.27–31.

53. Ibid., 188.4–8.

54. Ibid., 189.27–39. Luther had used this argument in briefer form in the *Proceedings at Augsburg*. See above, Chapter 3, n. 97.

55. WA 2, 190.37–40; 191.21–26.

56. Ibid., 189.35—190.4.

57. Ibid., 190.15–21; 191.34–35; cf. WA 2, 208.25–29: "Wherever the word of God is preached and believed, there is true faith; that rock is immovable. Moreover, where there is faith, there is the church. Where the church is, there is the bride of Christ. Where the bride of Christ is, there are all the things which belong to the bridegroom. So faith has all things in itself which follow upon faith: the keys, sacraments, power and all other things."

58. As claimed, e.g., by Th. Kolde, *Luther's Stellung zu Concil und Kirche bis zum Wormser Reichstag, 1521* (Gütersloh, 1876), pp. 44–45; Ernst Bizer, *Luther und der Papst* (Munich, 1958), p. 17.

59. WA 2, 195.16–28.

60. Ibid., 196.5–7; 196.9–19; 197.12–20; 197.30–33.

61. Ibid., 227.6–11.

62. In this sense, Luther had indeed "reached a new stage in his development," although much of his exegetical argument was contained in the *Proceedings at Augsburg*. See P. Fraenkel, "John Eck's *Enchiridion* of 1525 and Luther's Earliest Arguments Against Papal Primacy," *Studia Theologica* 21 (1967): 159. F. Rickers speaks of "a decisive turning point" in Luther's attitude toward the papacy in 1519: *Das Petrusbild Luthers: Ein Beitrag zu seiner Auseinandersetzung mit dem Papsttum.* Diss. (Heidelberg, 1967), p. 47. Luther's opponents attributed considerable importance to his *Explanation of Proposition Thirteen.* Rickers lists eleven works, published between

1520 and 1534, which in part or in toto sought to refute Luther's arguments in this treatise: *Das Petrusbild*, pp. iv–v.

63. WA 2, 239.23–24.

64. Selge, "Der Weg zur Leipziger Disputation," pp. 183–184.

65. For a detailed account of events leading up to the debate, see Selge, "Der Weg zur Leipziger Disputation," pp. 169–210. For a colorful account of the debate and its aftermath, see Fife, *Revolt*, pp. 327–394.

66. Papal authority was still a point of contention after Luther and Eck left proposition thirteen behind and debated the subject of indulgences. Eck took his stand on Leo's bull *Cum postquam* (WA 2, 344.28–34) and appealed to the impossibility that the whole church and its pontiffs had erred in issuing indulgences for the benefit of the faithful (WA 2, 346.10–23). Luther remained unmoved. The popes were human and could make mistakes, and in *Cum postquam* Leo had not proved one syllable of what he said (WA 2, 349.4–13). Against the various authorities Eck introduced, Luther resorted to the argument derived from Panormitanus that the decisive consideration was not *who* (pope, council, etc.) said something, but *what* was said. See U. Bubenheimer, *Consonantia Theologiae et Iurisprudentiae* (Tübingen, 1977), pp. 100–101.

67. WA 2, 239.23–27.

68. O. Seitz, ed., *Der authentische Text der Leipziger Disputation 1519* (Berlin, 1903), pp. 58–59. See S. H. Hendrix, *Ecclesia in via* (Leiden, 1974), pp. 80–82 and 230–232.

69. Seitz, *Der authentische Text*, p. 116.

70. For Eck's charge, see ibid., pp. 81–82.

71. Ibid., pp. 82–83. See Köhler, *Luther und die Kirchengeschichte*, p. 185.

72. Seitz, *Der authentische Text*, p. 87.

73. Ibid., pp. 87, 82.

74. Ibid., p. 87.

75. Ibid., pp. 92, 93, 99. The explanations were that impostors had inserted the true statements into the list of condemned articles and that not all the articles were classified as heretical, but variously as "erroneous," "blasphemous," "rash," "seditious," etc.

76. Ibid., pp. 99–100.

77. Ibid., pp. 119, 129.

78. Ibid., p. 67. See K.-V. Selge, "Die Leipziger Disputation zwischen Luther und Eck," ZKG 86 (1975): 32–36.

79. Seitz, *Der authentische Text*, p. 67.

80. WA 2, 225.24–28 (in the *Explanation of Proposition Thirteen*). Here Luther employs 1 Cor. 2:15 for the first time directly against the pope. The freedom of Scripture, which has thereby assumed such a dominant place within Luther's consensus of authorities, can still not be described as the desire to be "free from every authority," which Bäumer attributes to Luther from 1519 on: *Martin Luther und der Papst*, p. 45.

81. E var 3, 478.

82. These are listed by J. Metzler in *CCath* 2, 89–91.

83. *WA* 54, 183.17–18; *LW* 34, 333.

84. *WABr* 1, 452.12–15.

85. Ibid., 423.115–120.

86. On Emser, see G. Kawerau, *Hieronymus Emser* (Halle, 1898); F. X. Thurnhofer in *CCath* 4, 9–21. The dinner in Dresden had been the scene of an argument over indulgences and the papal ban. Luther had been among Emser's students at Erfurt in 1504.

87. *CCath* 4, 13.

88. Luther's attack appeared in September, Eck's defense in October, and Emser's rejoinder in early November: *CCath* 4, 15–21.

89. *WA* 2, 667.14–18. Compare his soft remarks on Tetzel in his reminiscence from 1545: *WA* 54, 184.31–36. In spite of his sympathy, Luther still calls Tetzel the "primary author of this tragedy."

90. See Oberman, *Werden und Wertung*, p. 334, n. 15.

91. In October 1520, Luther remarked to Spalatin: "Now that the die is cast, Karlstadt is summoning up courage against the Roman pope": *WABr* 2, 191.29–30. See Bubenheimer, *Consonantia*, pp. 163–165.

92. *Epistola de Lipsica disputatione*, 1519: *MStA* 1, 3–11.

93. *Defensio Phil. Melanchthonis contra Joh. Eckium*, 1519: *MStA* 1, 12–22, esp. 17.33—18.4.

94. On September 19, Melanchthon defended the authority of Scripture in his baccalaureate theses: *MStA* 1, 24.31–32; see Bubenheimer, *Consonantia*, pp. 160–161. Other humanists, such as Oecolampadius, took Luther's side, but Erasmus did not comment directly on the Leipzig Debate; see Fife, *Revolt*, pp. 415–435.

95. *WA* 2, 702.2–3.

96. *WABr* 1, 525.12–17; *LW* 48, 127.

97. Borth, *Luthersache*, pp. 70–71.

98. Höss, *Spalatin*, pp. 163–167.

99. See the summary by B. Moeller, *Deutschland im Zeitalter der Reformation* (Göttingen, 1977), p. 77. Frederick's interest in defending the prestige of the Ernestine house against Hohenzollern expansion in north Germany (represented by Albert of Brandenburg) is stressed by G. Mühlpfordt in his review of books by Borth and Olivier on Luther's trial in *Deutsche Literaturzeitung für Kritik der internationalen Wissenschaft* 95 (1974): 897–906.

100. *WABr* 1, 424.143.

101. *WA* 2, 677.3–14.

102. Ibid., 677.27–32.

103. Luther expressed appreciation for the corporate nature of the Christian life in sermons and in lectures which he delivered in 1519. J. Lortz conceded this appreciation, but argued that Luther's real concern did not revolve so much around the church as around the individual Christian: "Zum Kirchendenken des jungen Luther," in *Wahrheit und Verkündigung*, ed. L. Scheffczyk et al. (Munich, 1967), II, 971. Lortz's argument is hard

to understand in view of Luther's sermons on the sacraments in late 1519 and such passages as the one just discussed.

104. WA 54, 183.21—184.11; LW 34, 333–334.

105. E. Iserloh regards this as the real significance of Eck and of the Leipzig Debate: *HKG* IV, 65. Iserloh is seconded by Bäumer, *Martin Luther und der Papst*, p. 51.

106. WABr 1, 597.32–36 (December 18, 1519); *LW* 48, 138.

107. WABr 1, 611.37–46, 57–61 (January 14, 1520); *LW* 48, 146–148.

CHAPTER 5—OPPOSITION, 1520

1. Cf. the title of R. H. Fife's chapter, "The Rising Tide of Revolt," in *The Revolt of Martin Luther* (New York, 1957), pp. 463–478.

2. WABr 2, 42.22–29 (*c.* February 14, 1520); cf. *LW* 48, 153.

3. WA 5, 452.3–9. See S. H. Hendrix, " 'We Are All Hussites'? Hus and Luther Revisited," ARG 65 (1974): 146–147.

4. This was the second printing of Hutten's edition; the first printing appeared in 1518. W. Setz offers convincing reasons for this dating in his work: *Lorenzo Vallas Schrift gegen die konstantinische Schenkung* (Tübingen, 1975), pp. 159–166. Setz also argues that Hutten's preface addressed to Leo X was not sarcastic but genuine: ibid., pp. 155–159. Accordingly, Hutten's date on the preface, December 1, 1517, does not need to be considered as intentional backdating, as previous theories assumed. See, e.g., J. Benzing, *Ulrich von Hutten und seine Drucker: Eine Bibliographie der Schriften Huttens im 16. Jahrhundert, mit Beiträgen von Heinrich Grimm* (Wiesbaden, 1956), p. 3. See also Setz's edition of Valla's text (date: 1440): *Lorenzo Valla: De falso credita et ementita Constantini donatione* (Weimar, 1976).

5. WABr 2, 48.20—49.2 (February 24, 1520). Seventeen years later, in connection with the calling of a council at Mantua, Luther published a German translation and commentary on the *Donation* under the title: *One of the Chief Articles of the Papal Faith, Called the Donation of Constantine*: WA 50, 69–89. See Setz, *Lorenzo Vallas Schrift*, p. 167.

6. H. Preuss, *Die Vorstellungen* (Leipzig, 1906), p. 110.

7. WABr 2, 143.21–23 (July 14, 1520).

8. Ibid., 41.12—42.22 (*c.* February 14, 1520); *LW* 48, 152–153.

9. WA 6, 67.11–17; 67.28–33; 70.18–22.

10. According to the editors in WA 6, 61, and *Cl.* 1, 213. It is unlikely, however, that the decision to reedit the sermon in German in connection with the *Sermon on the Blessed Sacrament* had nothing to do with the negative reaction to the latter in Ducal Saxony. Luther's repeated reference to "bishops" and "officials" who misuse the ban calls to mind the mandate of the bishop of Meissen issued through the official of Stolpen. Luther responded to both by mid-February 1520.

11. WA 5, 404.23–25; 404.35—405.5.

12. Ibid., 407.33–38.

13. In the same vein, Luther protests against the condemnation of his views by the universities of Cologne and Louvain. The condemnation is another sign that the Antichrist is reigning. In response to their rejection of his views on confession, Luther writes that he does not deny the principle of examining consciences, but he does object to the butchering of consciences which forces the faithful to do the impossible task of enumerating all their sins: WA 6, 182.2–11; 194.10–16.

14. WA 6, 203.7–10.

15. See H. Dannenbauer, *Luther als religiöser Volksschriftsteller 1517–1520* (Tübingen, 1930).

16. WABr 2, 149.14–19 (July 28, 1520).

17. WA 6, 275.7–11.

18. WABr 2, 52.14–16 (February 25, 1520). Under heavy attack in Louvain as a sympathizer of Luther, Erasmus requested Luther not to mention his name in his works. In cautious fashion, he wrote: "If the matter promises tumult, I prefer someone else to be the author of the tumult. Nevertheless, I will not oppose your spirit lest, if it be led by the Spirit of Christ, I might oppose the latter": WABr 2, 157.64–69; 158.84–85 (August 1, 1520). In Freiburg, the humanist and lawyer Ulrich Zasius endorsed Luther's theology but advised moderation toward the papacy: WABr 2, 181–183 (September 1, 1520). Cautious appreciation was also expressed by John Fabri, episcopal vicar in Constance and later bishop of Vienna and opponent of Luther, in a letter to Vadian on May 12, 1520. Fabri stressed the danger of making Luther's views accessible to the laity, however, just as Luther's other opponents had done. See I. Staub, *Dr. Johann Fabri, Generalvikar von Konstanz (1518–1523)*, Diss. Freiburg (Switzerland) (Einsiedeln, 1911), pp. 124–125.

19. WABr 2, 120.3–15.

20. WA 6, 285.22–29.

21. Ibid., 286.22–26. The German version of Alfeld's treatise was entitled A *Fruitful and Useful Little Book About the Papal See, Saint Peter and the True Sheep of Christ*. Against claims that churches besides the Roman Church could be the true church, Alfeld offered seven reasons why the flock entrusted to Peter in John 21:15 ff., i.e., Christians under the pope, alone was the true church. This argumentation may have caused Luther to characterize the treatise as seductive. See L. Lemmens, *Pater Augustin von Alfeld* (Freiburg, 1899), pp. 33–34.

22. WA 6, 347.22–28. Fife notes that these words have often been cited to prove Luther's intolerant and violent nature, and that Luther apologists have just as often pointed to Luther's paraphrase of Ps. 58:10 to exonerate him: *Revolt*, p. 506, n. 85. For a recent, indirect example of the former, see R. Bäumer, *Martin Luther und der Papst*, 2d ed. (Münster, 1971), pp. 57–58. The context of the words provides the key to Luther's hypothetical and militant advice. If the Romanists do not permit a council to reform the church, then there is no other remedy against papal tyranny than for the secular princes to use force: WA 6, 347.10–20.

23. WA 6, 329.6–13, 17–19. In a papal breve dated July 21, 1520, Pope Leo X declared the works of Prierias against Luther "canonical." He placed the *Epitome* under his special protection and prohibited any unpermitted reprint under a heavy fine. Luther did not know about the breve until March 1521: WA 6, 326–327.

24. WA 6, 347.29—348.6.

25. Compare his statement of the issue at the beginning of the treatise: WA 6, 286.35—287.2.

26. Ibid., 321.31—322.1. See O. Starck, *Luthers Stellung zur Institution des Papsttums von 1520 bis 1546 unter besonderer Berücksichtigung des "ius humanum,"* Diss. Münster (Quakenbrück, 1930), pp. 45–48.

27. WA 6, 322.1–8, 19–21.

28. Ibid., 322.10–19.

29. Ibid., 406.21–29; 415.1–6.

30. Ibid., 415.29–31; 416.7–8.

31. Ibid., 453.10–14.

32. Ibid., 348.1; cf. WABr 2, 149.24; 151.13–14.

33. WABr 2, 125.5.

34. WA 6, 292.35—293.12; 297.36–40.

35. Ibid., 294.9–11. Alfeld did not deny that some prelates in Rome led immoral lives. He had admonished his readers only to obey what these prelates taught from Scripture, not to imitate their lives: Lemmens, *Alfeld,* pp. 35–36.

36. WABr 2, 138.40–46.

37. WA 6, 437.14–15, 31–32; 415.13–18.

38. Ibid., 312.31–35.

39. Ibid., 319.5–7. Against Luther's argument that the keys were given to all the disciples, Alfeld emphasized that John 21:15–17 was the proper basis of papal rule because these words were addressed to Peter alone: Lemmens, *Alfeld,* p. 38. Hence, Luther discussed the passage in detail: WA 6, 316.20—321.22.

40. WA 6, 331.12, 32–33.

41. MStA 7/I, 87.4–13.

42. WABr 2, 167.13–15 (August 18, 1520).

43. Ibid., 135.24–29.

44. In his reply to the bull published in November 1520, Luther summed up his opinion: "I am not completely persuaded that this bull is from the pope, but rather from the impiety of his apostle, Eck, who together with his own fathers hastens to devour me with his ferocious jaws": WA 6, 605.6–8; cf. WA 6, 597.16–20; 603.7–10. In 1521, the new convert to Luther's cause and preacher at the cathedral in Augsburg, Urbanus Rhegius, wrote a satirical pamphlet against the bull under the pseudonym Simon Hessus. Rhegius, a former pupil and admirer of Eck (see above, p. 79), attributed most of the articles to Eck's influence; in commenting on articles 2–4 condemned by *Exsurge Domine,* Rhegius wrote: "Not without good cause did the pope damn these three articles, since they are against Eck,

that strenuous guardian of the Roman see and most obvious author of the terrible bull. It was necessary to condemn certain articles as a favor to the Roman curia and other articles in gratitude to Eck without whom the bull would not properly have been put together." *Argumentum libelli: Simon Hessus Luthero ostendit caussas, quare Lutherana opuscula a Coloniensibus et Louvaniensibus sint combusta. . . .* (n.p., 1521), Aiii^{r-v}. Compare Melanchthon to Spalatin on November 4, 1520: "Martin responds to the bull, directing his case against Eck, who certainly for us is the author of so great a tragedy": *MStA* 7/I, 93.17–18. On the last stages of Luther's trial, see, in addition to the works of Kalkoff, K. Müller, "Luthers römischer Prozess," *ZKG* 24 (1903): 46–85; A. Schulte, "Die römischen Verhandlungen über Luther. 1520. Aus den Atti Consistoriali 1517–23." *Quellen und Forschungen aus italienischen Archiven und Bibliotheken* 6 (1904): 32–52, 174–176, 374–378; G. Müller, "Die römische Kurie und die Anfänge der Reformation," *Zeitschrift für Religions- und Geistesgeschichte* 19 (1967): 1–32.

45. See Eck's letter to the Elector Frederick on November 8, 1519: *WABr* 1, 495.597–599. For a comparison of this treatise with the sections on papal primacy in Eck's *Enchiridion* of 1525, see P. Fraenkel, "John Eck's *Enchiridion* of 1525 and Luther's Earliest Arguments Against Papal Primacy," *Studia Theologica* 21 (1967): 116–163.

46. In a letter dated May 3, 1520, from Rome to his friend John Fabri in Constance: *E var* 4, 256–258; 256. See Staub, *Dr. Johann Fabri*, pp. 126–127.

47. H. Roos, "Die Quellen der Bulle 'Exsurge Domine' (15.6.1520)," in *Theologie in Geschichte und Gegenwart: Michael Schmaus zum sechzigsten Geburtstag*, ed. J. Auer and H. Volk (Munich, 1957), pp. 909–926. The bull itself is printed in Mirbt-Aland I, 504–513; see esp. 507.

48. See above, Chapter 4, n. 33. In a letter to Bishop Christoph of Augsburg on October 29, 1520, Eck wrote that it would be a shame if Luther would make all of Germany into heretics and schismatics, but he admitted that the bishops and the pope were guilty in many matters: J. Greving, "Zur Verkündigung der Bulle Exsurge Domine durch Dr. Johann Eck 1520," *Briefmappe I*. Reformationsgeschichtliche Studien und Texte 21/22 (Münster, 1912), 215, no. 92.

49. E.g., articles 11, 13, 18, 20: Mirbt-Aland I, 506.

50. Mirbt-Aland I, 504.

51. Ibid., 507, 504.

52. Greving, "Zur Verkündigung," 202, 211.

53. See above, Chapter 4, n. 91.

54. See *WABr* 2, 192–193, n. 11.

55. *WA* 6, 497.7—498.9. The image of the hunt is taken from the treatises published by Emser and Eck in late 1519. They defended Emser against the "hunt" which Luther had undertaken against the "Goat Emser." For the titles, see G. Kawerau, *Hieronymus Emser* (Halle, 1898), p. 32; *WA* 2, 657.

56. WA 6, 501.24–26.
57. Ibid., 535.27–30.
58. Ibid., 537.5–12.
59. Ibid., 537.19–27. The "principle of freedom and subjectivity," which Starck stresses as the basis of Luther's strong opposition to the papacy, draws attention away from Luther's concern for the church and the effects of papal tyranny upon it. Otherwise, Starck's reconstruction of Luther's attitude at this point is helpful: *Luthers Stellung*, pp. 66–69.
60. WA 6, 504.21–25.
61. WABr 2, 189.22–24 (October 1, 1520); 191.15–22 (October 3, 1520).
62. Ibid., 195.22–23, 11–13, 19–20 (October 11, 1520).
63. Ibid., 184.12–15 (September 11, 1520).
64. Ibid., 195.28 (October 11, 1520).
65. Ibid., 66.50–54 (March 16, 1520). For the impact of Miltitz's argument on Luther, see H.-G. Leder, *Ausgleich mit dem Papst? Luthers Haltung in den Verhandlungen mit Miltitz 1520* (Stuttgart, 1969), pp. 46–49.
66. H. Jedin. *A History of the Council of Trent*, trans. E. Graf (London, 1957), I, 128, 132. For Leo and his reign, see L. Pastor, *Geschichte der Päpste seit dem Ausgang des Mittelalters* (Freiburg, 1906), IV, 1; F. X. Seppelt, *Geschichte der Päpste*, 2d ed., ed. Georg Schwaiger (Munich, 1957), IV, 408–426.
67. K. A. Fink in *HKG* III/2 (Freiburg, 1968), 676.
68. WA 7, 3.22—4.7; 6.35.
69. Ibid., 4.37—5.2; 5.32–33.
70. Ibid., 10.3–4; 10.13–16.
71. Ibid., 6.6–10; 5.34–37.
72. Ibid., 10.29—11.3.
73. Emphasized by Leder, *Ausgleich mit dem Papst?* pp. 49–53, 66.
74. WA 7, 6.38—7.5.
75. Ibid., 10.17–25. See above, p. 20–21.
76. MStA 7/I, 93.19–21.
77. WA 6, 576–577; 581.7–19; 584.7–11.
78. WA 7, 3.18–21.
79. The charge was made already by Luther's contemporaries. In 1521, Jerome Emser was particularly incensed by it in his response to Luther's *Address to the Christian Nobility*. Emser said it was a blatant lie that Luther did not intend to attack the person of the pope and accused Luther of being two-faced. Surprisingly, however, Emser himself defended the pope by putting the blame on the indulgence preachers. That was exactly Luther's procedure until he became convinced that the claims of papal authority prevented the preachers from being restrained. See *Luther und Emser: Ihre Streitschriften aus dem Jahre 1521*, ed. L. Enders (Halle, 1889), I, 53–54, 57.
80. WA 7, 5.2–6.

81. Ibid., 5.13–22.
82. Ibid., 9.25–38.
83. WATR 1, 294.19—295.5, no. 624.
84. Cf. Luther's characterization of his work in 1527: WA 23, 33.32–34.5 (*Auf des Königs zu England Lästerschrift Titel Martin Luthers Antwort*).
85. WA 7, 7.6–18. The remark was Luther's explanation of Thesis 22; see above, Chapter 4, n. 36.
86. WA 7, 49.7–12.
87. MStA 7/I, 93.24–25.
88. E.g., Leder regards the *Open Letter to Pope Leo* as the transition to Luther's final break with the papacy: *Ausgleich mit dem Papst?* pp. 60, 65. For Bizer, the appearance of *Grund und Ursach aller Artikel* (see below, n. 99) was the final evidence of Luther's break. Bizer sees Luther faced with a choice of alternative authorities: the church or his own teaching. *Luther und der Papst*, pp. 36, 40.
89. WA 6, 604.19–38.
90. When R. Bäumer attacks this appeal as "contradictory" and nothing but "pure maneuver," he joins two concepts which do not belong together in historical context. True, Luther did not believe in the infallibility of church councils, but neither did some conciliar theologians prior to Luther who supported appeals to councils. Conciliar appeals were a favorite legal tactic after 1460. Karlstadt and Luther were involved in the legal maneuvering at the electoral court, but that did not presuppose acceptance of conciliar infallibility. See Bäumer, review of *Luthers Konzilsidee* by Christa T. Johns, p. 200; Bubenheimer, review of *Nachwirkungen* by Bäumer, pp. 463–464. For a list of conciliar appeals after 1460, see A. Stoecklin, "Das Ende der mittelalterlichen Konzilsbewegung," *Zeitschrift für Schweizerische Kirchengeschichte* 37 (1943): 13–20.
91. WA 7, 183.8–9.
92. WABr 2, 234.4–10.
93. WA 7, 186.8–9.
94. Ibid., 162.8—164.7.
95. Ibid., 168.1–7.
96. Ibid., 180.4–7.
97. Preuss, *Die Vorstellungen*, p. 130; Bäumer, *Martin Luther und der Papst*, p. 63, and "Der Lutherprozess," pp. 47–48.
98. W. Borth, *Die Luthersache (Causa Lutheri) 1517–1524* (Lübeck and Hamburg, 1970), p. 89.
99. *Grund und Ursach aller Artikel D. Martin Luthers, so durch römische Bulle unrechtlich verdammt sind* (1521): WA 7, 309.7–15; 311.1–3.
100. WA 7, 317.10–24.
101. Ibid., 315.6–7. See H. Junghans, "Der Laie als Richter im Glaubensstreit der Reformationszeit," *LJ* 39 (1972): 46–53. Junghans emphasizes that by 1520 humanists had conceded to the laity the role of arbiter between Luther and Rome. Luther did not appeal specifically to the laity as

the arbiter of truth until after he was threatened with excommunication; but the theoretical basis of such an appeal was present in his ecclesiology from the time he acknowledged the superior judgment (based on 1 Cor. 2:15) of Christians who lived by faith and the spirit.

102. WA 7, 315.28—317.9.

103. Ibid., 313.17–29.

104. Ibid., 136.1–7.

105. Ibid., 135.23–24; cf. 431.31—433.7.

106. Ibid., 409.18–24.

CHAPTER 6—CONVICTION, 1521–1522

1. Mirbt-Aland I, 513.

2. WABr 2, 277.13–15 (March 6, 1521).

3. WA 7, 242.11–19.

4. Staupitz in a letter to Link, January 4, 1521, in A. M. Verpoorten, *Sacra superioris aevi analecta* (Coburg, 1708), p. 50. The roaring of the lion (*"rugitus leonis"*) is both a pun on the name of the pope and a quote from 1 Pet. 5:8.

5. WABr 2, 263.13—264.46 (February 9, 1521).

6. Ibid., 266.29–35 (February 17, 1521).

7. Reproduced at the end of WA 9. The introduction and captions are in WA 9, 677–715.

8. They may have been composed by Melanchthon with help from the jurist John Schwertfeger. For a discussion of the controversial passage in Luther's letter to Spalatin (*WABr* 2, 283.23–25) and of Luther's role in the production of the *Passional*, see *WABr* 2, 284, n. 11, and WA 9, 689–690.

9. WABr 2, 283.24–25 (March 7, 1521); 347.23–24 (May 26, 1521).

10. The captions: WA 9, 707.

11. WA 7, 148.14–29.

12. Ibid., 464.7–21; 465.11–17.

13. Ibid., 537.11–14.

14. WABr 2, 290.9—291.27 (March 22, 1521).

15. See F. Lauchert, *Die italienischen literarischen Gegner Luthers* (1912; reprinted Nieuwkoop, 1972), pp. 177–199, and MStA 1, 56.

16. WA 8, 235.26–29; 236.1–6.

17. WA 7, 636.31; 640.19; 641.2–3, 5–8; 644.2–3, 6, 26.

18. Ibid., 630.1–7; WA 8, 253.34–254.2.

19. WA 7, 645.7–27.

20. A full discussion of the work, its author, and its reception with a summary and reproduction of the text, in A. J. Lamping, *Ulrichus Velenus (Oldrich Velensky) and His Treatise Against the Papacy* (Leiden, 1976).

21. WABr 2, 260.11–13 (February 3, 1521).

22. WA 7, 673.1–2; cf. WA 54, 255.1–2.

23. WA 7, 673.12–27. Hence the decided opinion of Lamping (*Ulrichus Velenus*, pp. 141–142) that Luther was "essentially not interested in the

problem" and that the question of Peter's presence in Rome "in no way" influenced Luther's view that the papacy was not necessary to salvation needs to be qualified. The issue provoked keen interest in the 1520s, as Lamping's book itself testifies. Among the debaters were Jerome Aleander, John Cochlaeus, Emser again, John Fisher, the bishop of Rochester, and, in support of Velenus against Fisher, Urbanus Rhegius, writing under the pseudonym of Simon Hessus. For treatments of the question by these and other authors during the Reformation, see R. Bäumer, "Die Auseinandersetzungen über die römische Petrustradition in den ersten Jahrzehnten der Reformationszeit," *Römische Quartalschrift für christliche Altertumskunde und Kirchengeschichte* 57 (1962): 20–57. See also F. Rickers, *Das Petrusbild Luthers*, Diss. (Heidelberg, 1967), pp. 99–125.

24. WA 7, 686.5–8.

25. Ibid., 686.14–22.

26. Ibid., 686.29–36.

27. Ibid., 685.3–4.

28. Edited by Josef Schweizer in *CCath* 27 (Münster, 1956).

29. WA 7, 708.2–10.

30. Ibid., 708.15—709.33. Catharinus had devoted a sizable portion of his *Defense* to refuting Luther's earlier interpretations of this text: *CCath* 27, 95–152.

31. WA 7, 719.34—720.12.

32. Ibid., 720.32—721.14. See above, Chapter 1, n. 55.

33. Ibid., 721.15–21.

34. *CCath* 27, 157.14–27; 158.11–33.

35. WA 7, 721.29–34.

36. WA 8, 292.16–27.

37. Ibid., 293.4–5.

38. Ibid., 292.32–38.

39. On the course of the diet, see R. Wohlfeil, "Der Wormser Reichstag von 1521," in *Der Reichstag zu Worms von 1521*, ed. F. Reuter (Worms, 1971), pp. 59–154, 99.

40. *Die Depeschen des Nuntius Aleander vom Wormser Reichstage 1521*, ed. P. Kalkoff (Halle, 1886), p. 13.

41. WABr 2, 271.28–29 (February 27, 1521); 282.11–12 (March 7, 1521).

42. Ibid., 289.15–16 (March 19, 1521).

43. Ibid., 289.8–11 (March 19, 1521); 293.14–17 (March 24, 1521).

44. WA 7, 809.2–8.

45. WABr 2, 296.13 (April 7, 1521). Luther was fond of drawing parallels between the passion of Jesus and his own case. Already in Augsburg, in 1518, he had referred to his appearance before Cajetan as occurring "in the house of Caiaphas": WA 2, 7.11. And, upon his removal to seclusion after Worms, he quoted Jesus in John 16:16: "A little while, and you will see me no more; again a little while, and you will see me": WABr 2, 305.19–20 (April 28, 1521). A pamphlet published soon after the conclusion of the

diet, entitled *The Passion of Dr. Martin Luther*, compared Luther's appearance before the diet with the passion of Jesus. See Joachim Ufer, " 'Passion D. Martins Luthers'—Eine Flugschrift von 1521," in *Der Reichstag zu Worms von 1521*, pp. 449–458.

46. WA 7, 828.4–6.

47. Ibid., 829.5–17. For various explanations of Luther's request, see Wohlfeil, "Der Wormser Reichstag," pp. 115–116. The more probable explanations suggest that Luther may have expected a debate, was surprised by the demand to recant, and thought he might be able to persuade the diet to let him present his case if he had time to prepare an introductory speech. In spite of his oft-expressed determination not to recant and in spite of the fact that he was instructed beforehand only to respond to questions, he was still taken aback by the categorical answer required from him once he actually faced the diet.

48. Luther's speech as summarized here is found in WA 7, 832.1—835.18. Compare *LW* 32, 109–113. Many of the important primary sources have been made accessible by J. Rogge, ed., *1521–1971: Luther in Worms* (Berlin, 1971).

49. Von der Ecken's reply: WA 7, 835.23—838.24; cf. RTA-JR 2, 591.28—594.3. See K.-V. Selge, " 'Capta conscientia in verbis Dei': Luthers Widerrufsverweigerung in Worms," in *Der Reichstag zu Worms von 1521*, pp. 186–188.

50. WA 7, 838.4–9. The concluding words, "God help me," are better attested than the most famous statement: "Here I stand; I cannot do otherwise." See Selge, " 'Capta conscientia,' " p. 180, n. 1; *LW* 32, 113, n. 8.

51. See the summary of views in M. Baylor, *Action and Person* (Leiden, 1977), pp. 256–258.

52. WA 7, 833.10–13, 17–19. Selge has recognized the broader basis of Luther's concern: " 'Capta conscientia,' " p. 207. This broader basis is a necessary supplement to the emphasis on the religious nature of Luther's decision in Worms as expressed, e.g., by E.-W. Kohls, *Luthers Entscheidung in Worms* (Stuttgart, 1970), p. 31.

53. WA 7, 835.14–16. After Worms, Luther expressed relief that not all the princes and estates wanted him to recant. He would have been mortally ashamed of Germany if it had allowed the papal tyrants to make such a fool of it: WA 8, 211.15–18.

54. Baylor argues persuasively that both of these authorities, Scripture and evident reason, were clear, reliable, and objective authorities for Luther. They were not reducible to the certainty of Luther's own conviction, and hence Luther's appeal at Worms was not anticipating modern religious subjectivism: *Action and Person*, pp. 259–268. See Selge, " 'Capta conscientia,' " pp. 200–201.

55. RTA-JR 2, 594–596. See H. Wolter, "Das Bekenntnis des Kaisers," in *Der Reichstag zu Worms von 1521*, pp. 222–236.

56. RTA-JR 2, 609.19—610.2.

57. Ibid., 627.14–27.

58. Ibid., 640–659. For the questions raised by Paul Kalkoff about the legitimacy of the edict and a rebuttal, see P. Kalkoff, *Luther und die Entscheidungsjahre der Reformation* (Munich and Leipzig, 1917), pp. 253, 275–276; N. Paulus, "Zur Geschichte des Wormser Reichstages von 1521," *HJ* 39 (1918–1919): 269–273. Borth reaffirms the legitimacy of the ban; but he also points out how the ban placed the papal excommunication in its shadow and made imperial politics the stage for subsequent events: *Luthersache*, pp. 123–129.

59. WABr 2, 308.40–48; 308.66–70.

60. Ibid., 325.148–154 (May 3, 1521).

61. Ibid., 324.106–108 (May 3, 1521). On the question of popular unrest, compare Luther's words from the Wartburg: "Sedition is never less to be feared than when the word of God is taught": WA 8, 50.19–20.

62. WA 8, 47.27–34; 48.9–12.

63. Ibid., 49.24–26, 30–33. Compare Luther's contrast of the emperor, who is not concerned about consciences, with the pope, who refuses to let them be ruled by God and intimidates them with his own words and promises of eternal rewards and punishments: WA 8, 152.1–8.

64. Ibid., 49.33—50.9.

65. Ibid., 140.1–4.

66. Ibid., 341.26–29.

67. Ibid., 341.13–14.

68. Ibid., 152.29—153.20. See above, p. 16. Compare Luther's revealing exposition of Ps. 119:89–104 in WA 8, 196.29—197.3: "Here we note that there is much boasting in these verses: he [the Psalmist] has 'sought,' 'loved,' 'held,' etc. God's commandment, and similar statements. Still he asks that he continue to be willing and able to hold, love, know, and do it. That appears to be a contradiction. But we should understand it like this: When he stands up against his adversaries, who persecute him for the sake of God's commandment, he rightly boasts that his way is correct and good. But he asks that he might stay on it and, before God, increase in it even more. No one is too pious [to ask] for that."

69. WA 10/II, 194.35–39.

70. Ibid., 12.1–2.

71. See the accounts of the Wittenberg Movement by J. S. Preus, *Carlstadt's Ordinationes and Luther's Liberty: A Study of the Wittenberg Movement 1521–1522* (Cambridge, Mass., 1974); M. U. Edwards, *Luther and the False Brethren* (Stanford, 1975), pp. 6–33; N. Müller, *Die Wittenberger Bewegung 1521 und 1522*, 2d ed. (Leipzig, 1911).

72. WABr 2, 371.32–34 (August 1, 1521).

73. Ibid., 371.35–39.

74. On Karlstadt's biblicism, see Bubenheimer, *Consonantia*, pp. 230–250; and "Scandalum et ius divinum: Theologische und rechtstheologische Probleme der ersten reformatorischen Innovationen in Wittenberg 1521/22," ZSSR 90 [kan. Abt. 59] (1973): 263–342.

75. WA 10/II, 15.27.

76. Ibid., 25.11–25.

77. WA 8, 411.27—412.10.

78. WABr 2, 474.24–26 (March 17, 1522); cf. Luther's letter to Staupitz on June 27, 1522: WABr 2, 567.15–21.

79. WA 10/III, 18.12—19.3.

80. WABr 2, 336.13–14 (May 12, 1521).

81. Ibid., 333.18 (May 12, 1521); 348.67–73 (May 26, 1521).

82. WA 8, 44.32—45.10. Jonas himself sought and was finally granted a dispensation from lecturing on canon law and began to lecture on theology. The documents are contained in *Der Briefwechsel des Justus Jonas*, ed. G. Kawerau (Halle, 1884), I, 62–74.

83. WABr 2, 359.112–121 (July 13, 1521); LW 48, 262.

84. WABr 2, 503.3–8 (*c.* April 15, 1522).

85. Ibid., 580.5–6 (July 26, 1522).

86. Ibid., 478.16—479.21 (March 19, 1522).

87. Ibid., 406.25–26; 407.40–44 (December 1, 1521).

88. Ibid., 407.45–52.

89. WA 10/II, 105–158. For a discussion of the relationship between the two works, see G. Krodel, "*Wider den Abgott zu Halle:* Luthers Auseinandersetzung mit Albrecht von Mainz im Herbst 1521," *LJ* 33 (1966): 9–87, and his excursus in *LW* 48, 344–350.

90. WA 10/II, 109.27—110.7.

91. Ibid., 117.30.

92. Ibid., 138.31–32.

93. Ibid., 138.21–23.

94. *Briefwechsel der Brüder Ambrosius und Thomas Blaurer 1509–1548*, ed. T. Schiess (Freiburg, 1908), I, 52, no. 43.

95. *Assertio septem sacramentorum adversus Martin. Lutherum* (n.p., n.d.), p. 11.

96. WA 10/II, 196.31—197.2.

97. Staub, *Dr. Johann Fabri*, pp. 163–166.

98. J. Greving, "Verschiedene Briefe": in *Briefmappe* (Münster, 1912), I, 223, 225–228.

99. *Briefwechsel der Brüder . . . Blaurer*, I, 43, no. 38: Ulrich Zasius to Thomas Blaurer on December 21, 1521.

100. S. Ozment, *The Reformation in the Cities* (New Haven and London, 1975), pp. 47–120, 159.

101. WA 8, 575.27–29; LW 48, 335 (November 21, 1521): Luther's dedication to his father of his *Treatise on Monastic Vows*.

CHAPTER 7—PERSISTENCE, 1522–1546

1. See the judgment of Carolyn R. S. Lenz, who discovered a version of the prayer in which Luther's reference to the "insufferable pope" was omitted: "A Recently Discovered Manuscript Account of Luther's Last Prayer," ARG 66 (1975): 88. For the various versions, see Lenz, pp. 85–87; and Martin Ebon, trans., *The Last Days of Luther* (New York, 1970), pp. 45–103, esp. p. 73.

2. WA 54, 186.30—187.1.

3. See M. U. Edwards, *Luther and the False Brethren* (Stanford, 1975).

4. B. Moeller, *Deutschland im Zeitalter der Reformation* (Göttingen, 1977), p. 143.

5. H. Preuss, *Die Vorstellungen vom Antichrist im späteren Mittelalter bei Luther und in der konfessionellen Polemik* (Leipzig, 1906), p. 146.

6. Ibid. See J. Köstlin, *Martin Luther* (Elberfeld, 1875), II, 246, 388. WATR 3, 390.17–18, no. 3543A; LW 54, 227.

7. WA 51, 131.18—132.3.

8. See U. Pflugk, "Luther und der Papst," *Luther* 31 (1960): 135; F. Rickers, *Das Petrusbild Luthers*, Diss. (Heidelberg, 1967), pp. 56–57; R. Bäumer, *Martin Luther und der Papst*, 2d ed. (Münster, 1971), p. 98; E. Bizer, *Luther und der Papst* (Munich, 1958), p. 44; Preuss, *Die Vorstellungen*, p. 145.

9. Luther refers specifically to the *Papstesel*, the "pope-donkey": WA 30/III, 317.24. This term was derived from the portrayal of the pope as an upright donkey on the basis of a monstrosity rumored to have been born in Rome. It became known in Wittenberg by late 1522. Luther and Melanchthon published an interpretation of the *Papstesel* and of another alleged monstrosity in 1523. See H. Grisar and F. Heege, *Luthers Kampfbilder* (Freiburg, 1923), III, 1–13.

10. WA 30/III, 317.7–31.

11. Ibid., 317.9–10.

12. E.g., in 1545: WA 54, 215.17–25.

13. WA 26, 130.11–14 (*Ein gesichte Bruder Clausen in der Schweiz*, 1528); WA 30/III, 316.20–22.

14. WA 38, 250.27–32 (*Von der Winckelmesse*, 1533); WA 51, 545.3–6. The last quote: WA 51, 546.4–5.

15. WA 50, 250.12—251.14. For Luther's discussion of the papacy in Part II, see WA 50, 213.1—220.21. Attempts to separate the issue of authority from the doctrine of justification in Luther's break with Rome impose a distinction on Luther's thinking which would have been foreign to him. For example, Kolde argued that the question of authority and not the doctrine of justification was the "cardinal question between Protestantism and Catholicism": Th. Kolde, *Luther's Stellung zu Concil und Kirche bis zum Wormser Reichstag, 1521* (Gütersloh, 1876), p. 112. In fact, the issue of authority was the most important concrete application of the doctrine of justification.

16. WA 50, 193.17–21.

17. See ibid., 286 and LW 34, 234.

18. WA 50, 292.16–22.

19. Ibid., 215.8–13.

20. WA 23, 421.14–18 (*Tröstung an die Christen zu Halle*, 1527).

21. WA 50, 652.33—653.6 (*Von den Konziliis und Kirchen*, 1539).

22. WA 10/I/2, 97.12–26. This exposition was the basis of the apocalyptic speculation contained in the commentary on Daniel published by Melchior Hoffman in 1526. Apocalyptic concerns never dominated Luther's

theology as they did Hoffman's. See K. Deppermann, *Melchior Hoffman* (Göttingen, 1979), pp. 67–68.

23. WA 54, 187.3–5.

24. WA 26, 124.1–7.

25. K.-V. Selge, "Das Autoritätengefüge der westlichen Christenheit im Lutherkonflikt 1517 bis 1521," *Historische Zeitschrift* 223 (1976): 608–614. On the theme of the papal Antichrist in the Middle Ages, see B. McGinn, "Angel Pope and Papal Antichrist," *CH* 47 (1978): 155–173.

26. WA 30/III, 314.1–19.

27. WA 23, 405.1–2.

28. Ibid., 405.28–31.

29. Ibid., 377.24–28 (*Ob man vor dem sterben fliehen möge*, 1527). Bizer believes that Luther's polemic displayed a new intensity with his affirmation that the papacy came from the devil: *Luther und der Papst*, pp. 48–55.

30. WA 50, 62.18–24 (*Die Lügend von St. Johanne Chrysostomo*, 1537). A. Schnyder points out how Luther uses his comments on lying to build solidarity with his public against the common opponent of the papacy: "Legendenpolemik und Legendenkritik in der Reformation: *Die Lügend von St. Johanne Chrysostomo* bei Luther und Cochläus," *ARG* 70 (1979): 133.

31. G. Seebass, "Antichrist. IV: Reformations—und Neuzeit," *TRE* III, 31.

32. See WA 50, 5.6–14; WA 30/III, 301.23–26; Seebass, "Antichrist," 30.

33. E. Wolgast, *Die Wittenberger Theologie und die Politik der evangelischen Stände: Studien zu Luthers Gutachten in politischen Fragen* (Gütersloh, 1977), pp. 248–250; Seebass, "Antichrist," 30.

34. E. W. Zeeden, *Martin Luther und die Reformation im Urteil des deutschen Luthertums* (Freiburg, 1952), II, 4; cf. CR 11, 729–730. Melanchthon appealed here to the language of Erasmus. See Edwards, *Luther and the False Brethren*, p. 205.

35. Schiess, *Briefwechsel der Brüder . . . Blaurer*, I, 34, no. 31.

36. WABr 2, 563.26—564.2 (June 15, 1522).

37. Ibid., 580.13–16 (July 26, 1522); 594.29–30; 595.4–6 (August 28, 1522).

38. WATR 3, 391.1–2, no. 3543 A. For Mathesius, see E. W. Zeeden, *Martin Luther und die Reformation im Urteil des deutschen Luthertums* (Freiburg, 1952), II, 30.

39. E. Mülhaupt described the pictures ridiculing the pope and published in 1545 as filled with an "abysmal hatred": "Vergängliches und Unvergängliches an Luthers Papstkritik," *LJ* 26 (1959): 59, 60. Joseph Lortz maintained that vulgarity to the point of repulsive, irrational hatred against the papacy was one characteristic of Luther: "Martin Luther: Grundzüge seiner geistigen Struktur," *Reformata Reformanda. Festgabe für Hubert Jedin* (Münster, 1965), I, 222; cf. Lortz, *Die Reformation in Deutschland*,

4th ed. (Freiburg, 1962), I, 397; "Reformatorisch und katholisch beim jungen Luther (1518–1519)," *Humanitas—Christianitas: Walther v. Loewenich zum 65. Geburtstag* (Witten, 1968), p. 52, n. 21.

40. Bäumer uses the phrase "abysmal hatred," but as part of his evidence against Lortz's argument that Luther never completely cut his ties with the Catholic Church: *Martin Luther und der Papst*, pp. 98–99.

41. Lortz insisted that it was necessary to separate the objective content of Luther's polemic from his emotional reaction, including the hatred, which drove him forward: *Reformation in Deutschland*, I, 409.

42. K. Holl, "Luthers Urteile über sich selbst (1903)," *Gesammelte Aufsätze zur Kirchengeschichte*, I: *Luther*, 7th ed. (Tübingen, 1948), p. 409.

43. WA 51, 499.5—500.15.

44. Ibid., 501.16—504.9.

45. See B. Lohse, "Die Einheit der Kirche bei Luther," *Luther* 50 (1979): 13–14.

46. See J. Schutte, *"Schympff red": Frühformen bürgerlicher Agitation in Thomas Murners "Grossen Lutherischen Narren"* (1522) (Stuttgart, 1973), p. 68.

47. H. Jedin, *A History of the Council of Trent*, trans. E. Graf (London, 1957), I, 497–499; LW 41, 259–262.

48. WA 54, 346–373; Grisar and Heege, *Luthers Kampfbilder*, IV, 16–63, 73–113.

49. WA 54, 357–358.

50. Ibid., 354, 356.

51. Ibid., 215.11–25.

52. Ibid., 268.20–26; cf. WA 51, 492.14—493.8.

53. WA 54, 272.9–10; 250.23–25.

54. Ibid., 277.23–24.

55. Ibid., 262.12–16.

56. For example, in the same breath with the last quote: WA 54, 262.20–22.

57. MStA 1, 61.15 (*Didymi Faventini . . . oratio*, 1521).

58. Wolgast, *Die Wittenberger Theologie*, pp. 20, 285.

59. WA 10/II, 237.21–22.

60. WA 50, 62.6–24.

61. WA 51, 510.12—511.17.

62. WA 30/II, 483.36—484.14; LW 40, 348–349 (*Von den Schlüsseln*, 1530). Luther's defense of the literal meaning of the words of institution in the Lord's Supper was also made "for the weak and simple," just as his adamant rejection of the papacy: WA 23, 75.21–24; LW 37, 20. See Edwards, *Luther and the False Brethren*, p. 95. The consistency with which Luther expressed concern for others when defending his views provides important balance to the picture offered by Edwards of Luther's self-righteousness.

63. WA 50, 63.6–19.

64. WA 30/III, 309.2–6.

65. WA 53, 404–405 (*Neue Zeitung vom Rhein*, 1542).
66. WA 50, 209.12–17.
67. WA 51, 542.13—543.12.
68. WA 50, 218.6.
69. WA 30/III, 316.3–19; cf. WA 50, 342.24–40.
70. See the helpful distinction made by H. A. Oberman, *Werden und Wertung der Reformation* (Tübingen, 1977), p. 374. The distinction made by H. J. Urban is much less helpful. According to Urban, Luther's rejection of the pope's claim to authority by divine right was not a necessary consequence of Luther's insistence upon the independence of the word of God: "Der reformatorische Protest gegen das Papsttum: Eine theologiegeschichtliche Skizze," *Catholica* 30 (1976): 297–298. Urban's separation of the two themes results from his treatment of them at the theoretical level instead of at the practical level of their effect on the people where Luther dealt with them. Luther's interpretation of the "spiritual man" of 1 Cor. 2:15 not as the pope but as every Christian who judges by the word of God is a direct refutation of Urban's point. See Luther's reaffirmation of his interpretation of this key text for him in 1545: WA 54, 294.20–31. See also his rejection of the divine right of papal authority at WA 50, 343.1–12.
71. WA 54, 280.1–9; 294.20–31.

BIBLIOGRAPHY

SOURCES*

Altenstaig, Johannes. *Vocabularius theologiae*. Hagenau, 1517.

Biel, Gabriel. *Canonis misse expositio*. Edited by H. A. Oberman and W. J. Courtenay. 4 vols. Wiesbaden, 1963–1967.

Cajetan (Thomas de Vio). *Opuscula Omnia*. Lyon, 1562.

Eck, Johannes. *Epistola de ratione studiorum suorum (1538)*. Edited by Johannes Metzler. *CCath* 2. Münster, 1921.

Emser, Jerome. *De disputatione Lipsicensi, quantum ad Boemos obiter deflexa est (1519)*. Edited by Franz X. Thurnhofer. *CCath* 4. Münster, 1921.

Enders, Ludwig, ed. *Luther und Emser: Ihre Streitschriften aus dem Jahre 1521*. Vol. I. Halle, 1889.

Gess, Felician, ed. *Akten und Briefe zur Kirchenpolitik Herzog Georgs von Sachsen*. Vol. I: 1517–1524. Leipzig, 1905.

[Henry VIII]. *Assertio septem sacramentorum adversus Martin. Lutherum*. n.p., n.d.

Kalkoff, Paul, ed. *Die Depeschen des Nuntius Aleander vom Wormser Reichstage 1521*. Halle, 1886.

Kawerau, Gustav, ed. *Der Briefwechsel des Justus Jonas*. 2 vols. Halle, 1884, 1885.

Köhler, Walther, ed. *Dokumente zum Ablassstreit von 1517*. 2d ed. Tübingen, 1934.

————. *Luthers 95 Thesen samt seinen Resolutionen sowie den Gegenschriften vom Wimpina-Tetzel, Eck und Prierias und den Antworten Luthers darauf*. Leipzig, 1903.

The Last Days of Luther. Trans. by Martin Ebon. New York, 1970.

Politus, Ambrosius Catharinus. *Apologia pro veritate catholicae et apostolicae fidei ac doctrinae adversus impia ac valde pestifera Martini Lutheri dogmata (1520)*. Edited by Josef Schweizer. *CCath* 27. Münster, 1956.

[Rhegius, Urbanus]. *Argumentum libelli: Simon Hessus Luthero ostendit caussas quare Lutherana opuscula a Coloniensibus et Louvaniensibus sint combusta. . . .* n.p., 1521.

————. *Iudicium D. Urbani Rhegii de D. Martino Luthero*. In Urbanus Rhegius, *Loci theologici. . . .* Frankfurt, 1545, 215[v]–252[r].

Rogge, Joachim, ed. *1521–1971: Luther in Worms*. Berlin, 1971.

Scheel, Otto, ed. *Dokumente zu Luthers Entwicklung*. 2d ed. Tübingen, 1929.

Schiess, Traugott, ed. *Briefwechsel der Brüder Ambrosius und Thomas Blaurer 1509–1548*. 3 vols. Freiburg, 1908, 1910, 1912.

*See sources also in the section on Abbreviations at the beginning of the book.

Seitz, Otto, ed. *Der authentische Text der Leipziger Disputation 1519*. Berlin, 1903.

Setz, Wolfram, ed. *Lorenzo Valla: De falso credita et ementita Constantini donatione*. Weimar, 1976.

Soden, F. von, and Knaake, J. K. F., eds. *Christoph Scheurl's Briefbuch: Ein Beitrag zur Geschichte der Reformation und ihrer Zeit*. 2 vols. 1867; reprinted Aalen, 1962.

Staupitz, Johannes von. *Constitutiones Fratrum Heremitarum sancti Augustini ad apostolicorum privilegiorum formam pro Reformatione Alemanie*. n.p., n.d.

Verpoorten, Albert Meno, ed. *Sacra superioris aevi analecta*. . . . Coburg, 1708.

STUDIES

Aarts, Jan. *Die Lehre Martin Luthers über das Amt in der Kirche*. Helsinki, 1972.

Aland, Kurt. *Der Weg zur Reformation*. Munich, 1965.

Bäumer, Remigius. "Die Auseinandersetzungen über die römische Petrustradition in den ersten Jahrzehnten der Reformationszeit." *Römische Quartalschrift für christliche Altertumskunde und Kirchengeschichte* 57 (1962): 20–57.

―――. "Der junge Luther und der Papst." *Catholica* 23 (1969): 392–420.

―――. "Der Lutherprozess." *Lutherprozess und Lutherbann: Vorgeschichte, Ergebnis, Nachwirkung*. Edited by R. Bäumer. Münster, 1972, pp. 18–48.

―――. *Martin Luther und der Papst*. 2d ed. Münster, 1971.

―――. *Nachwirkungen des konziliaren Gedankens in der Theologie und Kanonistik des frühen 16. Jahrhunderts*. Münster, 1971.

―――. Review of *Luthers Konzilsidee* by Christa T. Johns. *Theologische Revue* 25 (1969): 198–202.

Bauer, Karl. *Die Wittenberger Universitätstheologie und die Anfänge der deutschen Reformation*. Tübingen, 1928.

Baylor, Michael G. *Action and Person: Conscience in Late Scholasticism and the Young Luther*. Leiden, 1977.

Beck, Hans-Georg et al. *Vom kirchlichen Hochmittelalter bis zum Vorabend der Reformation*. HKG III/2. Freiburg, 1968.

Benrath, G. A. "Ablass." *TRE* I, 347–364.

Benzing, Josef. *Ulrich von Hutten und seine Drucker: Eine Bibliographie der Schriften Huttens im 16. Jahrhundert, mit Beiträgen von Heinrich Grimm*. Wiesbaden, 1956.

Bizer, Ernst. *Luther und der Papst*. Munich, 1958.

Bornkamm, Heinrich. *Martin Luther in der Mitte seines Lebens: Das Jahrzehnt zwischen dem Wormser und dem Augsburger Reichstag*. Edited by Karin Bornkamm. Göttingen, 1979. (English edition forthcoming, 1983, Philadelphia, Fortress Press.)

BIBLIOGRAPHY

———. *Thesen und Thesenanschlag Luthers: Geschehen und Bedeutung.* Berlin, 1967.

Borth, Wilhelm. *Die Luthersache (Causa Lutheri) 1517–1524: Die Anfänge der Reformation als Frage von Politik und Recht.* Lübeck and Hamburg, 1970.

Brosse, Olivier de la. *Le pape et le concile: La comparaison de leurs pouvoirs à la veille de la Réforme.* Paris, 1965.

Bubenheimer, Ulrich. *Consonantia Theologiae et Iurisprudentiae: Andreas Bodenstein von Karlstadt als Theologe und Jurist zwischen Scholastik und Reformation.* Tübingen, 1977.

———. Review of *Nachwirkungen des konziliaren Gedankens* by Remigius Bäumer. ZSSR 90 [kan. Abt. 59] (1973): 455–465.

———. "Scandalum et ius divinum: Theologische und rechtstheologische Probleme der ersten reformatorischen Innovationen in Wittenberg 1521/22." ZSSR 90 [kan. Abt. 59] (1973): 263–342.

Campenhausen, Hans Freiherr von. "Reformatorisches Selbstbewusstsein und reformatorisches Geschichtsbewusstsein bei Luther 1517–1522." *Tradition und Leben: Kräfte der Kirchengeschichte: Aufsätze und Vorträge.* Tübingen, 1960, pp. 318–342.

Dannenbauer, Heinz. *Luther als religiöser Volksschriftsteller 1517–1520.* Tübingen, 1930.

Deppermann, Klaus. *Melchior Hoffman: Soziale Unruhen und apokalyptische Visionen im Zeitalter der Reformation.* Göttingen, 1979.

Dieckhoff, August Wilhelm. *Die Stellung Luthers zur Kirche und ihrer Reformation in der Zeit vor dem Ablassstreit.* Rostock, 1883.

Eckermann, Karla. *Studien zur Geschichte des monarchischen Gedankens im 15. Jahrhundert.* Berlin-Grunewald, 1933.

Edwards, Mark U. *Luther and the False Brethren.* Stanford, 1975.

Fife, Robert H. *The Revolt of Martin Luther.* New York, 1957.

Fraenkel, Pierre. "John Eck's *Enchiridion* of 1525 and Luther's Earliest Arguments against Papal Primacy." *Studia Theologica* 21 (1967): 110–163.

Grane, Leif. "Lutherforschung und Geistesgeschichte: Auseinandersetzung mit Heiko A. Oberman." ARG 68 (1977): 302–315.

———. *Modus loquendi theologicus: Luthers Kampf um die Erneuerung der Theologie (1515–1518).* Leiden, 1975.

Greving, Joseph. *Johann Eck als junger Gelehrter.* Münster, 1906.

———. "Zur Verkündigung der Bulle Exsurge Domine durch Dr. Johann Eck 1520" and "Verschiedene Briefe." *Briefmappe: Erstes Stuck.* Reformationsgeschichtliche Studien und Texte 21/22. Edited by J. Greving. Münster, 1912, pp. 196–235.

Grisar, Hartmann, and Heege, Franz. *Luthers Kampfbilder.* 4 vols. Freiburg, 1921–1923.

Günter, Wolfgang. "Die geschichtstheologischen Voraussetzungen von Luthers Selbstverständnis." *Von Konstanz nach Trient: Beiträge zur Geschichte der Kirche von den Reformkonzilien bis zum Tridentinum.*

Festgabe für August Franzen. Edited by R. Bäumer. Munich, 1972, pp. 379–394.

Haar, Johann. "Das Wort der Wahrheit." *Luther* 47 (1976): 5–22.

Hauffen, Adolf. "Husz eine Gans—Luther ein Schwan." *Untersuchungen und Quellen zur Germanistischen und Romanischen Philologie: Johann von Keller dargebracht von seinen Kollegen und Schülern,* Vol. II, Prag, 1908, pp. 1–28.

Hendrix, Scott H. *Ecclesia in via: Ecclesiological Developments in the Medieval Psalms Exegesis and the Dictata super Psalterium (1513–1515) of Martin Luther.* Leiden, 1974.

―――. " 'We Are All Hussites'? Hus and Luther Revisited." *ARG* 65 (1974): 134–161.

Hennig, Gerhard. *Cajetan und Luther: Ein historischer Beitrag zur Begegnung von Thomismus und Reformation.* Stuttgart, 1966.

Herrmann, F. "Miscellen zur Reformationsgeschichte: Aus Mainzer Akten." *ZKG* 23 (1902): 263–268.

Hinrichs, Diedrich. *Die Kirche in Luthers Vorlesung über den Römerbrief.* Mag. diss. Hamburg, 1967.

Holl, Karl. "Luthers Urteile über sich selbst (1903)." *Gesammelte Aufsätze zur Kirchengeschichte.* Vol. I: *Luther.* 7th ed. Tübingen, 1948, pp. 381–419.

Höss, Irmgard. *Georg Spalatin 1484–1545: Ein Leben in der Zeit des Humanismus und der Reformation.* Weimar, 1956.

Iserloh, Erwin et al. *Reformation, Katholische Reform und Gegenreformation.* HKG IV. Freiburg, 1967.

Jedin, Hubert. *A History of the Council of Trent.* Trans. by E. Graf. 2 vols. London, 1957, 1961.

Johns, Christa T. *Luthers Konzilsidee in ihrer historischen Bedingtheit und ihrem reformatorischen Neuansatz.* Berlin, 1966.

Junghans, Helmar. "Der Laie als Richter im Glaubensstreit der Reformationszeit." *LJ* 39 (1972): 31–54.

Kähler, Ernst. "Die 95 Thesen: Inhalt und Bedeutung." *Luther* 38 (1967): 114–124.

Kalkoff, Paul. *Forschungen zu Luthers römischem Prozess.* Rome, 1905.

―――. *Luther und die Entscheidungsjahre der Reformation von den Ablassthesen bis zum Wormser Edikt.* Munich and Leipzig, 1917.

―――. "Zu Luthers römischem Prozess." *ZKG* 25 (1904): 90–147, 273–290, 399–459, 503–603.

―――. *Zu Luthers römischem Prozess: Der Prozess des Jahres 1518.* Gotha, 1912.

Kawerau, Gustav. *Hieronymus Emser.* Halle, 1898.

Köhler, Walther. *Luther und die Kirchengeschichte nach seinen Schriften, zunächst bis 1521.* Erlangen, 1900.

Kohls, Ernst-Wilhelm. *Luthers Entscheidung in Worms.* Stuttgart, 1970.

Kolde, Th. *Luther's Stellung zu Concil und Kirche bis zum Wormser Reichstag, 1521.* Gütersloh, 1876.

BIBLIOGRAPHY

Köstlin, Julius. *Martin Luther: Sein Leben und seine Schriften.* 2 vols. Elberfeld, 1875.

Köstlin, Julius, and Kawerau, Gustav. *Martin Luther: Sein Leben und seine Schriften.* 2 vols. 5th ed. Berlin, 1903.

Krodel, Gottfried. *"Wider den Abgott zu Halle:* Luthers Auseinandersetzung mit Albrecht von Mainz im Herbst 1521." *LJ* 33 (1966): 9–87.

Lamping, A. J. *Ulrichus Velenus (Oldrich Velensky) and His Treatise Against the Papacy.* Leiden, 1976.

Lange, Irene. "Die kurfürstliche Universität und der Beginn der Reformation" and "Die Ablassdekretale Leos X. vom 9. November 1518." *Blätter für pfälzische Kirchengeschichte und religiöse Volkskunde* 44 (1977): 146–152.

Lauchert, Friedrich. *Die italienischen literarischen Gegner Luthers.* 1912; reprinted Nieuwkoop, 1972.

Leder, Hans-Günter. *Ausgleich mit dem Papst? Luthers Haltung in den Verhandlungen mit Miltitz 1520.* Stuttgart, 1969.

Lemmens, Leonhard. *Pater Augustin von Alfeld: Ein Franziskaner aus den ersten Jahren der Glaubensspaltung in Deutschland.* Freiburg, 1899.

Lenz, Carolyn R. S. "A Recently Discovered Manuscript Account of Luther's Last Prayer." *ARG* 66 (1975): 79–92.

Lindberg, Carter. "Prierias and His Significance for Luther's Development." *SCJ* 3 (1972): 45–64.

Lohse, Bernhard, ed. *Der Durchbruch der reformatorischen Erkenntnis bei Luther.* Darmstadt, 1968.

———. "Die Einheit der Kirche bei Luther." *Luther* 50 (1979): 10–24.

Lortz, Joseph. *Die Reformation in Deutschland.* 2 vols. 4th ed. Freiburg, 1962.

———. "Martin Luther: Grundzüge seiner geistigen Struktur." *Reformata Reformanda. Festgabe für Hubert Jedin.* Edited by E. Iserloh and K. Repgen. 2 vols. Münster, 1965, I, 214–246.

———. "Reformatorisch und Katholisch beim jungen Luther (1518/1519)." *Humanitas—Christianitas: Walther v. Loewenich zum 65. Geburtstag.* Edited by K. Beyschlag et al. Witten, 1968, pp. 47–62.

———. "Zum Kirchendenken des jungen Luther." *Wahrheit und Verkündigung: Michael Schmaus zum 70. Geburtstag.* Edited by L. Scheffczyk et al. 2 vols. Munich, 1967, II, 947–986.

McGinn, Bernard. "Angel Pope and Papal Antichrist." *CH* 47 (1978): 155–173.

Meissinger, Karl August. *Der katholische Luther.* Munich, 1952.

Moeller, Bernd. *Deutschland im Zeitalter der Reformation.* Göttingen, 1977.

Mühlmann, Sieghard. *Luther und das Corpus Iuris Canonici bis zum Jahre 1530.* Vol. I: *Prolegomena.* Diss. Leipzig, 1972.

Mühlpfordt, Günter. Review of *Die Luthersache* by W. Borth and of *Der Fall Luther* by D. Olivier. *Deutsche Literaturzeitung für Kritik der internationalen Wissenschaft* 95 (1974): 897–906.

Mülhaupt, Erwin. "Vergängliches und Unvergängliches an Luthers Papst-kritik." *LJ* 26 (1959): 56–68.

Müller, Gerhard. "Ekklesiologie und Kirchenkritik beim jungen Luther." *NZSTh* 7 (1975): 100–128.

―――. "Martin Luther und das Papsttum." *Das Papsttum in der Diskussion.* Edited by Georg Denzler. Regensburg, 1974, pp. 73–101.

―――. "Die römische Kurie und die Anfänge der Reformation." *Zeitschrift für Religions- und Geistesgeschichte* 19 (1967): 1–32.

Müller, Karl. "Luthers römischer Prozess." *ZKG* 24 (1903): 46–85.

Müller, Nikolaus. *Die Wittenberger Bewegung 1521 und 1522: Die Vorgänge in und um Wittenberg während Luthers Wartburgaufenthalt.* 2d ed. Leipzig, 1911.

Oakley, Francis. "Conciliarism in the Sixteenth Century: Jacques Almain Again." *ARG* 68 (1977): 111–132.

Oberman, Heiko A. "Reformation: Epoche oder Episode." *ARG* 68 (1977): 56–111.

―――. *Werden und Wertung der Reformation: Vom Wegestreit zum Glaubenskampf.* Tübingen, 1977.

―――. "Wittenbergs Zweifrontenkrieg gegen Prierias und Eck." *ZKG* 80 (1969): 331–358.

Ozment, Steven E. *The Reformation in the Cities: The Appeal of Protestantism to Sixteenth-Century Germany and Switzerland.* New Haven and London, 1975.

Pastor, Ludwig. *Geschichte der Päpste seit dem Ausgang des Mittelalters.* Vol. IV/1: *Leo X.* Freiburg, 1906.

Paulus, Nikolaus. *Die deutschen Dominikaner im Kampfe gegen Luther (1518–1563).* Freiburg, 1903.

―――. *Johann Tetzel der Ablassprediger.* Mainz, 1899.

―――. "Luther's Stellung zum Papstthum in den ersten Monaten des Jahres 1519." *Der Katholik* 79 (1899): I, 476–480.

―――. "Zur Geschichte des Wormser Reichstages von 1521." *HJ* 39 (1918–19): 269–277.

Pesch, Otto H. " 'Das heisst eine neue Kirche bauen:' Luther und Cajetan in Augsburg." *Begegnung: Beiträge zu einer Hermeneutik des theologischen Gesprächs.* Edited by Max Seckler et al. Graz, 1972, pp. 645–661.

Pflugk, Ulrich. "Luther und der Papst." *Luther* 31 (1960): 130–138.

Preus, James S. *Carlstadt's Ordinations and Luther's Liberty: A Study of the Wittenberg Movement 1521–1522.* Cambridge, Mass., 1974.

Preuss, Hans. *Die Vorstellungen vom Antichrist im späteren Mittelalter, bei Luther und in der konfessionellen Polemik: Ein Beitrag zur Theologie Luthers und zur Geschichte der christlichen Frömmigkeit.* Leipzig, 1906.

Rickers, Folkert. *Das Petrusbild Luthers: Ein Beitrag zu seiner Auseinandersetzung mit dem Papsttum.* Diss. Heidelberg, 1967.

Roos, Heinrich. "Die Quellen der Bulle 'Exsurge Domine' (15.6.1520)." *Theologie in Geschichte und Gegenwart: Michael Schmaus zum sechzigsten Geburtstag dargebracht von seinen Freunden und Schülern.* Edited by

BIBLIOGRAPHY

J. Auer and H. Volk. Munich, 1957, pp. 909–926.

Scheel, Otto. *Martin Luther: Vom Katholizismus zur Reformation.* 2 vols. Tübingen, 1916, 1917.

Scheurl, Siegfried Freiherr von. "Martin Luthers Doktoreid." *Zeitschrift für bayerische Kirchengeschichte* 32 (1963): 46–52.

Schlecht, Joseph. "Dr. Johann Ecks Anfänge." *HJ* 36 (1915): 1–36.

Schnyder, André. "Legendenpolemik und Legendenkritik in der Reformation: *Die Lügend von St. Johanne Chrysostomo* bei Luther und Cochläus." *ARG* 70 (1979): 122–140.

Schulte, Aloys. "Die römischen Verhandlungen über Luther 1520: Aus den Atti Consistoriali 1517–23." *Quellen und Forschungen aus italienischen Archiven und Bibliotheken* 6 (1904): 32–52, 174–176, 374–378.

Schutte, Jürgen. *"Schympff red": Frühformen bürgerlichen Agitation in Thomas Murners "Grossen Lutherischen Narren" (1522).* Stuttgart, 1973.

Schwiebert, E. G. *Luther and His Times.* St. Louis, 1950.

Seebass, Gottfried. "Antichrist: IV: Reformations- und Neuzeit." *TRE III*, pp. 28–43.

Selge, Kurt-Victor. "Die Augsburger Begegnung von Luther und Kardinal Cajetan im Oktober 1518: Ein erster Wendepunkt auf dem Weg zur Reformation." *Jahrbuch der hessischen kirchengeschichtlichen Vereinigung* 20 (1969): 37–54.

————. "Das Autoritätengefüge der westlichen Christenheit im Lutherkonflikt 1517 bis 1521." *Historische Zeitschrift* 223 (1976): 591–617.

————. " 'Capta conscientia in verbis Dei': Luthers Widerrufsverweigerung in Worms." *Der Reichstag zu Worms von 1521: Reichspolitik und Luthersache.* Edited by Fritz Reuter. Worms, 1971, pp. 180–207.

————. "Die Leipziger Disputation zwischen Luther und Eck." *ZKG* 86 (1975): 26–40.

————. *Normen der Christenheit im Streit um Ablass und Kirchenautorität 1518 bis 1521.* Habil. Heidelberg, 1968.

————. "Der Weg zur Leipziger Disputation zwischen Luther und Eck im Jahr 1519." *Bleibendes im Wandel der Kirchengeschichte: Kirchenhistorische Studien.* Edited by B. Moeller and G. Ruhbach. Tübingen, 1973, pp. 169–210.

Seppelt, Franz Xaver. *Geschichte der Päpste von den Anfängen bis zur Mitte des zwanzigsten Jahrhunderts.* Vol. IV: *Das Papsttum im Spätmittelalter und in der Renaissance von Bonifaz VIII bis zu Klemens VII.* Edited by Georg Schwaiger. 2d ed. Munich, 1957.

Setz, Wolfram. *Lorenzo Vallas Schrift gegen die konstantinische Schenkung: De falso credita et ementita Constantini donatione: Zur Interpretation und Wirkungsgeschichte.* Tübingen, 1975.

Sider, Ronald J. *Andreas Bodenstein von Karlstadt: The Development of His Thought 1517–1525.* Leiden, 1974.

Starck, Otto. *Luthers Stellung zur Institution des Papsttums von 1520 bis 1546 unter besonderer Berücksichtigung des "ius humanum."* Diss. Münster, 1930. Quakenbrück, 1930.

Staub, Ignaz. *Dr. Johann Fabri, Generalvikar von Konstanz (1518–1523), bis zum offenen Kampf gegen M. Luther (August 1522).* Diss. Freiburg (Switzerland), 1911. Einsiedeln, 1911.

Steinmetz, David. "Hermeneutic and Old Testament Interpretation in Staupitz and the Young Martin Luther." *ARG* 70 (1979): 24–58.

————. *Misericordia Dei: The Theology of Johannes von Staupitz in Its Late Medieval Setting.* Leiden, 1968.

Stoecklin, Alfred. "Das Ende der mittelalterlichen Konzilsbewegung." *Zeitschrift für Schweizerische Kirchengeschichte* 37 (1943): 8–30.

Tentler, Thomas. *Sin and Confession on the Eve of the Reformation.* Princeton, 1977.

Ufer, Joachim. " 'Passion D. Martins Luthers': Eine Flugschrift von 1521." *Der Reichstag zu Worms von 1521.* Edited by Fritz Reuter. Worms, 1971, pp. 449–458.

Urban, Hans Jörg. "Der reformatorische Protest gegen das Papsttum: Eine theologiegeschichtliche Skizze." *Catholica* 30 (1976): 295–319.

Vercruysse, Joseph. *Fidelis populus.* Wiesbaden, 1968.

Volz, Hans. "Erzbischof Albrecht von Mainz und Martin Luthers 95 Thesen." *Jahrbuch der hessischen kirchengeschichtlichen Vereinigung* 13 (1962): 187–228.

————. "Um Martin Luthers Thesenanschlag." *Luther* 38 (1967): 125–138.

Walz, Angelus. "Von Cajetans Gedanken über Kirche und Papst." *Volk Gottes: Festgabe für Josef Höfer.* Edited by R. Bäumer and H. Dolch. Freiburg, 1967, pp. 336–360.

Wohlfeil, Rainer. "Der Wormser Reichstag von 1521." *Der Reichstag zu Worms von 1521.* Edited by Fritz Reuter. Worms, 1971, pp. 59–154.

Wolf, Ernst. "Leviathan: Eine patristische Notiz zu Luthers Kritik des Papsttums." *Peregrinatio: Studien zur reformatorischen Theologie und zum Kirchenproblem.* Vol. I. Munich, 1954, pp. 135–145.

————. *Staupitz und Luther.* 1927; reprinted in New York and London, 1971.

Wolgast, Eike. *Die Wittenberger Theologie und die Politik der evangelischen Stände: Studien zu Luthers Gutachten in politischen Fragen.* Gütersloh, 1977.

Wolter, Hans. "Das Bekenntnis des Kaisers." *Der Reichstag zu Worms von 1521.* Edited by Fritz Reuter. Worms, 1971, pp. 222–236.

Zeeden, Ernst Walter. *Martin Luther und die Reformation im Urteil des deutschen Luthertums.* 2 vols. Freiburg, 1950, 1952.

INDEXES

PERSONS

PLACES AND SUBJECTS

BIBLICAL PASSAGES

DATE DUE